CONCEPTUALIZATION IN PSYCHOTHERAPY:

The Models Approach

CONCEPTUALIZATION IN PSYCHOTHERAPY:

The Models Approach

Fredric M. Levine

Evelyn Sandeen

 LAWRENCE ERLBAUM ASSOCIATES, PUBLISHERS

1985   Hillsdale, New Jersey   London

Lawrence Erlbaum Associates, Inc., Publishers
365 Broadway
Hillsdale, New Jersey 07642

Library of Congress Cataloging in Publication Data

Levine, Fredric M.
   Conceptualization in psychotherapy.

   Bibliography: p.
   Includes indexes.
   1. Psychotherapy—Methodology. I. Sandeen, Evelyn.
II. Title.
RC480.5.L48 1985   616.89′14   85-6957
ISBN 0-89859-549-5

Printed in the United States of America

10 9 8 7 6 5 4 3 2 1

To the E's and the M's

Contents

Preface

This book emerged from a dissatisfaction with the manner in which psychotherapists and clinical researchers were thinking and writing about clinical problems. In the professional lifetime of the senior author, there have been major and dramatic advances in knowledge about the nature of psychopathology and the techniques of intervention. However, it seemed clear that information on selection of treatment for a particular person was insufficient when compared to the great wealth of information on techniques of treatment. The process of conceptualization in psychotherapy was not being discussed adequately.

We saw this inadequacy expressed clinically by an overreliance on one's "school" of training and/or overreliance on diagnostic categories when selecting treatment for an individual. Thus, we would see clinicians treating all their clients in a manner congruent with their specific theoretical predilections, or alternatively, treating all persons who fit a particular diagnostic category using the same techniques. The lack of attention to conceptualization came out in clincial research by an overemphasis on "horse-race" comparisons[1] between one treatment and another administered to randomly assigned groups, with little concern about determining the characteristics of individuals for whom a particular treatment might be effective. The inadequate attention paid to conceptualization was perhaps expressed most lucidly in the training of clinicians. Students were taught piles of information on the techniques of assessment and therapy, but very little on how to conceptualize a case in a manner which would suggest the correct treatment to use. Over and over in supervision, students would be at a loss as to how to pick a treatment, or they would present a "shotgun strategy" of hitting the client with as many techniques as possible in the hope that one technique was on target. They were bright and were very sharp on research findings and techniques; however, they had had no training in how to apply this knowledge clinically. There appeared to be no systematic way of teaching conceptualization skills. This book is an attempt to articulate a system of conceptualization which acknowledges a wide variety of biological and psychological influences on human behavior.

---

[1] Beach and O'Leary (1985)

The basic assumption of the models approach is that human behavior is determined by a complex set of influences. At the most basic level, biological factors determine many aspects of human behavior. Due to a combination of biological and psychological factors, persons have limits on their capacities to change, and these limits influence their behavior in the world. Simple conditioning affects human beings, as do systems of reinforcement and punishment. We are thinking organisms, and our thoughts can affect our behavior enormously. Humans are social creatures as well, and our behavior cannot therefore be fully understood without taking into account the elaborate systems of family, class, and economic dependencies within which we exist.

Behavior which brings people into therapy is no differently determined than normal behavior. In order to intervene effectively, we must intervene at whatever level is relevant to the particular problem at hand. Central to the models approach to conceptualization is that various cases within a single diagnostic category may have very different causal mechanisms—what we have called *models*. Thus, behaviorally similar depressions may fit a biological model, an operant model, or may be the result of specific disruptive cognitions. Other cases of depression may be caused by a mismatch between the demands of the environment and the capacities of the individual, and yet other depressions may be the result of conflicting social demands placed on the person. In each instance, the treatment must be guided by the specific conceptualization of the individual's problem (according to model) rather than by the person's diagnosis of "depression".

We hope that this work lessens the gap in the field in the area of conceptualization. This is a book that we would have liked available for our courses in assessment, intervention, and abnormal psychology. We also hope that it fills a need felt by the professional. The majority of therapists define themselves as eclectic, and the models approach provides them (and others) with a system of conceptualizing cases according to psychological principles leading to a variety of interventions.

We have also tried to make this book fun. We have often illustrated the models we present with clinical cases. More importantly, it is our hope that the book succeeds in transmitting our excitement about the potential of psychological knowledge in reducing human suffering. We had fun and felt excitement in writing this book.

Fredric M. Levine
Evelyn Sandeen

Acknowledgments

We are grateful for the stimulation, the comments, and the criticisms of many people. This book evolved from both a graduate course in therapeutic intervention and years of clinical supervision by the senior author, and was greatly modified during the 4 years of our collaboration. We were also influenced by the response of several generations of students. Those having the largest influence were Steven Beach, Ileana Arias, Joan Broderick, and Marvin Lee.

Many helpful comments were generously given by Ronald Friend, Marvin Levine, Howard Rachlin, Michael Simon, and Ira Turkat. Our editor, Brendan Maher, was particularly helpful in making this book more comprehensible. Although we were unaware of his enormous influence until the book was completed, we have a major intellectual debt to the late Gardner Murphy.

Finally, we are appreciative of the organizational help given by Leigh Liagre, who kept the book and our sanity intact.

Levine and Sandeen: Flowchart for THE MODELS APPROACH

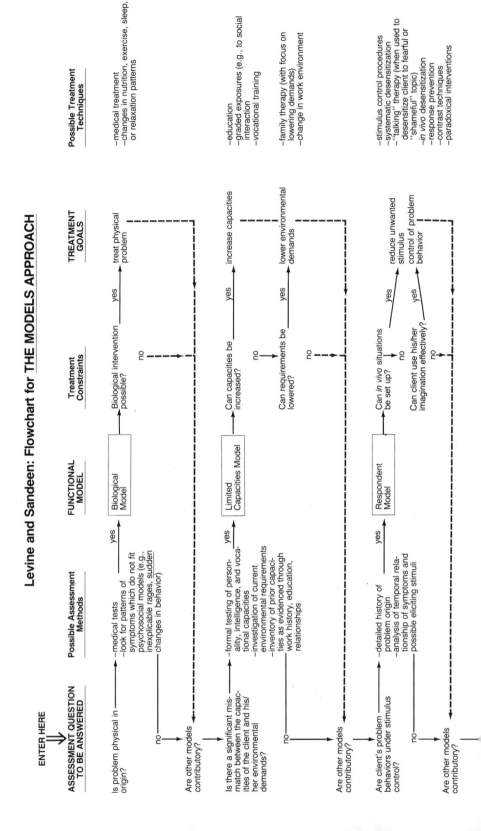

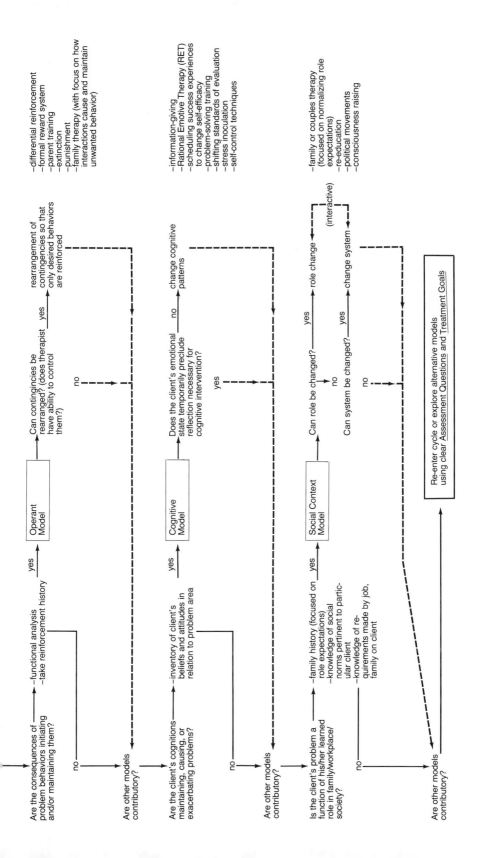

1 Introduction

A 42-year-old married female client enters the therapist's office and describes herself as having a "phobia of leaving the house." She states that she has had various fears since shortly after she was married 20 years ago, but that these feelings of anxiety surrounding leaving her home have become so intense that she has rarely left the house in the last 3 years. How does the therapist go about determining the appropriate treatment for this client? Certainly most therapists would agree that further information-gathering about the woman's situation is necessary. But how does one go about assessment in a systematic manner so that the information obtained can lead to treatment decisions? In the current stage of the development of psychotherapy, the crucial work of selecting a treatment for a particular client is, unfortunately, frequently based on a combination of one of two factors: the diagnostic category into which the client's symptoms fall, and the theoretical predilections of the therapist. Thus, many therapists would diagnose this woman's problems as "agoraphobia," and, depending on their theoretical affiliation, they would select a treatment popularly acknowledged (within their affiliation group) to be effective with "agoraphobia."

THERAPEUTIC APPROACHES

The therapist trained in the Freudian psychoanalytic approach may see the woman as suffering from an unconscious conflict about sexuality; since sexual impulses may emerge by being exposed to the outside world, she reduces her anxiety by avoiding going outside. The analytic therapist would select intensive psychoanalysis to make this woman aware of her currently unconscious motivations as the therapy of choice. If the therapist is a medically-oriented psychiatrist, the physical components of the anxiety as well as the woman's suitability for medication will be thoroughly assessed, and the treatment of choice will probably center on medication to combat the anxiety keeping her in the house.

To those therapists trained in a Pavlovian classical conditioning approach, the woman is assumed to have had an anxiety-provoking experience out of the house. This has caused her to become conditioned to not only the specific stimuli associated with her trauma, but through stimulus generalization, to other situations occuring outside of the house. Such a therapist would recommend a counterconditioning procedure such as systematic desensitization or *in vivo* desensitization to treat this problem.

The therapist with a Skinnerian-operant approach to therapy may look for the reinforcers that keep this woman in the house. She may hate shopping and her phobia then would serve to help her avoid this unpleasant task; she may have a jealous husband who questions her in great detail after each trip out of the house in an aversive and punishing manner; or in combination with the Pavlovian explanation, she may be reinforced by the anxiety reduction that takes place by avoiding a situation that had previously been associated with anxiety. Thus the preferred treatment of a Skinnerian therapist would be a contingency-management program in which the woman was rewarded for going out of the house while not rewarded for remaining inside.

A cognitive therapist would be selectively interested in the woman's dysfunctional cognitions which maintain her fear and avoidance, and would treat her by attempting to change these cognitions to more functional ones. Therefore, a cognitive restructuring program would be instituted with this client.

On the other hand, the therapist with a social perspective may ask about the conditions outside of the house; this woman may live in a high-crime area. She may be at real physical risk by leaving the house since her neighborhood is replete with incidents of mugging and rape. This therapist then concentrates on concrete strategies the woman could use to increase her safety.

An eclectic therapist may choose some sort of treatment "package" for agoraphobia, including elements of most or all of the above mentioned treatments. Frequently this choice is made by searching the therapy literature for "agoraphobia treatments" and picking one with the greatest researched effectiveness. However, the therapy literature says very little about the *type* of person who will benefit most from a particular treatment, so this choice would be made independently of specific client characteristics other than symptomatology.

This case shows that there is not a single treatment for agoraphobia, since in psychopathology, unlike medicine, accurate diagnosis does not dictate treatment. In fact, we have seen cases of people who fit the diagnostic category of agoraphobia who have met each of the descriptions given above, and responded to the appropriate treatment. It is the role of the therapist to carefully assess the facts surrounding the specific case, and make a conceptualization of *what psychological process* is producing the symptomatic behavior. Only after an accurate conceptualization has been made can a treatment be effectively selected for an individual. The important question of how to conceptualize in terms that will lead to treatment decisions has been largely ignored. This book is an attempt to guide therapists in the essential task of conceptualization in psychotherapy. We shall briefly explore the historical pressures which have led to the failure to address conceptualization before explicating our approach.

The Problem of Therapeutic Schools

As the practice of psychotherapy enters its second century, a large number of therapeutic approaches have been established. The very fertility of the field threatens to impede its progress. We are exposed to a wide variety of approaches to treatment with each claiming superiority over the others. Although many of these approaches are based on important theories, there seem to be few attempts to define the limits of the theory. Instead, therapists identify with a given treatment technique, or set of techniques, and attempt to expand the area of applicability of these techniques. For example, reinforcement procedures were initially found to be powerful interventions of changing disruptive behavior of psychotic patients on hospital wards (e.g., Ullman & Krasner, 1965). Proponents of the operant approach then applied their therapeutic viewpoint to problems of weight control (Ferster, Nurnberger, & Levitt, 1962); smoking (Ober, 1968); depression (Lewinsohn, 1974; Lewinsohn & Atwood, 1969; Lewinsohn & Graf, 1973; Lewinsohn & Libet, 1972); and marital problems (Azrin, Naster, & Jones, 1973; Jacobsen & Margolin, 1979). Therapists who follow the cognitive approach, in a similar manner, try to expand their "domain." There are cognitive approaches to similar problems (e.g., Baucom, 1981; Beck, Rush, Shaw & Emery, 1979; Ellis, 1972, 1977a; Emery, Hollon, & Bedrosian 1981; Meichenbaum, 1977; Shaw & Beck, 1977).

Clinical research is often directed at obtaining data supporting the superiority of a given technique. Frequently, there is selectivity in the gathering of such data. Thus, in a process labeled "academic tribalism" by DiLoreto (1971), different "schools" of therapy have historically generated data supporting their beliefs (e.g., Bandura, Blanchard, & Ritter, 1969; Paul, 1966; Rogers, 1967; Sloane, Staples, Cristol, Yorkston, & Whipple, 1975). Such "comparative" research projects were not designed to elucidate, as much as to confirm what was already believed (e.g., that behavior therapy is superior to insight therapy).

In a review of outcome research in marital therapy, Beach and O'Leary (1985) state their opinion that such " 'horse race' comparisons [between different treatment approaches] could lead us to inappropriately discard therapeutic approaches which are valuable for some subgroup . . .

[p. 771]." We feel that this is indeed what has occurred with this approach to outcome research. Additionally, research *within* schools usually has not challenged the prevailing assumptions of the school. Research is typically published only in journals which share the theoretical predilections of the researcher. Therefore, different schools of therapy evolved with little or no thought as to how each might fit with other established schools. Practitioners often feel allegiance to a particular therapeutic tribe, and are likely to treat all their patients according to the lore and data of that modality (Kelly, 1961). London (1964) clearly articulates the dilemma produced by such a state of affairs:

> Now if this plentitude of treatments involved much variety of techniques to apply to different persons under different circumstances by different specialists, there would be no embarrassment of therapeutic riches here, just as there is not within the many specialties of medicine or law or engineering. But this is not the case. . . . One hardly goes to a psychoanalyst to be cured of anxiety and a nondirective therapist to be treated for homosexuality, as he might to a cardiologist for one condition and a radiologist for another. Nor does the same doctor use Freudian therapy for psychogenic ulcers and Rogerian treatment for functional headaches, as a physician might use medicine for one ailment and surgery for another. On the contrary, being a certain kind of psychotherapist has little bearing on treating a certain kind of problem, but refers rather to the likelihood of treating all problems from the vantage of a certain system [pp. 30–31].

The current state of psychotherapy is comparable to what Starr (1982) describes as the situation in medicine between 1850 and 1900. During this chaotic time, there were feuds between the allogenic and homeopathic schools of treatment. The homeopathic school believed that the body had natural healing mechanisms, such as fever, which medicines should promote, while the allogenic school felt that these processes were abnormal and should be suppressed. The theoretical convictions on both sides of the debate prevented each one from asking the question of, for example, under what circumstances is fever healing, and under what circumstances must it be controlled. Parenthetically, as is occurring in psychotherapy today, there were intense disputes during that tumultuous period regarding the necessary training and educational requirements for membership in the healing profession.

The Rise of Eclecticism

Recently, grumbling has been heard within the psychotherapeutic community, indicating dissatisfaction with a "schools" approach in treating clinical problems. Garfield and Kurtz (1974), in a survey of clinical psychologists, found that—compared to an earlier survey (Kelly, 1961)—fewer clinicians identified themselves exclusively with the psychoanalytic, neo-Freudian, or Sullivanian schools of therapy, and more were self-identified "eclectics." Therapists of many orientations have been confronted with the inadequacies of a narrow, monolithic approach to therapy (Franks, 1976; Goldfried, 1980; Goldfried & Padawer, 1982). This dissatisfaction has expressed itself in different forms.

Some therapists respond to the inadequacies of a narrow ideological stance by greatly broadening the techniques they are willing to use and the forms of behavior and experience they will investigate (e.g., Lazarus, 1970, 1981). Others advocate "rapprochement," attempts to identify the commonalities between different theoretical schools and to incorporate these commonalities into a new and improved therapeutic system (e.g., Goldfried, 1982; Marmor & Woods, 1980; Wachtel, 1977). Many of these innovative thinkers identify themselves as "eclectics," as do a surprisingly large number of practicing clinicians: 55% of those surveyed by Garfield and Kurtz (1974). There have been attempts at structuring the eclectic approach (e.g., Beutler, 1983; Dimond, Havens, & Jones, 1978; Goldstein & Stein, 1976). We view these moves as positive responses to the rigidity of the previous therapeutic *zeitgeist*. However, while the weakening of dogmatic schools is doubtless a positive occurrence, eclecticism without theoretical guidelines is incomplete.

One problem of eclecticism is that once the theoretical underpinnings of a "school" are taken away, leaving the practitioner with a purely pragmatic stance, the ability to understand and predict the effect of interventions can be attenuated. The clinician may be reduced to an attempt at matching a patient's diagnosis (e.g., "depression") to treatments for that disorder which have been reported in the psychotherapy literature (e.g., increasing reinforcement experiences, Lewinsohn, [1974]; attribution retraining, Abramson, Seligman, & Teasdale, [1978]; cognitive restructuring, Beck et al., [1979]). Such treatment reports tend to be technique-oriented without giving information on how to determine whether such an intervention would be appropriate in a given case (Meyer & Turkat, 1979). Although it is undoubtedly true that successful eclectic clinicians evolve their own "theory" (cf. Garfield & Kurtz, 1977), one can only speculate about the efficacy of those who are not capable of doing so. As Goldstein & Stein (1976) point out, it is a difficult task to develop and practice a "skilled eclecticism." Without the theoretical background provided by a school of therapy to guide them in making treatment decisions, eclectics must rely on trial and error, attempting to match a patient's disorder (e.g., "depression" or "phobia") with a treatment technique.

A second problem of eclecticism is actually one faced by all psychotherapy: What is the method for selecting treatments? Some therapists would recommend substantially similar treatments for all clients. As an example, traditional psychoanalysis may differ in content for different individuals, but would be the treatment of choice for all patients, according to some analysts. Even those who employ a variety of treatment techniques (such as behavior therapists) have failed to clearly state in what cases different techniques are to be used (Meyer & Turkat, 1979).

Eclecticism emphasizes freedom in the choice of treatments. While we agree with that concept, simply expanding our selection of treatment techniques still leaves us with the fundamental question: Under what conditions are we to use a given technique? In order to answer this question, it is important to first direct attention to the problem of conceptualization in psychotherapy. This book is a guide to *conceptualizing* clients' problems in the terms of established psychological principles. Its purpose is to help the therapist go beyond treatment by diagnosis or treatment by ideological predilection and instead, conceptualize cases in a manner which will generate effective points of intervention.

The strategy presented is idiographic because each case is analyzed individually, and treatments are designed to fit the particular person's problems. In this respect, it bears similarities to the behavior-analytic approach (Flasher, Maistro, & Turkat, in press; Meyer & Turkat, 1979; Turkat & Maisto, in press; Turkat & Meyer, 1982). Since the strategy is idiographic, we would assert that diagnosis per se should never dictate the treatment. The categorization of persons according to the third Diagnostic and Statistical Manual (DSM III) (American Psychiatric Association [APA], 1980) is of little help in guiding treatment, especially for non-psychotic disorders. At best, a DSM III diagnosis gives the therapist clues to what should be investigated closely during assessment. Although diagnosis has a function in aiding communication between professionals (Spitzer, 1975), the fact that a client meets the criteria for a certain diagnostic category should not, in itself, determine what treatment strategy should be taken. For example, depression is a disorder that is beginning to be viewed as a heterogeneous category (Beach, Abramson, & Levine, 1981). From our clinical experience, we have seen that some depressions are biological and respond to drugs or diet changes; some are related to boredom and respond to increasing environmental reinforcers; some depressions are related to cognitive deficits subsumed under "learned helplessness"; some are a result of dysfunctional handling of anger; some are manipulations of the environment; some are due to grief. It would obviously be foolish to treat these disparate problems—all correctly labeled "depression"—with a single treatment (e.g., antidepressant medication) and expect the same recovery pattern from each.

THE MODELS APPROACH

The systematic approach we propose for conceptualizing clinical cases we call the *models approach*. We define a *model,* as used in the context of psychotherapy, as a sufficient explanation of the data of a client's situation based on empirically tested psychological principles. A model is the *psychological mechanism* behind a particular symptom or set of symptoms. The model refers to the process by which a symptom is developed and maintained. In the following chapters we will discuss several models that we have found to be present (singly or multiply) in most clinical cases, and will demonstrate how conceptualizing these cases in terms of models guides the therapist to which interventions to use with which client.

The models we present are: the biological, which emphasizes the role of biological functioning upon behavior; the limited capacities, which emphasizes the match between what the person is capable of and the demands of the environment; the operant, which emphasizes the role of reinforcement upon the problem areas; the respondent, which views associations of experiences in the development and maintenance of problems; the cognitive, which looks at how thoughts and beliefs influence the person; and the social-context model, which emphasizes the effects of social forces on the individual. The models discussed in this book are intentionally broad in scope. They were chosen on the basis of their combined explanatory capability, in our experience, when applied to clinical cases, and on the basis of their empirical support. It is certainly true, however, that a models approach could be employed using different or more specific models. The concern is with the approach—i.e., systematically conceptualizing cases in terms of psychological principles—rather than the choice of a particular model.

Within the models approach, the task of assessment is to find which model fits the data of the case best to direct us in our intervention strategy. Thus, assessment and therapy become a process of testing hypotheses about what factors are maintaining the problem behaviors and what factors we as therapists can introduce to produce change.

A flowchart of the conceptual analysis approach to assessment and intervention within the models approach has been included. (See p. xii–xiii at the beginning of this volume.) It is designed to provide rough guidelines for the therapist in determining points of intervention. Although the order of assessment generally goes from internal determinants of behavior (i.e., the biological and limited-capacities models) to more situational determinants of behavior, the experienced therapist will often shorten the procedures. Frequently, the therapist will quickly pick up information that allow rapid assessment without systematically having to rule out alternative models. The flowchart should be used as a guideline for the development of conceptual hypotheses. Once a model has been hypothesized to be active in a given case, the therapist must look at the capacities of the client for change, in the direction dictated by the model. As an example, a client may be depressed because of a stressful and unrewarding job. The limited-capacities model would suggest that this stress be eliminated by finding a new job. However, the client may have limited options vocationally and may become even more depressed without a job. Often stressful situations represent the best available opportunity for individuals at some point in time. Once the model, the treatment goal, and the individual's capacities for change are determined, the flowchart points out some of the many therapeutic techniques available to achieve the therapeutic goals.

A model is initially chosen because it "fits" the data of the case relatively well and the data are congruent with the given model. The model then serves as a working hypothesis with which we collate further data and initiate intervention. Our original conceptualization of the problem is retained or changed to another model (working hypothesis) on the basis of the client's response to intervention, as well as on the basis of other data gathered. The best treatment in a particular case may be one commonly acknowledged to be effective with the diagnostic entity the person displays; or it may be a totally different treatment, depending on the model operating behind the set of exhibited symptoms.

Phobias, for example, are frequently treated by systematic desensitization, a counterconditioning technique with a demonstrated treatment effect. The classical conditioning model is the implicit model that is assumed when this treatment is used. The phobic object has become a conditioned stimulus for fear and avoidance. The models approach here would give theoretical reasons for using other treatment strategies, depending on the facts of a particular case. As in the case of agoraphobia presented previously, a number of phobias have strong operant components. The phobic behavior is being inadvertently reinforced. In such a case, unless the operant component of the problem is addressed and contingencies are changed, desensitization may work initially but not be stable. The models approach requires conceptualizing behaviors according to psychological principles rather than to diagnostic categories.

To have various psychological models in mind while performing the hypothesis-testing serves the very important purpose of preventing it from being a random process, directs assessment, and also serves as a guide which lets the therapist predict reactions to interventions. For example, conceptualizing a "phobia" as fitting an operant model (the phobic behavior is maintained by the consequences—such as attention and comfort—that it obtains for the individual) leads to specific predictions about what affects the problem behavior. It can be predicted that if the consequences of the phobic behavior are changed (for example, by the client's family giving love and attention only in the absence of phobic responses) then the phobia should decrease in intensity. The phobic behavior will be extinguished by withdrawing the factors that had been reinforcing and maintaining it.

However, we also know from operant psychology that there frequently are brief increases in a behavior—called "extinction bursts"—when reinforcement is withdrawn. Operant psychology also informs us that the more sources of reinforcement a person has in his environment, the less dependent he or she is on any one source (McDowell, 1982). In this case, we can put together these facts to predict that we should give the client other sources by which to obtain reinforcement besides acting fearful, and to inform the client's family to expect a temporary increase in the phobic behavior due to an extinction burst. If these conditions are met, then we can predict with reasonable certainty that the phobia can be eliminated through extinction and differential reinforcement. If there is no ameliorative effect of the operant intervention, it tells us that the operant model is not the correct psychological process behind the symptom constellation for this case.

In one case, a 4-year-old girl was having intense temper tantrums in which she hit her older sister and her mother as a way of getting attention. It was determined that the temper tantrums were an operant. A time-out procedure was set up by having the mother and the sister lock themselves in their rooms when she hit them. (The youngster wasn't isolated in her own room because she resisted being there, and getting and keeping her there required attention. Since time-out is a period of time without reinforcement, operant theory leads to the prediction that either having the child isolated from her sister and mother *or* having the sister and mother isolate themselves from the little girl would work equally well if attention was the reinforcer). Initially, as predicted, an extinction burst occurred and the behavior became worse. As also predicted by the operant model, after 1 week, the temper tantrums significantly decreased. The results were, in a way, a test of the hypothesis that the girl's temper tantrums were operant.

Conceptualizing in terms of models also helps the clinician by giving an explanation of the problem which can be shared with the client and which can help the client simply by putting the problem in a rational perspective. Therefore, the girl's parents were told how the temper tantrums were reinforced and why consistency was critical to avoid intermittent reinforcement. The explanation helps the parents justify the intervention.

The clinician should be careful not to become overly enamored of the search for a "perfect" model, one which fits all aspects of a case. The job of the clinician is to look for points of intervention.[1] By *point of intervention* we mean the condition surrounding the problem behavior which (1) is in the here and now; (2) we have the potential ability to change; and (3) if changed, will have a positive effect on the problem. The point of intervention should be that place in the behavioral sequence which, if changed, will maximize therapeutic change.

In the process of choosing a point of intervention, it is important to be realistic about the resources available. The choice of a point of intervention has nothing to do with "blame" and everything to do with pragmatism. As an example, in the case of children who are teased by their peers, it is usually necessary to change the teased child's behavior. Although some may claim that this smacks of "blaming the victim" (Ryan, 1971), the therapist cannot afford the indulgence of merely being correct. Although most of us would be in agreement that the victim's behavior does not warrant the abuse, it is of little service to simply attribute fault. The job of the clinician is to use points of intervention to help the teased child. It is usually the teased child who comes into therapy and not his persecutors. Choosing a point of intervention, then, involves finding that entry point into the behavior sequence which will give the maximum change and which we have a realistic possibility of changing. In some cases of teasing, entry into the school is possible and a different point of intervention becomes feasible: having school personnel warn and punish the persecutors.

It is frequently useful to talk about the *etiological* and *maintaining* models of a case as separate entities. An etiological model is that model which best fits the data at the time of the origin of the problem, whereas the maintaining model fits the current data surrounding the problem situation. Take an example of a male client with erectile failure. The assessment has determined that the problem began several years ago while taking a drug to control his hypertension. (Antihypertensives are known to cause erectile problems in some men.) Furthermore, the assessment informed us that his relationship with his wife was, at that time, quite good. Suppose that the current situation is different. He has now been off the antihypertensive agent for a year. However, his relationship with his wife has seriously deteriorated to the point that she is threatening him with divorce. He is experiencing a great deal of anger and resentment toward her. In this case, it appears that the etiological and maintaining models of this man's erectile dysfunction are probably different. Originally, the etiological model appears to be a biological one, in which a drug caused impotence in an otherwise well-functioning man. With the removal of the etiological factor and the addition of other variables, the

[1]Lee Sechrest, personal communication.

current data of the case no longer fit a biological model. They could, however, fit an operant model (in which case he might be punishing his wife by denying her sex), a cognitive one (in which negative thoughts and expectancies become self-fulfilling prophecies), or a respondent model (wherein anxiety has become conditioned to feelings of sexual arousal). Further detailed assessment—guided by the models mentioned above—would be required to determine which model(s) best fit the data.

It is also possible for the etiological and maintaining models to be the same. On the condition that the client's erectile problem started when he began an antihypertensive drug regime, and was still taking the medication when he came into therapy, both the etiological and maintaining models would appear to be biological. If an assessment turned up no other significant factors, it could be assumed that the etiological and maintaining models are the same.

Although the clinician is usually primarily concerned with fitting the current data to a maintaining model (because this process serves to clarify points at which direct intervention is possible), etiological models are helpful in giving the clinician data that can be used in choosing interventions. If the assessment determined that the etiological and maintaining models were different, knowledge of the etiology of the dysfunction guides the clinician in determining the intervention. Knowledge of the man's history with drug-induced impotence helps the clinician by supplying more data. If the man was never informed by his physician that the antihypertensives were likely to produce impotence (as is frequently the case), he may still harbor cognitions that he has "lost it," or that he's "over the hill." In addition to an intervention based on the maintaining model, a cognitive intervention of supplying the patient with accurate information about the etiology of his problem will be helpful. Knowing that the cause of his impotence was biological will help reduce personal feelings of inadequacy by changing the "responsibility" for the problem, and could lead to increased motivation for therapy. This knowledge can shift the burden of responsibility from oneself to the medication. Therefore, the impotent man would not blame himself for his problem.

Intervening to change the etiological factors themselves may be the preferable strategy in some cases (such as reducing the dose or changing medication in the case of the impotent man who was still on antihypertensive drugs when entering therapy). Often, it is not possible to change etiological factors, as when cases involve physical or psychological trauma. In other cases, the etiological model provides the therapist with points of intervention. When etiological factors have become maintaining factors, and are accessible to change, they should be prime targets of intervention.

A kindergarten teacher contacted us regarding an extremely aggressive child in her classroom. Observation of the child's classroom behavior showed that his aggression was not rewarded by undue attention or social gains. What was striking during the observation period was that the boy, who was from a family on welfare, wolfed down his food at snack time. It seemed to us that this youngster was hungry and irritable. Our first intervention, based on the facts fitting into a biological model (and the lack of fit with another model), was to allow him larger breakfast snacks each day to ensure that he was not hungry. His behavior improved when he was given more food. Although using reinforcement principles may have changed his behavior (as might play therapy or a Rogerian approach), the change could have been unstable unless the chronic etiological factor of hunger was addressed.

The data surrounding any clinical case may be complex enough to allow a good fit with more than one model. To employ the models approach most successfully in actual practice, the various models should not necessarily be seen as competing. Usually it is helpful conceptually to view a case in terms of as few models as necessary to adequately explain the major facts of the case. However, several different models may fit different aspects of a single problem, and all may be useful to the clinician. In the case of children who have "homework problems," there are often several models operating simultaneously. A child may be getting reinforced (usually by increased parental and teacher attention) for not completing his homework independently (the operant model). Concurrently, the child may have a learning or perceptual problem which makes the homework aversive (the limited-capacities model). At the same time, the child and the parents may be unaware of the power of stimulus-control procedures—such as having a quiet place used only for studying—in aiding study behavior (the respondent model). A clinician must address all of the psychological processes relevant to a particular case in order for change to occur and be maintained.

The chain of causality of a behavior will certainly include some influence of genetic and early experiential factors. However, the clinician should use the models as guidelines for finding places where change can be accomplished. It is impossible to change one's genetic or early history, but by knowing something about the contributory role of these factors, practical points of intervention may become perceptible. As an example, someone having difficulty with authority may trace it back to a relationship with his or her father. Knowing this by itself is of some, though limited, value. The person would still have to learn to recognize what is and what is not an appropriate expression of anger, how to recognize early signs of anger, and most importantly, how to express anger appropriately. As another example, there is the aforementioned case of the child with homework problems. While the etiological problem is frequently one of capacities (e.g., a learning disability), change can be accomplished in the present by addressing other models which may be contributing to the problem (the operant and respondent), or by addressing the etiological model as directly as one can in the present. In this case, special placement or individualized instruction plans may be necessary to aid the child in overcoming or coping with a disability. The assessment should look, using psychological models as a guide, for interventions which can be accomplished in the here and now.

A models conceptualization will ideally aid the clinician by providing appropriate assessment questions, treatment goals, and point of intervention. Although treatment goals are clearly the priorities of the client, the models approach may help the client understand what is feasible. For example, there are times the client should be aware that limited capacities exist that may interfere with a goal. A parent may want his or her child to be in an advanced class, while intellectual testing may indicate the child would be better in a regular classroom placement.

Our intention in this book is to delineate a system for conceptualizing clinical cases and guiding treatment decisions. We do not intend this to be a sourcebook on assessment or therapy techniques, as there are many good texts on these subjects. Such techniques are mentioned but are not, in most cases, explicated fully. Additionally, as the various models are discussed, we touch on large bodies of psychological data. We do not intend to perform the herculean task of reviewing and evaluating all psychological evidence having to do with biological factors, operant conditioning, respondent conditioning, limited capacities, cognition, and social learning. It is our intention to demonstrate how a selective application of basic and applied psychological knowledge in these areas can benefit the psychotherapy process. We now discuss some general issues of therapy which transcend the models approach.

DEFINITION OF THERAPY

We define *psychotherapy* as the deliberate and conscious use of psychological technology to treat emotional distress or loss of adequate functioning. We stress the "technology" part of the definition because that is what separates our professional abilities from the often quite real help which is given by the friends and relatives of a troubled person. It is important to know the psychological technology and to keep active in both its development and consumption. In many respects, the craft of psychotherapy is similar to the craft of engineering; we must apply the knowledge of our basic field to the real-life problems that people present to us. Just as engineers utilize knowledge derived from the basic sciences of physics, chemistry, and geology in order to solve practical problems, clinicians need to be acquainted with basic information concerning human functioning, culled from the fields of physiological psychology, perception, cognitive science, social psychology, and abnormal psychology, in order to aid clients with their problems in living.

Thus, it is not enough to only know the techniques of intervention. In order to adequately perform a models conceptualization, one must be familiar with tenets of basic psychology. Throughout this book we have attempted to bring principles of experimental, social, physiological, and developmental psychology to bear on clinical problems.

The tools available include the principles of operant psychology, particularly in the assessment of what is reinforcing a behavior and how to change contingencies; the principles of respondent or Pavlovian psychology; a variety of approaches from cognitive psychology, particularly concerning the development of standards and in the use of the "Blank Trials Law" in problem solving. Feedback from a credible source is an extremely valuable tool in our kit. There should be an awareness of theories of perception, especially adaptation-level theory, in that the judgment of an event is influenced by the standard used for comparison; we should know ethology enough to know that cues people emit influence how others respond to them; we should know a wide variety of motivational theories; we should have familiarity with economic theory and be capable of aiding clients in placing their problem in a sociological perspective when appropriate; and, quite importantly, have an awareness of the profound influences that biological factors have on behavior. Each of these are discussed at greater length in succeeding chapters. We should also have enough life experience to have common sense to help people. This, of course, does not require an advanced degree, but there are times when common sense transcends all technical knowledge.

THE TECHNOLOGY OF INTERVENTION

Once we have determined points of intervention to reach treatment goals, it is necessary to decide on techniques of intervention which will be effective in achieving these goals. It is important that allegiances to certain types of techniques not restrict the resources viewed as "appropriate" interventions. Thus, if a models analysis has determined that a child's temper tantrums fit an operant model (that is, they are maintained by the results obtained for the child), the treatment goal is to rearrange the contingencies operating in the child's life so that tantrums are no longer so rewarding, and so that other activities are more rewarding. Theoretically, there is no one intervention technique which is necessarily superior over another in accomplishing this. Contingencies could be rearranged by using a token economy to reward the absence of tantrums, by punishing the tantrums, by rewarding appropriate assertion, or by rearranging parental attention so it is not contingent on misbehavior. The details of the treatment will be determined by the specifics of the case.

The important point, however, is that once a treatment goal is determined, the appropriateness of various treatment techniques becomes readily apparent. There is nothing sacred about a particular technique since techniques are only the tools used to achieve goals. As London (1964) said, "the same theory may suggest several techniques and a single technique be deduced from many theories [p. 32]." It is the appropriateness of the selection of a technique in a given situation which determines efficacy, not some inherent quality of the technique alone.

The models conceptualization should make clear what a treatment goal is to be. At that point, a treatment technique may be selected from among the many which abound in the literature, or a treatment may be specially designed to fit a particular client's situation. It must be pointed out that, although conceptualization skills are essential in psychotherapy, techniques must also be applied skillfully, and we should not underplay the importance of learning a given technique well. Many techniques (e.g., those of cognitive therapy) take a long time to be mastered. No technique, however skillfully applied, is going to be effective without a valid conceptualization of the case.

Any factor affecting the behavior of people which may have a role in malfunctioning is potentially part of our technology. Since the range of what affects behavior is so vast, it is obviously beyond the scope of any one therapist to know all aspects of this technology. We should know enough to make referrals to physicians, lawyers, vocational counselors, or others when appropriate. However, there is available a powerful psychological technology, of which we should be in sufficient command to be able to utilize for behavioral or emotional change. It is important to be aware that our technology represents tools that can be used to reduce suffering. There is no sympathy for those who claim to be strict adherents to one tool over another, because it is felt the use of tools must be determined by the characteristics of the problem. Certainly all craftsmen develop preferences for certain tools because of familiarity with the tool or a history of success with them. It is hard to imagine any plumber, for example, trying to use his favorite screwdriver to unplug a toilet. We must know when to use which tool. As Maslow (1966) pointed out, if the only tool a person has is a hammer, everything is likely to be treated as a nail.

CREATING A THERAPEUTIC CLIMATE

Before we are able to apply a models approach to the dynamics of a case, our knowledge of psychological principles must be used to maximize the atmosphere of comfort, trust, honesty, and work orientation between the client and therapist. It is widely believed that if a good therapeutic relationship is absent, therapy does not occur or is seriously compromised (e.g., Frank, 1961; Goldfried & Padawer, 1982; Rogers, 1951; Snyder, 1961). What are the essentials of the therapeutic relationship?

The Therapeutic Alliance

The nature of the therapeutic alliance should be defined in the first session. The client must understand that therapy involves effort and that it involves changing oneself. All too often, people enter therapy believing it to be a process where support is given for living in a cruel and unfair world. Frequently clients expect unconditional approval for whatever nonfunctional behavior they exhibit. Invariably, therapy must address change of these nonfunctional behaviors. Some schools of therapy (the nondirective and the "insight" schools,) will let the client determine the rate of change. The findings on learning without awareness showed that those subjects who were aware of the reward contingencies they were operating under revealed much greater learning (Hilgard & Bower, 1975). We advocate giving a clear agenda to the client as early in therapy as possible. By setting the rules and expectations early on, the therapy process should be accelerated.

For example, upon entering therapy, one woman presented her difficulties as being caused by her role as a giving person in a cruel world. She related several situations in which, despite her kindness, people consistently took advantage of her. She was involved in a variety of radical causes and could not comprehend how people she yearned to help could attack her. She volunteered to work in a reform school for girls. At one point soon after she began working there, the girls decided to play "under the mill" with her. This game required that she go through the residents' legs while they beat on her backside. She was, of course, very hurt that they responded to her altruistic motives as if she were just another uncaring person.

As she told these stories, it was apparent that she desperately wanted the therapist to say, "Isn't it awful that such a giving person as you should be treated so cruelly by our society." However, what was said was, "We have to begin work on changing your behavior which leads people to respond to you as a victim." Her response was a stunned silence, after which she started crying. She subsequently did extremely well in therapy, becoming appropriately assertive and not allowing herself to be treated like a doormat. One of the reasons for her improvement, was the message she was given that she had control over her situation. She found that the response of people to her was, to a large degree, something which she could change. It is important that the client leave the first session with this information. It is becoming apparent that feeling "in control" is an important aspect of psychological well-being (e.g., the areas of learned helplessness [Abramson et al., 1978] and locus of control [Rotter, 1966]). Increasing clients' perception of control of their environment, therefore, is an important goal of therapy.

By setting the terms of the therapeutic alliance early (preferably during the first session), the client does not feel betrayed when change is required later on. We have made this mistake and seen clients act as if we had violated a contract when we pointed out areas that they needed to change. It is as if we had endorsed inappropriate behavior by not directing attention to it. As is known from the Blank Trials Law (which will be explicated more fully in the next section), no feedback is frequently taken by people as confirmation that their behavior is correct.

It is important that the expectation on the part of the client that therapy is hard work be set as a standard as early as possible (See the discussion of adaptation-level theory in chapter 6). Although it is difficult to isolate the essential ingredients of the therapeutic alliance, the client must perceive that the therapist is on the client's side. As vividly illustrated by the nondirective approach, a completely nonjudgmental, nonevaluative atmosphere may be necessary for therapy to occur. The therapist cannot sit and evaluate whether the client is a "good" or "bad" person, but must communicate an attitude of positive regard for the client. This must be distinguished from communicating an attitude of acceptance of problematic behavior, which the therapist does not want to do.

The client also contributes to the therapeutic relationship and the client must be motivated to change. Sometimes clients are "assigned" to therapy by the courts or are in therapy to assuage the feelings of someone else such as a parent or spouse. These involuntary or semivoluntary clients may prevent the relationship from developing and thereby prevent therapy from occurring. Therapy requires an alliance whereby the therapist and the client are congruent in the direction the client is seeking. In our experience, the absence of a therapeutic alliance often means the absence of therapy. We have found it considerably more efficient to discuss these issues immediately rather than waiting to "seduce" the client into wanting therapy.

For example, one sixteen year old youth was reluctantly brought into therapy by his parents because of a pattern of acting-out behavior which lead him into contact with the law. Prior to the initial session, he had stated his motivation for therapy by informing his parents that he "didn't want to see no asshole shrinks." When this was brought up in the first session, we immediately asked the parents to leave and discussed this with him. Our response was to point out his history of problems, the personal cost to him, and the clear fact that therapy would be a waste of our time, and his time and money if he were not willing to work. It was further pointed out to him that therapy would require hard work; that changing oneself is very difficult and could not occur without effort. Finally, we suggested that he might be able to work with us even if we were "asshole shrinks." Given these options set under his control, the therapeutic alliance was quite secure and we began work.

These issues of definition of therapeutic goals and the ways to meet the goals should be candidly discussed very early in therapy. The initial treatment plan will be incomplete and sometimes incorrect, but the fact that therapy involves a commitment to work and to change and general approaches should be openly discussed in the first session. In one instance, a professional married man with chronic anxiety stated that a variety of people and events were hassles for him. He stated that he couldn't trust his wife and became very irritated when she violated rules he had set up, such as her drinking "his" beer. He explained that he bought her her own supply of beer so that she would leave his supply intact. He said that although he loved his wife and she was wonderful, he was planning to leave her because his goal was to streamline his life by eliminating all hassles. His goal was directly challenged by our statement, "One of the objectives we will work toward in therapy will be for you to handle differences without experiencing them as hassles." We then discussed the implications of the goal in an open manner early in therapy. Rate of timing of interventions will be determined by the client's rate of assimilation.

Feedback from a Credible Source

In a series of classic experiments in problem solving, Marvin Levine has shown that, in the absence of feedback, people act as if their approaches to problems are the correct ones (M. Levine, Leitenberg, & Richter, 1964; M. Levine, 1966, 1971). He called this the "Blank Trials Law." The implications of the Blank Trials Law for human functioning are enormous. Due to the prevailing attitude in our society that personal criticism should be avoided, individuals who behave in nonproductive, offensive ways frequently do not receive feedback on their actions. According to the Blank Trials Law, these people can believe that their nonproductive behavior is socially correct. In the absence of feedback, they believe that their solutions to problems are perfectly adequate. When given feedback, their performance improves. For therapists, the problem lies in creating a climate in which the therapist is a credible source of such feedback.

The attitude change literature has shown that credibility has several important components. Two that are generally thought to be especially potent are the perceived expertness and trustworthiness of the persuader (e.g., Aronson, Turner, & Carlsmith, 1963; Cohen, 1964; Kelman, 1961;

Mehrabian & Williams, 1969). Certainly, there is a mystique about the therapist by virtue of advanced degrees and position of wisdom, which gives credibility. However, that is clearly not enough. The therapist must demonstrate that, in addition to listening and understanding the client, he or she has suggestions and recommendations that are helpful and make sense to the client. The therapist must show an understanding of the client's position which is more useful than the client's own ideas. The therapist must help the client find a way out of the client's dilemma which is not apparent to the client. Beutler, Johnson, Neville, Elkins, & Jobe (1975) demonstrated that therapist credibility did have an effect on the outcome of therapy.

Safe Haven

One reason the therapeutic relationship is therapeutic may be its function for the client as a safe haven. The therapeutic climate of acceptance can provide conditions under which the client is able to explore previously feared aspects of his or her life or experiment with new behaviors while feeling in a secure atmosphere.

Exploratory behavior of both humans and monkeys has been shown to increase when there is a safe haven to which they can return. Ainsworth and Bell (1970) found that the presence of a 1-year-old child's mother in a novel environment increased exploration greatly over what it was when the child was alone in the new setting. Additionally, the presence of the mother inhibited crying and other indices of hyperemotionality in the babies.

Harlow and his associates (Harlow & Suomi, 1970; Harlow & Zimmerman, 1959) found that a surrogate terry-cloth mother of rhesus monkeys served the same function for rhesus infants. In their famous series of experiments investigating infant monkey's behavior when raised apart from their natural mothers and given inanimate wire or cloth surrogates instead, the investigators found that the infants responded to the cloth surrogate with a great deal of emotionality and attachment behavior. Harlow and his associates found that the cloth surrogate gave the infant a sense of security and that the surrogate's presence enabled the infant to explore and play. The sense of security imparted to the infant from the cloth surrogate was also great enough for the infant, after contact with the cloth mother, to investigate and attack a stimulus designed to be fear provoking. Within the therapy situation, the importance of a secure therapeutic relationship in providing a catalyst for patient change has been investigated. Rogers (1961, 1967) reports research which shows that clients' perceptions of a therapist's acceptance, genuineness, and understanding were positively related to therapeutic change.

These citations from the human and animal literature concerning the role of a secure relationship in facilitating exploration and adaptive behavior should not be taken to mean that the therapist/client relationship should be a static, dependent one. On the contrary, there are findings in the developmental literature indicating the function of a "safe-haven" relationship in the achievement of independence and competence. Hay (1977) investigated the function of 9- to 12-month-old human infants following their adult companions. She found that infants following adults could function as a form of exploration. The infants were more likely to independently explore an environment similar to one they had previously explored while following an adult, than if they had never had such experience. Thus, having a safe base can actually facilitate growth and exploration, rather than foster dependence.

The therapist, by providing an accepting safe haven for the client, can help the client explore and try out new behaviors without fear of disapproval. The client can either attempt these explorations in the "real world" and return to the therapist with a progress report, or the therapist and client can go through a "dry run" of novel or feared situations in the office, employing the techniques of role-playing or systematic desensitization. These explorations can in turn help the client improve functioning and achieve independence from the therapist.

WHO NEEDS THERAPY?

Because of the fashionable nature of psychotherapy among the upper and middle classes, and because third-party payments have made the costs of psychotherapy within the budget of the motivated, it is important that we try to deploy our therapeutic resources where they are of highest social value. Psychotherapy should be provided to those who need it. Despite the apparent obviousness of that statement, it is difficult to tell someone who is asking for help that it is unnecessary. This difficulty is compounded by contingencies of the therapist. That is, the therapist also has financial and emotional needs that are satisfied by the client. Schofield (1964) asked social workers, psychologists, and psychiatrists to describe their "ideal patient." They described a young, attractive, verbal, intelligent and successful person. Schofield coined the acronym "YAVIS" to refer to this type of preferred consumer of psychotherapy. It is easy to restrict one's practice to the YAVIS clientele. They are more pleasant to work with and can afford to pay the bill. However, that is not enough social justification for therapy.

Therapy should be provided for those with nonfunctional syndromes which are crippling their lives. In our experience, it is difficult to get qualified psychotherapists to work in institutions and clinics where the client population is often very slow to respond to the services offered and where the therapeutic technology is simply inadequate to deal with the enormity of the problems. Psychosis has generally been refractory to psychological interventions (O'Leary & Wilson, 1975; Rachman & Wilson, 1980), and many therapists find it frustrating to work with psychotic populations. However, many behavioral programs can produce changes in psychotic patients' functioning.

In addition, therapy should be provided to those people who have characteristic *patterns* of maladaptive behavior or emotional distress which compromise their lives. The word "patterns" is emphasized because there is a functional difference between an incident and a pattern. Most people will experience a number of incidents of depression or anxiety and sometimes these occur without apparent reason. However, most of these incidents are self-limiting and will respond well with time. Incidents are also often situation-specific while patterns of problems occur in widely different situations. This is important for assessment. The recommendation of therapy has the connotation that the person is "sick" and in need of treatment. Telling people that the discomfort they are experiencing is natural and within reasonable limits is often considerably more therapeutic than treatment.

For example, a young man came to us complaining about sleepless nights and frequent moments of intense despair. His 25-year-old wife had just died after a gruesome yearlong battle with cancer, leaving him with two children to raise. In addition, his wife's parents were trying to get custody of the older child who was from a previous marriage. After assessment of his style and range of coping with these real and very intense problems indicated that his patterns of coping were clearly adaptive, he was told his reaction was a perfectly understandable and predictable one under the circumstances. He did not need therapy but needed time to grieve and to be relieved from stress. A follow-up phone call indicated that the intensity of the client's emotional response was diminishing and he was feeling more comfortable. The important point in determining whether therapy was called for was whether his response was part of a pattern of despair or whether it was an appropriate response to the situation. This particular client felt relieved when he was pronounced "normal."

The people who would benefit most from therapy are highly motivated people seeking changes in patterns in their lives. The areas of malfunction tend to center around, as Freud put it, *Lieben und Arbeit* (love and work). The personal cost of a life without intimacy, without closeness, without giving and getting support and love from others is immeasurable. The cost of losing jobs and fearing responsibility can also be crippling. Certainly these statements are value judgments; there are people who prefer to avoid closeness and there are those who decide that responsibility is a silly burden. We are referring here to those who desire intimacy and success, yet who have developed patterns which prevent the achievement of these goals. Therapy should be addressed to changing the patterns which prevent satisfaction in the areas of *Lieben und Arbeit*.

2 The Biological Model

Most, if not all, maladaptive lifestyles can be caused by biological factors. Hypoglycemia, a metabolic condition of low blood sugar, can produce symptoms virtually indistinguishable from an anxiety attack, allergies can cause depression, drugs certainly can cause patterns of behavior parallel to psychosis. It is difficult to demonstrate social skills when one is in pain from an ulcer just as it is difficult to develop intimacy with someone who is in intense pain. In most cases the therapist sees, there is not a strong biological component. We chose to place the biological model first, however, to reflect our belief that it should be the first model considered in the clinical assessment process. If the behavioral problem were caused by biological factors and this were missed, therapy would needlessly prolong discomfort.

ASSESSMENT

The clinician should be alert to biological problems as early in the therapy process as possible. If a biological problem is causing the psychological complaints, it may be possible to intervene directly with the biological problem and eliminate or greatly reduce the need for psychological assistance. In addition, the biological problem could also be life-threatening. We have been aware of cases in which cardiac problems were treated as anxiety, and brain tumors causing behavioral problems were not detected while the behavior problem was being treated. There is considerable overlap between physical and psychological problems. It has been shown in a recent study that about 9% of psychiatric outpatients had a medical problem which was causing their psychiatric symptoms, while about 30% of medically ill patients display some psychopathology (Martin, 1983). The issue of physical ailments being involved in emotional/behavioral problems needs to be addressed. As indicated in the flowchart (p. xii–xiii), the assessment question in the biological model is: Is the problem physical in origin?

It is impossible for the nonmedical therapist to be able to diagnose the vast array of biologically determined emotional or behavioral responses. As is the case with all models, however, the more factual information a therapist has at his or her disposal, the more effectively can the possibility of a biological model be recognized. For this reason, later in this chapter we will review some common biological problems which may manifest themselves as psychological dysfunctions. In general, though, a nonmedical therapist must be conservative in order to avoid mistakes in misdiagnosing physical problems.

A good general rule is that bodily complaints may have biological causes unless a psychological model clearly fits better. When we say a model "fits better" than other models, we are saying that this model provides the best explanation of the facts of the client's distress. That model must be consistent with more of the behaviors and circumstances of the client than alternative models in order for us to say it "fits." For example, anxiety certainly can have biological mediators. If, though, the anxiety is seen only when the person is taking an exam or only when going on a date, it is extremely improbable that this is biologically determined; the symptoms seem related to psychological rather than biological variables. In other words, a psychological model fits better. When in doubt it is wiser to seek medical evaluation.

Another general rule is for the biological model to be investigated thoroughly when psychological interventions are not working. Most depressions are amenable to psychological intervention. However, biological factors do contribute to some and cause others. When psychological models have been tested and eliminated, the therapist should be aware of the possibility of biological factors as causal agents. The following is a firsthand account of a graduate psychology student's hypoglycemic depression:

I have not been a person who typically responds to stress by becoming depressed or unhappy. I have experienced many life events that were extremely stressful but was always capable of handling them with a minimum of anxiety and unhappiness. Thus when I began to experience short periods of anxiety and sadness in my third year of graduate school I searched my environment for reasons that would explain the depression. Aside from the fact that I was in graduate school geographically separated from my husband, I could identify no other situational factors. However, I had been in graduate school, living away from my husband for 3 years; why the depression and anxiety now? Within a month of the onset of the symptoms, my depression deepened. I had overwhelming feelings of sadness, unconnected to any situational event. In other words, I was not sad *about* anything, I was simply overwhelmingly utterly sad. I experienced suicidal thoughts frequently revolving around my wish not to experience this sadness any longer. During my deepest depression, I lay in bed all day, staring at the furnishings in my apartment, simply wanting to die. I made no suicide attempts because I could not arouse myself long enough to sustain the effort. I experienced perceptional distortions as well. Bright lights and unusual sounds bothered me tremendously. I felt as if someone had turned the screws a little too tight! In addition, prior to the onset of the depressive symptoms, I had experienced several nightly episodes of uncontrollable muscle spasms, racing violent thoughts and tachycardia. As my depression and anxiety worsened, my physical symptoms became more frequent. However, I had noticed that having some fruit juice generally helped relieve the symptoms. Finally, I consulted a psychologically astute physician who told me he suspected hypoglycemia. That, he said, would explain my physical symptoms (the muscle spasms and tachycardia are caused when a release of epinephrine is triggered by low blood-sugar levels) and the relief I experienced after drinking fruit juice. A 6 hour glucose tolerance test confirmed an acute case of reactive hypoglycemia. I am now on a diet free of all simple sugars and rich in protein and complex carbohydrates. Within 3 weeks, I noticed an improvement. My depression, anxiety has dissipated and I have had no recurrence of the physical symptoms in 4 months. I feel cheerful again and capable of handling my life. However, at times when I become overly anxious or tired, or when I haven't eaten in 4 hours, I notice the depression returning. A good meal and 20 minutes of relaxation exercises relieve the symptoms.

As stated previously, an important part of the assessment of whether a given pathological behavior is biological or not is accomplished by a process of exclusion. Often we cannot find a psychological model which fits the behavioral pattern. The depressions of the graduate student were not related either to antecedent conditions or to consequences of the depression. There were no precipitating life events which were nearly in proportion to the intensity of the response of severe, sometimes suicidal depression. There was no evidence of a previous pattern of cyclical depression. Indeed, her life history was one of strong coping skills which had allowed her to handle both the stress of graduate school and the stress of separation from her husband. Although it may be argued that these stresses would have a cumulative effect, the rather rapid onset and the intensity of the depression makes this seem less likely.

Other psychological models that will be covered in this book did not seem to fit. She had accurate information and standards about important areas in her life, so the cognitive model did not appear to be applicable. In fact, the student was able to perceive that a cognitive model was not of use in explaining her situation. (Of course, if she *were* having problems with cognitive distortions, she may not have been able to realize the nature of her problem.) Having ruled out common psychological models which could account for her problems, the model of best fit was the biological. In the absence of a relatively clean psychological model that can explain and predict the behavior, the therapist should be careful to assess for biological causes, especially when somatic symptoms are present.

The usefulness of the biological model often lies in indicating behavioral interventions which take biology into account. Many times biological interventions are not possible although the etiology of a disorder may well be, at least in part, biological. As indicated in the flow chart, other models may, and often are, operating even when a biological model is well established. It is important to know, for example, the client's attitudes and feelings towards the biological factor. There are times when these cognitive factors are very important.

SUBTLE BIOLOGICAL EFFECTS ON BEHAVIOR

There are some psychological disorders which are largely or totally biological in nature. These will be covered later in this chapter. There are also more subtle physical factors which can contribute to psychological problems and which, because of their relative subtlety, the clinician may fail to check out. The two factors we have found especially pertinent in clinical practice are temperament and a group of biological stressors we call "biological irritants."

Temperament

Thomas, Chess, and Birch (1968, 1970) produced evidence that children display individual differences in temperament which emerge during the first few weeks of life and tend to persist over the years. These differences, because they appear so early, may be seen as at least partially biological in nature. For this reason, their study illustrates a particularly useful way to employ biological information clinically. Thomas et al. obtained behavioral information on 141 subjects over a period of years. Although the investigators found that 35% of the children could not be categorized, they were successful in grouping the remaining 65% into three persistent behavioral types. They categorized these children as "easy," "slow to warm up," or "difficult." These categorizations were made on the basis of a 9-point classification system. The points that differentiated the types most clearly were mood, adaptability, intensity of reaction, regularity of bodily processes, and whether the child typically approached or withdrew from novel situations. The broad "personality types" extracted from the behavioral information appeared to have external validity, since in the course of the longitudinal investigation 70% of the "difficult" children developed behavior problems, whereas only 18% of the "easy" children did so. These authors concluded that there are persistent patterns of temperament that are biologically determined and that these patterns are discernable very early in life.

Thomas et al. (1970) make some suggestions for practical applications of their findings: *biological* information can help direct *behavioral* intervention. These authors advise parents that while "easy" children may not require special attention to avoid serious problems, "difficult" children demand much consistency on the part of the parents. "Difficult" children may require more persistence and imagination from their parents, and parents (and clinicians) should be aware of that fact. The authors also point out that the children labeled "slow to warm up" needed a delicate balance of encouragement to try new things and understanding that they must progress at their own pace. In general, Thomas et al.'s investigation demonstrates the potential usefulness of biological information for assessment and intervention. The point here for the psychotherapist is to work with biology, and not to deny biological influences.

Biological Irritants

As part of the assessment process, a therapist should attempt to get a good, detailed description of the client's living patterns. Factors such as sleep and work schedules, diet, exercise, or the presence of chronic physical or emotional stressors can act to exacerbate or cause psychological problems. These "biological irritants" have the effect of lowering the threshold of irritation or stress of the person in a manner that increases vulnerability to common stressors often difficult to avoid. The irritants themselves are not the problem, but they leave the client selectively vulnerable.

Fatigue. Most people are aware that even mild sleep deprivation can lead to decreases in alertness and performance. However, simply changing a person's timing of sleeping without altering the amount of sleep can have detrimental effects. There is some evidence to indicate that workers who work rotating shifts (sometimes working at night, sometimes during the day) have more health problems than those who have regular schedules (Luce, 1971). The lifespans of mice have been shortened in the laboratory simply by inverting their light-dark cycles once a week. People also show individual differences in their daily periods of best functioning, with some working best in the morning, others after midnight. A client who complains of problems concentrating on the job may be attempting to work against biology. Finding a job which demands alertness during a period of the day synchronous with that person's time of optimal functioning may alleviate many problems. Sleep deprivation has been found to increase irritability while decreasing work productivity (Foulkes, 1966). This clearly sets the stage for further problems.

Knowing the client's capacity for fatigue (the concept of limited capacities will be more fully developed in Chapter 3) may help in programming the timing of treatment interventions. For example, many working people come home from a hard day's work and they simply need time to relax and unwind before they are able to meet any domestic responsibilities. While they are fatigued, they will have a reduced threshold for irritation and tasks requiring cooperation will be doomed until after a rest period.

Children also are susceptible to fatigue (perhaps even more so than adults). Goodenough (1931) found that temper tantrums occurred consistently during times when children were tired, such as just before nap or bedtime. We see many marital cases in which the partners have their biggest arguments before dinner. Often, both partners are tired and hungry and they try to discuss differences at that time. Adults may not throw temper tantrums, but their threshold for irritation may be low when they are tired and hungry. We advise these couples to discuss differences after dinner.

Diet.   Hunger as a biological irritant can clearly decrease the threshold for anger. Certain diets are also reported to have the same effect. One of the most dramatic examples we have seen of behavior change related to diet is one that occurred in an 8-year-old with uncontrollable seizures who was put on the ketogenic diet. The ketogenic diet is a severely restricted diet with large amounts of fats to turn the body more acidic. The youngsters' behavior could not be controlled at home or in school by anyone. The principal had war stories of how resistant this youngster was to discipline. When the youngster was sent to the principal, she was entirely unaffected. She continued to disobey and be aggressively defiant by doing things that did not endear her to the authorities, such as kicking the principal. Although this may have endeared the girl to some of the teachers, her behavior was a major problem for both her parents and her classroom teacher. Not only did this diet control her seizures, but the youngster was simply a different child in terms of temperament. She became warm, friendly, and cooperative. Her tested IQ went up 15 points. Although the ketogenic diet is quite extreme (and could not be maintained for this youngster) it illustrates the profound potential that diet can have in anger control. The clinician should look for diet extremes, or sometimes for possible allergic reactions to food.

Some clients are on weight-loss diets which simple leave them hungry all the time. One such client described herself as always being a fat girl until the age of eighteen. She lost weight successfully on a diet which led to her becoming glamorously thin. Her life changed in the way many obese people fantasize but seldom achieve: she married a very wealthy, attractive, and kind man. However, she was chronically irritable. The marriage ended, for this and other reasons, and she still pursued the thin life. At forty, her mood was still irritable and anxious.

The assessment for the appropriate model was very difficult because the effects of being on a sustained diet are not very frequently seen in therapy. Essentially, this hypothesis was arrived at by a process of elimination. The information that was obtained while investigating the client's history seemed applicable to her current problem of irritability. We attributed at least part of this to her being hungry all the time. Although she chose to be hungry, her knowledge that this was related to her mood took some of the edge off her irritability. It is difficult to simultaneously maintain an artificially low weight and obtain enough nutrition. Additionally, it has been suggested that people differ in their "set point" or natural weight level (Nisbett, 1972) and that attempts to lower weight below this point lead to behavior similar to that of a starving person (Wooley, Wooley, & Dyrenforth, 1979).

General nutrition influences psychological processes profoundly. It is well documented that starvation has profound detrimental effects on psychological functioning (Brozek, 1955; Keys, Brozek, Henschela, Michelson, & Taylor, 1951). Weinberg, Mandel, and Miller (1979) reported on the change in MMPI scores which came about during the semistarvation experiments of the 1940s. At the outset, all subjects had normal scores, but by the end of the period of food restriction, they showed MMPI profiles resembling hypochondriacs, depressives, and hysterics. Sterner and Price (1973) showed that prolonged dietary B-vitamin restriction produced significant change in 5 subscales of the MMPI (hypochrondiasis, depression, hysteria, psychopathy, and hypomania). Significantly, these changes did not reverse rapidly during a repletion period. These changes occurred in the absence of clinical physical deficiency symptomatology; that is, psychological effects occurred before any medical ill effects were noticeable. Weinberg et al. found a significant relationship between nutritional factors and specific MMPI subscales in psychiatric inpatients, psychiatric outpatients, and normals.

Several investigators have pointed to the role of allergies in producing behavioral problems (King, 1980). Feingold (1973) reports that the syndromes of fatigue, listlessness, irritability, and behavior disturbances may indicate allergy problems in children. Feingold also believes the behavioral syndrome usually referred to as hyperactivity is an allergic reaction, mainly to synthetic flavors and colors in food, and recommends a diet free of these additives for children who display hyperactivity. Such allergic reactions are not restricted to children. Feingold reports a case history of a 40-year-old woman who had been under psychiatric care for 2 years for her problems of hostility and inability to hold a job. After going on an additive-free diet, her psychological complaints totally left.

Strickland (1979) reports allergic reactions to common food items or environmental pollutants mimicking severe psychological symptoms such as suicidal ideation, bursting into tears, or hearing voices. Ossofsky

(1976) recruited 96 children and adults who were referred for depression and tested them for allergy as well, whether they showed allergic symptoms or not. Ninety-three of these were shown to be allergic. In a single reversal design, O'Banion, Armstrong, Cummings, and Stange, (1978) showed dramatic increases in disruptive behavior as a consequence of ingestion of foods such as wheat, corn, tomatoes, sugar, mushrooms, and dairy products in an 8-year-old autistic boy.

Fitness Level. Exercise, especially aerobic exercise, has been implicated in enhancing general well-being and psychological adjustment (Bailey, 1977; Cooper, 1968; Young & Ismail, 1978). Regular exercise has been shown to increase people's sense of personal worth and physical self-image (Hoiberg, 1978; McNamara, 1978). There are data suggesting the positive effects of exercise on postpartum adjustment (Dargis, 1978), frequency of sexual behavior in older males (Katzman, 1977) and alleviation of tension, depression, and listlessness in the elderly (Tredway, 1978). Clinically, we have used exercise as part of a treatment program for some depressed clients with success. Several investigators are now using aerobic exercise as a treatment for depression, with reports of moderate to good success rates (Brown, 1978; Higdon, 1978). Since exercise makes people stronger, it seems plausible that exercise will increase tolerance for stress.

Stress. One biological stressor that is central in dynamic theories of neuroses is the role of sex. Freud considered *coitus interruptus* to be a causal factor in the development of the neuroses. Although, to our surprise, we were unable to find data on the role of sexual satisfaction on the level of people's functioning we have seen some clients who report a change in their mood as a function of how satisfactory their sex life is.

It is extremely important to assess for general levels of stress, either physical (as in a chronic illness) or psychological. Although it is a truism that all disorders are caused by some type of stress, sometimes general, chronic stressors can lead to specific psychological problems indirectly. Selye (1976) cites the following diverse psychological problems as being among possible indications of overly high general stress levels:

1. Irritability, hyperexcitation, or depression.
2. Impulsive behavior.
3. Inability to concentrate.
4. Overpowering urges to cry, to run and hide.
5. Free-floating anxiety.
6. Insomnia.
7. Bruxism.

8. Feelings of unreality, weakness, dizziness.
9. Headaches.
10. Increased substance abuse.

Given the wide range of problems associated with high levels of stress, the therapist may decide to give attention to redesigning the client's life to minimize the biological irritants before moving on to more "psychological" interventions.

In cases where the level of stress is higher than the client seems capable of dealing with, the therapist may wish to use some of the recommendations discussed in the limited-capacities model (see Chapter 3). We do believe that the therapist should be aware of the possible role of biological irritants in lowering the client's capacities and ways in which he or she can intervene by recommending appropriate ways of "strengthening" the client. As shown in the flowchart (p. 000), a variety of recommendations that are biologically mediated can increase resistance to stress.

Drugs. It is imperative that the therapist know which medications a client is taking. A large number of drugs lower the threshold for anger control (or change mood). Among those which have an effect on anger are the barbituates and some antipsychotic drugs (viz. Taractan). Hypnotics taken to help people sleep are, with repeated usage, the single largest cause of insomnia. It is wise to check the *Physician's Desk Reference* (*PDR*, 1984) to obtain information about side effects of drugs. However, the *PDR* may simply list "emotional change" as a general category of side effects.

Sometimes trial and error in collaboration with a physician may be necessary. We have seen three youngsters on the same epilepsy medication make suicide attempts in ways so similar that it is unlikely they were coincidental. They all tried jumping out the window. The *PDR* did not report that Mysoline, an anticonvulsant, could be involved. Informal discussion with several neurologists indicated that they had seen this same pattern previously with Mysoline. The test of whether the drug has an effect is to change medication. Some drugs take longer than others to leave the body. We have, however, seen dramatic improvements in anger control as some medications have been changed.

COMMON PSYCHOLOGICAL PROBLEMS WHICH MAY HAVE BIOLOGICAL CAUSES

In addition to the subtle effects of temperament and biological irritants on behavior, there are many physical disorders which can convincingly mimic psychological problems. Although some of these may be relatively rare in terms of the numbers seen by a therapist, it is our purpose simply to point out the possibility of such relationships between physical and psychological difficulties. This information will be especially helpful if one is confronted with a case which does not fit a psychological model or which, although it may fit a model, does not respond as expected to intervention based on that model. In such cases, the relatively uncommon biological model must be seriously considered. The following list is by no means an exhaustive one, and again, we want to stress the necessity of the nonmedical therapist to be conservative. Whenever a biological problem is suspected, make a referral to a medical colleague.

Anxiety

People frequently enter therapy with problems of either primary anxiety (anxiety which dominates their lives and inhibits comfortable functioning in virtually all situations), or secondary anxiety (anxiety which accompanies various problem areas of their lives). For example, many people are anxious mainly in specific situations, usually involving either social interactions or evaluations. The first assessment problem is to rule out biological determinants of the anxiety.

Anxiety is mediated by the sympathetic nervous sytem and produces a group of symptoms which include a high degree of muscular tension (with different people having different characteristic muscular-tension patterns), a high respiration and heart rate, patterns of profuse clammy sweating, and often diarrhea and stomach distress. Clients who are anxious often complain about feelings of imminent doom and worry about their impact on the world and the world's impact on them.

It is absolutely essential to get a detailed description of what the client feels before advancing any model of therapy. All too often clients will report that they feel "anxious" when in fact they feel depressed or, even more often, state that they feel "depressed" when they are anxious. A "tour of the body" should be taken with special emphasis on those activities which involve the sympathetic nervous system. The tour should include detailed questions about where in the body the client feels the disorder. Since clients are not used to thinking this way, conducting the tour takes skill. The client should be given direction in stating what the important symptoms are. Questions like, "Do your hands sweat a lot?" and others relating to sympathetic activity should be asked. Different people will have different patterns of muscular expression of anxiety and this may be important for future therapy. Some people, for example, will experience headaches in the temples. Often these headaches are the result of their characteristic muscular pattern of anxiety in which they clench their jaw. Clenching the jaw leads to temporal headaches. Others will tighten their grips, tense their necks, or hunch their shoulders. For future therapy a detailed description of the characteristic pattern of tension is necessary. When desensitization is discussed, the utility of a specific description of anxiety will become more apparent (see Chapter 4).

Hyperthyroidism.   Among the biological determinants of anxiety is hyperthyrodism (Martin, 1983). Hyperthyroidism is a disease caused by overactivity of the thyroid gland. Its physiological symptoms are identical with anxiety with three exceptions (Bockar, 1976). Patients report being hot and sweaty rather than complaining of the cold clammy sweat or anxiety; they lose or maintain weight while increasing in appetite; and the anxiety state is constant rather than related to specific times or situations. In addition, the hyperthyroid patient may have a change in hair texture to a finer level and may have bulging eyes.

Cardiac Conditions.   Symptoms of a cardiac condition can sometimes resemble acute or chronic anxiety. For obvious reasons, it is important to recognize the difference. The early warning signals of an impending heart attack include intense pain, pressure or burning sensations centering in the chest and sometimes extending into the jaw, shoulder, back, or arm. The pain may leave and return. Often people who have had heart attacks will clench their fists while describing the sensation. Any such intense discomfort lasting 2 minutes or more may be a heart attack. Other symptoms of a heart attack are sweating, nausea, palpitations, shortness of breath, and feeling of impending disaster (Effront, 1978). These occurrences are identical with some anxiety states. The presence of pain or a history of heart disease in the presence of these other symptoms indicates a thorough medical examination, including an electrocardiogram.

Hypoglycemia.   Another disorder with symptoms difficult to distinguish from anxiety are those produced by hypoglycemia. Hypoglycemia is a condition of *low* blood-sugar level in which the body attempts compensation by a sympathetic reaction. Here, it is important to determine what time of the day the anxiety attacks occur. Hypoglycemic attacks usually occur after sleep because that is the longest period between meals, leading to low blood-sugar levels. Some patients report that anxiety decreases after consuming orange juice or some sweet. Others may report a characteristic time of day when they experience symptoms, which may be related to diet habits. For those who do not make the connection spontaneously, it is important that metabolic factors be ruled out by the therapist. One client with hypoglycemia described her condition as experiencing variable periods of anxiety which she could not understand. They often came while she was being productive or enjoying an activity. They also occurred during periods of tension, especially with her mother-in-law. Since she did not understand her symptoms, which included trembling, fearful mood, cold sweat, and diffuse muscular tension, she was anxious about the next period of anxiety. Almost as an aside, she mentioned that orange juice helped her mood. We did not schedule a second session until after a glucose tolerance test. The results indicated no need for a second session. This case is discussed more thoroughly in Chapter 8.

Although this is a controversial point, we have seen clients who scored within the normal range in glucose tolerance tests who had a reduction in their experienced anxiety level after their diets were modified. The traditional method of diagnosing hypoglycemia is to classify those people whose responses to the glucose tolerance test fall within a "clinically positive" range as hypoglycemic, while those who fall outside that range, even slightly, are not diagnosed hypoglycemic. Real diseases, however, rarely have bimodal distributions; they are usually continuously distributed. We have seen some people who do not test within the clinical definition of hypoglycemia, yet who reported that their mood improved after their diet was modified. It seemed as if their threshold for stress tolerance increased after their diet was changed. Suggestions were made that they try to change their diet as an experiment when other forms of intervention were not working.

Depression

When people suffer, they frequently say they are depressed. The clinician must discriminate between depression and other states of suffering. As in anxiety, a tour of the body is necessary for the clinician to get a good picture of the problem.

Endogenous Depression.   Depressed people who are said to have *endogenous depression* tend to report combinations of the following symptoms: sadness, psychomotor retardation, disturbance of sleep patterns (usually inability to fall asleep or early morning waking), disturbance of eating patterns, and apathy. It is well established that some depressions respond dramatically to antidepressant medication and therefore those should be referred to a physician. The endogenous depressions simply look different from those that react to the environment. They are characterized by changes in sleeping and eating patterns, a hopeless grim mood in which weeping is often seen, and by very low energy levels that interfere with social and vocational functioning. Patients in this group generally report a very high level of penetration of the disorder; i.e., the depression invades virtually every area of their lives with relatively homogeneous intensity. Even good news brings about a morbid reaction. Additionally, a history of periodic serious depressions unrelated to environmental events leads to the categorization of a depression as endogenous and biologically mediated.

One young man came in displaying all these signs and could not explain the black cloud that hung over his head. He had been successful in college, had no specific problems with his girl friend, still participated in sports, but could not enjoy any of these activities. His judgment was sound and he clearly did not have an overly negative view of himself. He recognized that he sometimes did not do well on tests and that did not make him a terrible person, nor was it upsetting if people did not like him. However, he was depressed. After psychotherapy was getting nowhere, we recommended he see a psychiatrist for medication; he was not depressed after 2 weeks of Tofranil therapy.

Parenthetically, this client awakened the senior author to the fact that a strictly behavioral approach had limitations. At that time, early in the evolution of behavior modification, it was the senior author's conviction that knowledge of behavioral principles was sufficient to intervene effectively in virtually all cases. When the senior author was beginning to find the sessions with this client aversive (because of the lack of progress and the therapist's inability to choose a new route for therapy), the referral was made to a psychiatrist out of frustration. The same type of cases are now referred with the confidence that this is the necessary route for service to the client.

Hypothyroidism   Depressions are also caused by underactivity of the thyroid gland. Signs of hypothyroidism include a deepening of the voice, gaining of weight, chronic fatigue, and loss of leg hair and hair on the outer third of the eyebrow. The hypothyroid person complains about his or her depression and describes the mood state in a way quite similar to those of endogenous depression.

Psychosis

Although there is still controversy about the relative role of heredity versus environment in the determination of the psychoses, we choose to discuss them in the biological model because there is evidence that they contain a large biological component. In fact, the classic studies of the genetic influences on schizophrenia by Kallmann (1953)—which showed that identical twins had concordance rates (i.e., the rates at which they both received the same diagnosis) between 69% and 86%—have been quite reliable and have been replicated with considerably more sophisticated studies (e.g., Gottesman & Shields, 1972; Kety, Rosenthal, Wender, & Schulsinger, 1971). Neale & Oltmanns (1980) conclude, "The controversy surrounding genetic studies in schizophrenia has subsided . . . there is general agreement that genetic factors do play an important, though not exclusive role in the etiology of the disorder [p. 215]."

There is comparable evidence that there is a genetic component of the affective disorders (e.g., Hays, 1976, Winokur & Clayton, 1967). The therapist is more concerned with treatment than with etiology (although knowledge of etiology can guide treatment). The more important question for the therapist here is whether the psychotic disorders respond to biological intervention. At this point the evidence is clear that the neuroleptics have a major role in the control of schizophrenia and some of the affective disorders, and there is evidence that electroconvulsive shock therapy is effective with certain types of depression (Klerman, 1972). In addition, antidepressant medications and the use of lithium in the treatment of the manic psychosis is well established. Because of the preponderance of evidence that biological interventions have been effective in reducing psychotic symptoms, it is essential that the nonmedical therapist consult with a medical colleague when treating clients with psychoses.

Simply because there is a biological component to the psychoses does not mean that there is no room for psychological interventions. Although paraplegia is a symptom of a largely irreversible spinal cord injury, for example, there are any number of psychological interventions that are helpful in adjusting to or overcoming primary physical loss. In fact, it is common for a rehabilitation unit to have a psychologist and/or a social worker on the staff for counseling and therapy. In the same way, there is a role for psychological interventions with any number of biological disorders. However, the therapist should be familiar with the limitations that the physical conditions presents. We are dubious that psychotherapy will cure psychosis, but feel that there have been any number of psychological programs that have effectively increased the level of functioning of psychotic patients (e.g. Atthowe & Krasner, 1968; Ayllon & Azrin, 1965).

When the biological model is determined to be the best fit for the facts of a particular case, it is important for the therapist to become knowledgable about the particular physical disorder that the client has. Often the therapist must read the appropriate literature about the disorder itself and also the treatments used. Most psychoactive drugs have side effects that have to be monitered. These side effects can become worse than the original disorder. For example, the neuroleptics not only can reduce symptoms of psychoses, but they can cause tardive dyskenesia. Tardive dyskenesia is a disfiguring motor disorder where the mouth and the tongue make uncontrolled movements, leading to grotesque appearance. This disorder occurs in 77% of the patients treated with phenothiazines. In addition, there is evidence that prolonged use of the major tranquilizers can lead to basal ganglia damage, which in turn, can lead to losses of higher mental functioning (Lidsky, Labuszewski, & Levine, 1982). It is important for the therapist to be aware of both the therapeutic effects and the side effects of whatever medication the client is taking.

Anger Control

Many people, especially children, are referred to therapy because of problems of anger control. They act out in ways which are destructive to them and often to the people around them. As with anxiety, the clinician should be aware of biological factors which contribute to anger-control problems.

Brain Injury. One of the behavior signs of organic pathology is a problem with impulse control. Frequently people coming out of comas after brain trauma have irrational temper tantrums that they feel they cannot control. Certainly the frustration of losing control over bodily functions contributes to the problem, but often temper tantrums of a childlike quality are exhibited, and the patient reports feeling that these displays are uncontrollable. Other emotions may also be expressed too freely, such as grief or sexual acting out. However, controlling anger is a common problem in a rehabilitation unit.

Emotional lability is also seen with brain tumors and with the evanescent category of minimal brain injury. Charles Whitman, the mass killer from the Texas Tower, was found to have a brain tumor in the amygdala. In the case of brain injury, other signs are frequently present. They include errors in judgement, problems in either fine or gross motor movements, and/or intellectual changes. It is important that neurological referrals be made when this is suspected. It is also important to recognize that the treatment may still be psychological: although the neurological lesion had an effect, the lesion only *lowered* the threshold for anger. Psychological techniques may still be the best intervention for raising the threshold.

We have set up programs of anger control for patients with neurological lesions who have come out of comas. One such patient was a 20-year-old man who was comatose after a motor vehicle accident. When he came out of the coma, he had a pattern of behaviors in which he became increasingly agitated with any interaction with the staff. When we consulted them, the nurses and aides showed us their bruises. However, the referral was not made until the patient grabbed his neurologist by the tie, pulled him forward, and punched him in the face. When we saw the patient, he repeated words in ever increasing speed as he became more agitated. He said that he did not like it when he became so angry and that he would try to stop. We stood very close to him, touched him gently on his shoulder and talked very quietly as we tried teaching him relaxation exercises. He tried breathing slower.

In what seemed like a more powerful approach, we used an operant intervention. We recommended to the nursing staff that they leave the room as he became agitated and tell him they will return after he calmed down. We explained to the client we were doing this. The nursing staff carried out the recommendations. He was incident free after 1 week. It is also quite possible that neurological recovery was involved in his improvement. This case illustrates the point that, although a disorder may be biological in etiology, psychological interventions should not be dismissed. It must be remembered that *all* behavior is neurologically mediated, but we can still change behavior by use of psychological procedures.

Epilepsy

Therapists must also be aware that some seizure disorders present themselves as behavioral problems. One problem the therapist should be alert to is attention disorders in children. Petit mal seizures are characterized by brief pauses in attention and responding that simply may look like an extended eyeblink. Other seizures may be as undramatic, yet have the effect of interfering with attention or performance. One physician we saw in therapy was unable to recognize letters for a week after she had a grand mal seizure. When parents complain that their child has mastered material one day but cannot do simpler material the next day, we wonder about seizures.

Seizures often occur in the body and some stomach aches are seizure equivalents and respond to anticonvulsive medications. In addition, seizures may occur at night and not be noticed during the day. Many people with noctural seizures will describe waking up with a headache and feeling weak. What makes diagnosis difficult is that seizures are also responsive to stress. There are times when we have recommended that anticonvulsant medication be given diagnostically. If the behavior (like the stomach ache) improves, we assume that it was related to a seizure. The diagnosis is considerably less difficult when the performance deficits we have mentioned occur without any special environmental reason.

Psychomotor seizures are difficult to diagnose because the behavior may be ordinary, although not appropriate to a given situation. For example, the person may walk around a room, or unbutton and button a top button of a shirt. Usually, although not always, the person is unaware of the behavior and the environment during these periods. The therapist should recommend a neurological evaluation for inexplicable losses of attention.

Sexual Problems

There are several biological factors which may directly cause or interact with psychological variables to produce sexual dysfunction. Masters and Johnson (1966) indicate that sexual dysfunction can be the result of any acute or chronic problem, either psychological or physical in nature. It is important to note, however, that an organic disease, if present, is not necessarily the cause of a sexual problem (Bockar, 1976). Often, psychological processes may maintain a sexual disorder originally caused biologically. A man may attempt intercourse after a night of heavy drinking. Alcohol, like other Central Nervous System (CNS) depressants, can have a detrimental effect on erection in the male. The man finds himself unable to have intercourse that night, much to his shock and dismay. The next time he attempts to have sex, several days later and without the influence of alcohol, he is again unable to perform. If this pattern continues, he may label himself impotent. In this case, the biological factor initiated the disorder, but psychological factors maintained it (and would be the best targets for intervention). Of course, if the man is a chronic alcoholic, the biological factors may have to be addressed first during intervention.

Other drugs beside alcohol can lead to sexual problems. It is always a good idea to assess for drug use, but it is imperative in the case of sexual dysfunction. Any CNS depressant may have a detrimental effect on men's erectile capacity and the major tranquilizers and antidepressants may lead to a decrease in vaginal lubrication in women (Bockar, 1976). In addition, antihypertensive and diuretic medication can cause erectile failure (LoPiccolo & Hogan, 1979). Illicit drug use may also interfere with sexual functioning. Anecdotal evidence to the contrary, cocaine and LSD may sometimes block sexual responses and opiates like heroin and morphine can eventually lead to erectile failure (Jarvik & Brecher, 1977).

Some medical problems commonly associated with secondary impotence are diabetes, multiple sclerosis, spinal cord injury, heart disease, and advanced kidney disease (Bockar, 1976; LoPiccolo & Hogan, 1979; Masters & Johnson, 1966). A clinician working with persons with such medical problems must assess how much the organic disease is affecting sexual response, and how much the secondary anxiety about performance vis-a-vis the disease is affecting it. This assessment may be aided by the use of standard behavioral sex-therapy techniques designed to reduce performance anxiety. Complete medical examinations of the neurological and vascular systems involved in arousal and orgasm may be necessary.

Once the physiological capacity of a client is determined, the therapist's job may be one of education in sexual techniques possible within that person's capabilities (LoPiccolo & Hogan, 1979).

Chronic Pain

Simply because pain may be biological in origin, does not mean that psychological techniques are not called for. Often it helps a person to understand that pain affects mood, and that periods of pain will affect emotional response. Rather than blame other people, the patient should be aware of the cause of the dark mood, and perhaps avoid outside contact during periods of biologically based lowered thresholds for irritability. A number of relaxation procedures or operant procedures may help biologically based pain become reduced. In addition, Fordyce (1976, 1978) has shown that expressions of pain can be controlled by contingency management approaches that differentially reinforce "well" behaviors. Patients so treated increased activity and level of functioning.

Keefe and Brown (1982) have applied the "Learned Helplessness Model" to pain. These authors hold that prolonged pain with limited help from either drugs or rehabilitation produces a state of depression. The therapist should therefore stress areas of life that the patient can control in order to reduce the feelings of helplessness these patients experience.

FINAL CONSIDERATIONS

In using the biological model, it is important to consider two factors. Often the biological model should be reviewed in the absence of specific body symptoms when the psychological models do not apply. For example, if the person describes becoming angry in situations which do not fit into a psychological pattern (e.g., there are no precipitants, there is no "payoff," cognitions are not distorted, anger has not been modeled by others), the biological model must be reviewed.

We are currently reviewing a case of a 16-year-old girl who is being seen for problems of self-esteem and for potential alcoholism. The client also reported that she has periods of uncontrolled anger which she cannot understand. These periods of uncontrolled anger are preceded by a state of confusion accompanied by headaches. They occurred with sufficient frequency to be regarded as clinically significant. We considered the fact that the neurological examination is expensive and that the parents are struggling financially. It was our opinion that she have a neurological examination even though the probability of a positive finding would be low. Before making this recommendation to the parent, we checked with a clinic to see if the fee could be put on a sliding scale. At this moment, we do not know how the parents will respond nor the outcome to the neurological examination. Again, we want to emphasize that part of the process of conceptualizing a case as biological must be done by process of elimination, by finding the model which best fits the facts of the case, and thereby eliminating several psychological models.

A biological conceptualization of a case does not preclude a psychological intervention. As previously mentioned, brain injury may decrease the threshold to anger, but the threshold an be increased by psychological treatment. Many years ago, the first patient treated by us in an operant manner was a young man coming out of a 6-month coma following an auto accident. His speech was incomprehensible, he was hemiplegic, disfigured, and used a catheter to urinate. He became angry and negative when asked to participate in most rehabilitation activities and was therefore progressing slowly. When many hours of conversations with him did not lead to behavior change, we decided to use an operant approach. A rehabilitation team meeting was set up and strict rules were laid down to eliminate his temper tantrums and, more importantly, reinforce positive movement. He was told that no matter what he did, he was going to continue his therapies for the prescribed times; he had a choice of making this time productive or not.

After he screamed all the way to his first appointment of speech therapy, he started rocking his wheelchair. We trembled, as did the speech therapist, but we ignored his negative behavior. The patient threw himself on the floor and yelled while we read magazines. He pulled out his catheter and urine spilled out on the floor. There is no doubt that our positions would have been difficult to defend if a hospital administrator came into the room and witnessed this sight. At the end of the allotted period we picked him up, talked to him about his choice of reading materials, and agreed to get him his choice, *Playboy* magazine. He threw no further temper tantrums and became motivated in therapy, despite the role that the brain injury had in his reduced threshold of anger. This experience has been duplicated by recovering trauma patients many times; they have responded to contingencies. Also, to be candid, we would handle this man differently now. With experience, we are no longer as committed to treatment purity. We would pick the man up, but not speak to him or make eye contact until he was positively involved in rehabilitation.

Psychological problems can also benefit from biological interventions. There are times when the therapist may wish to refer the client for a biological intervention even when the disorder is due to a psychological precipitant. There are people who experience a panic reaction to situations of stress. This is often seen when relationships are dissolving or when trauma such as losing one's job occurs. The panic response is extremely dominant and often may lead to use of alcohol or other drugs to reduce the suffering. The individual may not be able to function effectively without medication. This may lead to a different set of problems which can compound the stress.

As an example, one man was in a turbulent relationship which started after his wife's early death. The relationship was initially characterized by his being dominant and his clearly not wanting long-range involvement. He felt that their needs, temperaments, and interests were unresolvably different. As the relationship continued, he became increasingly dependent upon the woman. She no longer pleaded for his forgiveness or initiated one of the many reconciliations which characterized this turbulent couple. He found that he was pleading for her forgiveness, even though he recognized that the relationship was destructive to both of them. The intensity of his needs disrupted his work, as well as his social and family responsibilities. He was in a state of panic. He was afraid that he might marry the woman to decrease the panic, even though he was absolutely convinced that the marriage would be a disaster. Although psychotherapy had the prominent role in helping this man conquer his intense feelings of dependency, antianxiety medications limited the panic which could have led to a more inextricable situation. In this case, the man had experienced a very prolonged and intensively stressful period which made him considerably more vulnerable than he may have been otherwise. The biological intervention of drugs helped him to get to a state in which he could benefit from psychotherapy and avoid making unwise decisions which would further complicate his situation.

The therapist should be aware of the array of available medications and their use. There are times when suffering is needlessly prolonged when it can be reduced by the use of appropriate medication. Also, biological predispositions, whether genetic or not, may have led the person to be selectively reactive to situations in a way that may be destructive. Knowledge of these biological factors may lead to points of intervention of considerable utility.

3 The Limited-Capacities Model

The concept of limited capacities can be used by the therapist within the therapy situation as well as be utilized as a model of dysfunctional behavior. Within the therapy situation, the therapist should always be aware of the client's capacities when performing interventions within any model. In this sense, then, the concept of limited capacities, rather than being a model of the dynamics of a problem, leads us to a series of caveats for the therapist. On the other hand, when used as a model of dysfunctional behavior, limited capacities of clients can be the causal and/or maintaining factors present in many problem situations. Since everyone is limited in many ways, the limited capacities of clients only take on dysfunctional properties when there is a significant mismatch between the demands of a person's environment and the limitations of that person.

Wallace (1966) proposed an abilities conception of personality in which he set out a structure for understanding personality based on abilities rather than underlying dynamics. Wallace recommended that psychologists begin to think of personality traits in terms of the capacity of the person to perform in a given manner in a particular situation, rather than in terms of their underlying predisposition to perform in a certain way. Thus, Wallace suggested that the clinician must examine the ability of a person acting in a dysfunctional manner to behave in any other way. For example, persons who are labeled "shy" may not be acting reclusive because of their needs or traits, but because they are incapable of acting otherwise in a given situation. Wallace's view is in some ways a "skills" conception of personality. Thus, Wallace was in the forefront of rejecting traditional intrapsychic notions of personality and attempting to initiate a more skills-oriented, parsimonious system. Apart from the issues of personality theory and assessment that Wallace raises, his emphasis on the importance of looking at the capacities of individuals behaving in a dysfunctional manner is a point well taken.

The therapist should be aware that identical therapeutic tasks are not the same in terms of the amount of effort needed to complete them by different clients. For some clients with social anxiety, the task of going to a group meeting will be relatively easy; they may not feel uncomfortable as long as there are no specific demands placed upon them. For other clients, this same task may be extremely difficult. They may feel self-

43

conscious and experience high levels of anticipatory anxiety for fear that attention will be focused on them. The therapist must always keep in mind that the experience of the task is mediated by the capacities of the client.

We first explore the considerations for therapists which emerge from the concept of limited capacities, and following that, we will delineate the model of limited capacities as it describes certain problem dynamics.

CAVEATS FOR THERAPISTS

Therapists must be cognizant of their clients' capacities for change. Change, in some manner, is a universal goal of all therapy, yet individuals differ greatly in their inherent capability to change many of the problems brought into therapy. Some may be able to do this readily, while others may be really incapable of change in certain areas. Far more common are the clients who fall somewhere in the middle range. The rate of change initiated in therapy must be dictated by the client's capacity for change, or no real progress can be made. The client will feel overwhelmed and misunderstood if change is required at a rate above that which he or she is capable of incorporating. The cues to the therapist will generally be the response of the client to past assignments and suggestions. If the client is responding well, the pace can be kept up or accelerated, while the pace should be slowed if the client is not changing. Too often the therapist views lack of change as being resistance when it is, in fact, a function of the capacities of the client. By attempting to be aware of clients' capacities, errors in this area can be reduced.

The therapist should be aware that the acquisition of new skills, be they interpersonal or emotional, requires practice. Anderson (1982), as will be discussed more fully in Chapter 6, claims that it requires at least 100 hours of practice before a cognitive skill is acquired. By keeping the capacities of the client in mind, individual adjustments can be made.

Areas of Limited Capacities Affecting the Therapy Process

Cognitive Capacity.   Within much of psychotherapy, a prime vehicle for change is language. Most psychotherapy is "talking therapy," regardless of the content of that talk. Thus, the cognitive capacities of the client are extremely important in gauging the sophistication of the presentation of content in psychotherapy. Therapists must be sure that their language makes sense to the client. This may be fairly obvious when working with individuals of low intellectual functioning, but is especially important to keep in mind when dealing with children. The cognitive limitations of children can be handled by knowing developmental norms, so that therapy can proceed at the appropriate pace. One Spanish-speaking therapist had a good deal of difficulty speaking to children in therapy. Adults only required that he translate his thoughts into English, which he did quite well, but translating into "child-English" really tested the therapist's language capacities. This therapist's difficulty in translation to children is indicative of the problem that exists for all therapists. We simply need to be aware of, and change our presentation according to, the linguistic capacity of those we see in therapy.

Cognitive capacity does not only refer to intellectual or linguistic ability. A person's cognitive style also determines, to a large extent, their ability to change. A rigid, inflexible cognitive style makes the therapeutic-change process much slower. Some people experience change itself as being delightful, while other people are uncomfortable when they are either exposed to different situations or when they are expected to respond in a different manner.

Intellectual ability is to a large extent reflected in linguistic ability. During therapy the therapist must not only be aware of the level of the language that is being used, but must also recognize the conceptual level of the communication. Interpretations and summary statements must be especially monitored for this and adjusted to the client's conceptual level. A statement that might really "hit home" for an "intellectual" person might only confuse or anger a more concrete individual. A good deal of irony is usually used in therapy; e.g., when clients tell us things such as how good it felt when they exploded at their spouses, we may say, "Yes, and I'm also certain that it made your spouse feel warm and receptive when you later asked to make love." Although the irony may emphasize the problem we wish to direct attention to with some clients, it is counter-productive with others. Rather than say that the client should develop a sense of irony, we must adjust our statements to the client's capacities.

Formal psychological testing can prove most useful in providing cues about clients' cognitive capacities. Verbal ability, conceptual ability, and cognitive style can all be assessed via traditional tests. Also, other strengths which may be used during therapy can become apparent during such assessment. Frequently the most important information gained during such structured assessment sessions is not that which is scored and normed, but the general working style of a person when confronted with a structured task. Thus, a therapist is able to learn a great deal from the clients reactions to failure and success during testing, as well as to their style of working (impulsive versus methodical). Social-evaluation fears are also readily displayed in such settings. Testing with these goals in mind can be viewed as looking at the test as a sample of typical behavior rather than a sign of some underlying trait.

Emotional capacities.   It has been proposed that different people may have different inherent emotional capacities for reasons that may be genetic. As mentioned in Chapter 2, researchers have presented evidence that certain aspects of temperament may be genetically determined, present from birth, and may influence development throughout a person's lifetime (Buss & Plomin, 1975; Thomas & Chess, 1977; Thomas, Chess, & Birch, 1968). These researchers present evidence that adaptability, regularity of bodily functions, level of activity, quality of mood, and persistence, among other characteristics, are qualities that can differentiate children at a young age and persist throughout a child's life. Further, these characteristics have an impact on the incidence of behavioral problems and success in school. Thomas, Chess, and Birch were able to categorize 65% of their sample as belonging to one of three temperamental "types" which they labeled "easy," "difficult," and "slow to warm up" children. These three types required individual treatment in order to perform up to their capacity.

In the therapy situation, the therapist must be aware of the temperamental characteristics of the client, in order to present material at an appropriate pace and to correctly interpret reactions on the part of the client. Also, knowledge of these inherent temperamental tendencies may allow the therapist to set reasonable therapeutic goals by taking into account a client's longstanding temperament. It is unlikely that a therapist could ever change a withdrawing, moody, persistent person into a cheerful, carefree extrovert. Radical temperamental change is not a realistic goal for psychotherapy. A goal is often to held people accept their capacities. There is a cultural goal of the extrovert being the model of mental health. We taught a course on psychological adjustment where students replied to a questionnaire about their adjustment problems. They indicated that a large majority of them wanted to be more extroverted. When we discussed this at length, it seemed as if they had assimilated the notion of the extrovert being the model of mental health. We then talked about how introversion and extroversion may represent personal preferences rather than values of health. The goal in therapy is often to help people be comfortable in accepting their range of temperamental capacities.

In dealing with psychotics, the issue of emotional capacities becomes especially difficult. Most schizophrenics are characterized by withdrawal. Frequently the patients avoid external stimulation and are more comfortable by themselves. Levine and Tursky (1972) found that chronic schizophrenics had reduced levels of electrodermal responses during sensory deprivation sessions of 45 minutes duration as compared to normal controls. That is, in a situation which is relatively stressful for most people, the schizophrenics were relatively less stressed by the absence of stimulation. F. M. Levine (1966) found that chronic schizophrenic patients avoided external auditory stimulation as compared with controls. Although the decision regarding what level of stimulation and information input the psychotic client can deal with must be individually determined by the client's capacity, the therapist must keep in mind that the psychotic client may not be able to handle the "normal" social demands others may be comfortable with. The therapist should work within the limits of the client's capacities by not promoting activities that would be overly stressful to the psychotic client.

Although there are limitations in the capacities of the psychotic client to deal with many situations, especially those requiring social interaction, the therapist can help the client find situations that are less socially demanding. In one psychiatric hospital where we worked, one patient, who had great difficulty dealing with interacting people, was extremely good at analyzing polygraph records. The demands of analyzing polygraph records were well matched with the need to decrease stimulation. Most nonpsychotic people would find it aversive to do the repetitive operations involved in scoring those records. Her response, of course, does not mean that all psychotic patients would respond in a similar way. What it reflects is that the therapist can be involved in designing an environment that is a better match for the capacities of the client only after the capacities of the client are recognized.

Financial Capacities.   Another reality which the therapist must recognize is the financial capacities of the client. Private psychotherapy is quite expensive and may create financial hardships for some clients. The therapist should discuss the costs of the proposed therapy program before the client becomes committed to therapy. If the client cannot afford the program, the therapist should be willing to either reduce or defer fees, or to make an outside referral to a public-service agency. It is often of no service for clients to have to compromise other important areas of their lives in order to afford therapy.

Therapists should also be aware of the profound effect client financial capacities can have upon the ability to change in ways that the therapist may designate as therapeutically desirable. As an example, there are large numbers of clients who may reach the conclusion along with their therapists that their marriages are unsalvageable. However, they are locked into a bad marriage because they simply cannot financially afford the cost of separating from their spouse. To some extent, then, divorce is determined by economics. (This situation may be changing, however, as more women enter the work force, thereby increasing the opportunity of meeting potential new mates, as well as making the prospect of divorce economically feasible). These economic factors are well-structured in the decision making matrix of many clients. In a recent discussion, an English psychologist from Liverpool pointed out that she made errors in treatment by not keeping the financial capacities of the client in mind. She was treating agoraphobic clients from an area of high unemployment and recommended that they practice their relaxation skills while traveling progressively further distances from home by taking trips on a bus to nowhere in particular. Several replied that they could not afford the "luxury" of the bus trip.

Any therapeutically desirable change suggested by the therapist should be examined for its feasibility given the client's financial capacities. While many people have unhappy vocational adjustments, they also realize that they must work to survive. Archibald (1978) reported that while 15% of the Canadian work force reported being dissatisfied with their jobs (a figure which he later concluded may be a gross underrepresentation of true opinion), 30% say they work more because they have to than because they want to [p. 125]. It is important that the therapist avoid a myopic definition of the client's "problem," and refrain from making suggestions or gear the therapy in a direction that is not consistent with the client's financial status.

It has been asserted that some physicians may be more concerned with the treatment of the symptom than with treatment of the patient. Unless the therapist is aware of the clients' symptom picture within a broader framework including the clients' limitations, that same allegation may be warranted.

LIMITED CAPACITIES AS A MODEL OF DYSFUNCTIONAL BEHAVIOR

Apart from affecting the process and outcome of psychotherapy itself, the limited capacities of clients may lie at the heart of the problems which they bring into therapy. Limited capacities become a model of problem dynamics when the capacities of the client are incompatible with the requirements of the environment. It should be emphasized that it is the *mismatch* between personal capacities and environmental demands which characterize the limited-capacities model. Limits in and of themselves are not problematic; it is only when they are not respected in some way that they present trouble.

The "mismatch" between person and environmental demands does not only designate the case in which the person has lower capacities than those required by the situation; being "overqualified" can also lead to problematic mismatches. As the early sensory-deprivation experiments demonstrated, lack of adequate stimulation can be quite stressful (Bexton, Heron, & Scott, 1954; Heron, Doane, & Scott, 1956). Gruneberg (1979) asserts: "One factor which may affect the relationship between intelligence and job satisfaction is role overload and role underload, where giving the individual too much or too little to do in terms of his capacities causes frustration and job stress [p. 144]."

We have seen a substantial number of housewives who suffer from intellectual deprivation, and wonder if this contributes to the higher rate of certain psychiatric problems among women. Many of these women report that they are stressed all day with the children and chores, but have little intellectual stimulation. They report that the chores become routine and that there are few challenges in their lives. Chesler (1972) reported statistics showing a much higher rate of depression in women than in men at all ages, and Bart (1971), in a study of middle-aged depressed women, concluded that these women were depressed because they had completely accepted the feminine role. They were, at this point in their lives, no longer fulfilling their role, because their children had grown up and left. The women could be seen as suddenly being in a nonstimulating environment. Cited in Chesler (1972), Farberow and Schneidman (1965) in a statistical study of suicide found that housewives were the group comprising the largest number of both attempted and successful suicides. Although depression and suicide among women are certainly multidetermined, we wonder if lack of adequate meaningful stimulation among those who stay at home is a contributory factor.

In one case that we saw, the client was the wife of a famous artist. There was no economic incentive for her to work, but her affect was bland and it was concluded that she simply needed stimulation. Although she seemed quite content with tending the garden and maintaining their collection of art, there was not enough aggravation in her life. We recommended that she begin working outside the home, and that any job would be helpful in beginning development of work habits. She took a job as a salesperson in a department store. The job itself was entirely nonfulfilling, but she became considerably more animated. Because of increased stimulation, she was more able, at that point, to see the humor and the absurdity of the human condition. In a relatively short time she left and was able to get more intrinsically satisfying employment. Beginning work had helped this woman by improving the match between her capacities and the demands of the environment.

Areas Commonly Affected by Limited Capacities

Vocational area.   When there is a mismatch between the capacities of the person and the demands of the environment, there is an increased probability of higher stress, discontent with the situation, and lowering of self-esteem. Nowhere is this potentially more true than in the vocational arena. Job stresses and satisfactions are central to one's level of adjustment, and in fact play a principal role in how one defines oneself. A number of studies have found a relationship between occupational stress and physical and emotional dysfunction (e.g., Cooper & Marshall, 1976). Palmore (1969), in fact, found that work satisfaction was the single best environmental predictor of longevity. The correlation between longevity and work satisfaction was .26, which although not startling, was even higher than the negative correlation found between longevity and use of tobacco. When one takes into account the effects of the Peter Principle (Peter & Hull, 1969) in the corporate job structure (according to which everyone is promoted until they reach a level in which they are incompetent), the stress caused by mismatches between ability and job demands can be rampant. A particular job may require skills a client does not have, but does *not* imply that the client is without skills; only that the match between this person and the job is a poor one.

For example, we have seen several graduate students who felt they were under enormous pressure as beginning therapists. The interpersonal demands of doing therapy were more than they were able to meet. They became dubious of their own worth and were somewhat chronically depressed. When they switched into other clinical fields, they again became more confident and simply better adjusted. In one case, the student entered the field of neuropsychological assessment, where he was quite well regarded and which suited his ability to do detailed work; another student went into environmental psychology and also was successful.

It is important that the therapist avoid the mistake of attributing problems arising from a mismatch between personal capacities and job demands to purely intrapersonal sources. The stress caused by an inappropriate job can lead to personality disturbances, just as easily as personality problems can lead to job difficulties. When assessing for the applicability of the limited-capacities model, the therapist must investigate the strengths and weaknesses of the client. It is important that the therapist also get a good idea of the particular array of skills demanded by the client's job. Apart from interviewing the client extensively regarding these two areas, the therapist would also do well to get outside sources of information from family, friends, and employer, if the client is agreeable. Formal vocational testing may also be helpful to the therapist in determining strengths and weaknesses of the client which are pertinent to job competence.

In a series of experiments by Schönpflug and his colleagues in Germany (Schönpflug and Schulz, 1979; Schulz and Schönpflug, 1982; Schulz, 1979), it was found that the match between capacities and demands that produced the highest levels of stress, as indicated by both physiological and questionnaire data, was when there was a high correspondence between the capacities of the person and the demands of the task. This high correspondence required that the worker be vigilant at all times, because errors would occur if the person was not working at capacity. If the work was too demanding, the worker would make more errors, but would emotionally "withdraw" and feel that the demands were unreasonable. If the work was below the capacity of the worker, there would be fewer errors and less stress. This research is surprising from the traditional point of view; normally it was thought that stress would be highest if workload exceeded capacities.

Educational capacities.   Many child clients enter therapy because of a problem which parallels the match between adults and their job demands discussed previously; the problem being the match between the abilities of children and the demands of school. Often a great deal of assessment is required to determine the applicability of the limited-capacities model to children with school-related difficulties. The "typical" case involves a child who is not performing well in school. Although the number of models that may potentially "fit" the facts of this case is large, among the models to be investigated early on is the limited-capacities model. The immediate question is whether the youngster has sufficient intellectual resources to meet the requirements of the classroom. A large armamentarium of tests exist to assess this possibility. Once again, there are any number of good books that detail the specifics of the intellectual-assessment process (e.g., Anastasi, 1982).

It should be emphasized that although low intellectual level is mainly responsible for problems of mismatch between child and school demands, there are also a great number of children with school problems for whom the pace of the school program is too slow. In this case, behavior problems may develop because the child may be more advanced than his or her peers and may be bored by school. In many of these cases the major problem is that there are limited alternative resources for the youngster. In some cases, the parents could afford private schools and the child has done quite well. In other cases, the schools able to individualize programs. Frankly, we have seen a number of cases in which the schools could not provide for the special needs of the child and adjustment was a matter of waiting for the demands of school to catch up to the capacities of the child; i.e., the intellectual demand on the child in the lower grades was not high enough but the demands increase as education progresses. There are often more educational options for the youngster in the senior grades. Sometimes, however, this means that the child fails to develop sufficient work habits to maximize performance when the demands of school do become more in line with the youngster's capacities. In some cases, this catching up does not occur until college, when it may well be more difficult because poor works habits have developed.

The clinician must assess several aspects of the child's capacities when investigating the applicability of this model to school problems. In addition to assessing global intelligence, the clinician must assess specific academic areas as well. Deficits in school performance are often associated with specific learning disabilities. The most frequently seen of these deficits is a reading disability, which may be related to a visual problem. In addition, we have seen any number of auditory or visual-memory problems play a role in poor school performance. In virtually every case, the child has learned to view himself or herself as being "stupid." The therapist provides a service by explaining what a learning disability is and the implications of the specific learning disability to the youngster's educational functioning. There is a controversy about the role that special education has in overcoming specific learning disabilities. However, if the nature and the specificity of the youngster's learning disability is explained to the child and family, dramatic improvements in mood can occur. These youngsters no longer think they are "stupid" if they cannot perform at grade level or are placed in special classes. They are told about how some children have good vision while others need glasses; how some run fast while others can run long distances; and how they have difficulty in specific areas that requires them to work harder in these areas, while also having strengths in other areas.

Another area in which there is a mismatch between the youngster and the demands of school is in the interests of the child. School curricula are generally fixed. Many youngsters are interested in auto mechanics, for example, and are taught Shakespeare. These same youngsters can achieve when they are given a curriculum which matches at least some of their interests. Having part of the school day be interesting can alleviate some general behavioral problems associated with school as well. The clinician should be able to assess the child's interests by interview or formal interest inventories. While resources of the school may limit the opportunity for change, many schools can accomodate what they regard as justifiable flexibility in the educational program, especially if it may help calm a problematic child. School can become a powerful source of reinforcement once a program is better matched to the child's interests.

Yet another important capacity of the child which affects school performance is the tolerance for various methods of presenting academic material. Some youngsters thrive on a highly structured program, while others need individual room for exploration. Educators frequently get involved in arguments of the virtues of the open versus the closed system of education. When viewed from a models approach, the question becomes: Which children will benefit from which system? Thomas and Chess (1977) reported data on the relationship between temperamental characteristics and school functioning. They found that, while temperamental types did not differ in IQ, they differed radically in the environment which was most conducive to academic success. Thomas and Chess found children to differ in persistence, activity level, attention span, and distractibility (among other temperamental characteristics). They reported that highly active and distractible children fared poorly in permissive, unstructured school settings. Persistent children with a long attention span were ideally suited for such an environment, and would rebel at structure which forced them to drop an activity to go on to something else.

Slow activity level could also be a problem for a child in a highly structured setting, as their slowness is made conspicuous in such an environment, which may make others irritated and impatient with the naturally slow-moving child. Children with short attention spans tend to have trouble in school settings in general, because prolonged concentration is usually stressed. Thomas and Chess (1977) point out that continued pressure from teacher and parents on the child to do what is impossible for him or her (concentrate for long periods of time) only led to "anxiety, self-derogation, and defensive techniques to avoid any difficult task performance [p. 101]." Short attention spans can be effectively dealt with if tasks are structured in such a way that they do not exceed the limited concentration capacities of the child. We do not know of any formal assessment devices for helping determine the best level of structure for a child, but often close discussion with the parents and the child, focusing on the areas of temperament formulated by Thomas et al (1968, 1970) can give the information to aid in this decision. Once again, we have seen children who languish in one type of educational system thrive in another, and have seen it work both ways: Those who failed in the open classroom succeeding in a military academy and some who did poorly in a structured system doing extremely well in a more open system.

Interpersonal capacities.   In many ways, marriage is the most intense interpersonal relationship. Within it, the mismatch between the values, temperament, and abilities of the two partners can easily lead to difficulty in the relationship. Again, the problem is one of matching a person's capacities to the situation (which in terms of a marriage is the other person, or the other person's set of capacities).

Any two persons are bound to differ on many opinions, values, or ideas. Within marriage, it is how these differences are handled, not whether they exist, that determines much of the emotional tone of the relationship. We have seen a couple who have been fighting for over 26 years over the issue of saving money. His attitude toward money is relatively conservative. He stated that he did not mind spending it, but abhorred anything he considered "waste" and strongly resisted going into debt. The wife felt that, since they both worked, they could afford some debt, and that the pleasure of enjoying an object immediately outweighed the relatively insignificant interest payment. In session, she screamed that he was a "cheap bastard," while he felt she was an absolute spendthrift who would drive them to the poorhouse. They reported intense fights over whether to set the thermostat at 67° or 69°. These were two very bright, reasonable people in other aspects of their lives.

What makes this example so cogent is the smallness of their actual differences in the face of the intensity and duration of their struggle over them. After therapy concentrating on increasing communication skills (e.g., Gottman, Notarius, Gonso, & Markman, 1976) they were able to become more empathic with the other's point of view, and, more importantly, to realize that the other person was entitled to a different point of view. Although the differing criteria for their financial behavior persisted, and conflicts over finances came up repeatedly, they were able to resolve them by realizing that they differed but that both had reasonable positions. The meaning of the differences was de-escalated from an indication of the basic sanity or kindness of the partner to a simple preference or style. By emphasizing their conflict in terms of their preferences, it allowed them to focus on addressing the problem rather than addressing the person. They could focus on the thermostat rather than "winning the war."

An area that is somewhat more difficult to handle in marital therapy is that of mismatches between the basic temperaments of the partners. Duhl and Duhl (1975) discuss marital problems as resulting from differences in the cognitive styles of the partners. They describe cognitive style as the characteristic patterned way in which information is taken in and processed by an individual. They metaphorically present two opposites in terms of cognitive style as "hedgehogs" and "foxes." The hedgehog is characterized as slow, methodical, and persistent, preferring to process information in a sequential manner. The fox, on the other hand, is quick and somewhat impulsive, able to process information on several levels simultaneously. Of course, people can also fall somewhere in the middle. Duhl and Duhl point out that the labeling of people's cognitive styles—the process rather than the content of the internal lives—can be the first step toward differentiating the two partners. Lack of differentiation and respect for the different temperamental styles the two partners bring to the marriage can lead to major conflicts. Labeling the differences as innate styles that are resistant to change can also help shift expectations from a "curing" to a "coping" model in terms of marital differences and disagreements. This is certainly a more reality-based expectation.

Another area of mismatch occurs when there are differences in abilities between the two partners in important areas. One area that can produce significant disturbance is when the partners differ in intelligence. We have seen a number of such couples for whom communication has become difficult since they are not relating on the same intellectual level. However, there may certainly be other factors which attentuate the importance of the difference within the entire marriage. He may be a great father and lover though not as bright as she. She may have great sexual ability and be able to cook gourmet meals that delight his palate, although she never reads. Often the less bright partner may compensate for intellectual deficiencies by being more creative or more stable. However, many of the marriages the clinician sees have come to a point where such differences in abilities may have become a source of stress. The sole shared interest one couple had was a passion for remodeling houses. The wife complained that he never talked to her except about this issue. The husband could not bring himself to say that he did not talk to his wife because she was unable to relate to him on an intellectual level he found satisfying, but this became evident as he discussed his varied interests. The pattern that they had adopted was to buy a house, remodel it, sell it, and buy another. The couple was unsuccessful in developing alternative ways of relating to each other, and were constricted in this because of their differing intellectual levels. Although this marriage continues, the difference in abilities remains at best a significant vacuum in their lives.

INTERVENTION WITHIN THE LIMITED-CAPACITIES MODEL

The dynamics of problem situations which fit the limited capacities model have been defined as a mismatch between the person's capabilities and the demands of the particular environment surrounding that person. Thus, there are three areas of intervention open to the clinician: changing the client's abilities, changing the environmental demands, or aiding the client's acceptance of the mismatch and supporting the client in coping with the concomitant stress.

Changing the Client's Capacities

Capacities are not fixed, but are to some degree a reflection of the training and experience of the client. Certainly some capacities are easier to change than others; it is easier to become an acceptable bridge player than to become taller. However, people often look at their "givens" as being cast in concrete and immutable when they are not. We have seen several "homely" men and women talk about how their appearance is their albatross, that they are simply too plain to be attractive to members of the opposite sex. More often than not, this type of statement masks other dynamics, such as a fear of failure in general or fear of the opposite sex in particular (for reasons that a full assessment should determine). Other times, such feelings can reflect a simple misbelief about the modifiability of physical attractiveness. By attention to grooming and fashion, attractiveness can be greatly enhanced. Men who are quite ugly can easily grow a full beard and look like everyone else with a full beard. Women, by diet and dress, can significantly improve their appearances. More importantly, being attractive is considerably more than the physical impact one makes, as other factors contribute to one's social impact. For example, perceived competency is a factor in how attractive a person is (Mettee & Wilkins, 1972). Also, it may be the case that physical attractiveness is only an important factor in the early states of interaction, and that with other personality information, the influence of physical attractiveness on liking drops in importance (Berscheid & Walster, 1974).

In the case of mismatch between the client and his or her job situation, the immediate point of intervention would be for the therapist to recommend that the client receive appropriate training in order to function well in the job.

It is not the purpose of this book to get into the day-to-day ingenuity that the clinician needs in order to intervene effectively within a given model. In general, though, it is often an effective point of intervention when the case fits the limited-capacities model to help the clients to develop skills or characteristics so that their capacities better fit the demands of the environment.

Changing the Client's Environment

Serious sources of stress occur as a result of mismatches between the person's capacities and the requirements of the environment. These are generally in areas that are profound in one's life: work, school, or marriage. Because of the importance of these areas, the decision concerning whether or not to change the environment in these situations is a difficult one. The question is not only one of the match between the current environment and the person, but also of the match between the available alternatives and the person. A bad marriage may be better than no marriage, and can well be better than the next marriage. In terms of work and school, the client may be able to get information about the alternative environment, but there will still be large areas of ambiguity about the alternative. As we know, ambiguity leads to stress (as in experimental neurosis, which will be explored more fully in Chapter 4) and these decisions require support from the therapist and the social-support network. A general rule for the therapist is that the client should not be encouraged to simply leave an environment, but should be able to replace the unsuitable environment.

In terms of marriage, these decisions are even more difficult since all members of the family are involved. Therapists frequently observe people in relationships that are extremely destructive because the alternative seems worse. We supervised a graduate student who saw a woman in therapy who was terribly abused by her husband. He had beaten her, made her drive her car nude at gunpoint and display herself nude to his friends, and tried to force her to have sex with his friends (which she refused). Although this woman despised her husband, she chose staying with him for two reasons: the fear of what he would do to her if she left him, and the fact that there were no clear safe alternatives. Her decision was complicated by having children who were old enough to resist leaving. She would feel like she had abandoned her children if she left her husband. Although we offered support to the woman, including a referral to the local agency for helping "victims," she chose to stay with her husband.

In cases where changing the environment is a viable alternative, it is not clear to us what the special role of the therapist is. We can give counsel, but it seems that our chief role is to help clarify the consequences of the alternatives and to help the client articulate what she or he really wants. For example, we have advised several parents of severely retarded children that residential treatment would be the best available alternative for the child. Hearing the professional articulate this can significantly reduce guilt in this value-laden area and may enable parents to then decide more rationally whether they want their child at home and whether they will be able to care for him or her. People often have trouble articulating the fact that they want a divorce, and come into therapy for help to do so. Frequently people cannot admit that their job is not for them, because they feel too much like a failure if they consider that conclusion. They may need a therapist's help to face their limits and change the situation. The therapist must be alert to latent messages of the client. The actual recommendation, however, often can be given just as well by a friend or other social-support person. The therapist has added status to "authenticate" the recommendation. The role of a counselor can be an important function of the therapist. The concept of "quitting" often has strong negative connotations; people are reluctant to leave situations that are not matching their capacities or are too stressful. The change in situations is often the most powerful of available interventions.

One man we had seen in therapy had a history of several psychiatric hospitalizations. He was in constant stress over his job in a factory. He described his boss as always tormenting him with accusations of not doing enough work and with repeated racial slurs. He was degraded constantly both vocationally and personally. It did not seem like the work demands of the supervisor were fair. It was also a point of enormous pride to this man that he was employed, so he endured these pressures. We worked on the possibility of his obtaining alternative employment and we were unable to do better. This man was limited by racial prejudice, by his psychiatric history, and by his limited vocational skills. Therapy then focused on his becoming less bothered by his supervisor and by ways he could perform his job with less emotional interference. The client came to realize that his supervisor had serious personal limitations and that he should work on not allowing his supervisor's limitations to become so upsetting to him. Although he showed improvement in this area and was not as bothered by the slurs, when therapy ended he was still receptive to changing jobs.

Accepting the Situation

The intervention most often used by the therapist is helping the client accept the small mismatches between the client's capacities and the demands or expectations of the environment. The method through which acceptance can be achieved is often the use of rational-emotive approaches (Ellis, 1962, 1970). As will be discussed in Chapter 6, the therapist may be of service when the client is helped in accepting conditions which cannot be improved. This is certainly true within marriage. When, as Ellis points out, the client realizes that the partner does not exist for his or her gratification, but as an independent person with faults (some of them major faults), the client need not get angry about this. As Ellis points out, we live in an irrational world with irrational people, and demanding that people behave in a rational way and act the way they *should* simply leads to disruption. The outraged partner frequently spends a good deal of time and effort convincing the other of how terrible they are. The client should be helped to elevate his or her tolerance for differences and realize that the other person has faults and weaknesses, and that that is simply a condition of life.

For example, recently one husband told us about how sloppy his wife was. He documented, in great detail, a compelling case that she left a trail of garbage behind her. She never washed dishes, swept, or did laundry, and when she did cook she left a terrific mess. He pointed out that he did his share of domestic chores and would also cook and clean, but that she created work for him which he resented. Our comment was, "Right, your wife is a slob. Now that we are convinced, how do you expect a slob to act?" He agreed that slobs act slovenly. We then went on to say that he has done everything he could to change her, but that his repetition of angry criticism was obviously ineffective. We told him that he cannot get surprised or outraged when his wife, whom we agreed was a slob, acted in a slovenly way. He had to accept the situation or design a system in which she had fewer opportunities to be sloppy. He decided that he could not design a system with fewer opportunities, and he accepted the situation. To his surprise, she really did do considerably more housework after he stopped most of his criticism, although she was still a weak housekeeper. Because he was less angry and hostile towards her, she was no longer reinforced by his irritation over what she considered trivia. She became more reinforced by positive relating with her husband. He also had to understand her perspective. Being a housewife was not high on her priority list, as she had a professional career that she was developing and just was not concerned with the traditional values of cleanliness. After the "righteousness" of the client is ventilated, the client can often accept the fact that the other party has limited capacities in some area(s).

The same principles can be applied to help a client accept his or her own limitations. Ellis (1962, 1970) documents one basic irrational belief: one must perform well at everything one does. Ellis points out that all evaluations are relative, and that one can very easily keep expectations of one's performance higher than one's ability. In addition, there is almost always someone better with whom to compare oneself. The goal is to accept oneself with full knowledge that one cannot be perfect.

Getting clients to accept the fact that there are mismatches between their capacities and the demands that the environment (or they themselves) place on them is not easy; however, it is a very necessary step in a large proportion of therapy cases. We all have to work within our capacities. Unless the limits of our capacities are tested, we may work below the appropriate level. Some failure is a positive sign of exploration of one's limits, and should be presented to the client in that light.

4 The Respondent or Classical-Conditioning Model

The respondent model focuses on maladaptive behaviors which are acquired or maintained by classical, or Pavlovian, conditioning. In this model the key concept is *contiguity;* stimuli which are close to each other or close to a response in either space or time have the ability to become associated. The basic assessment question, as indicated in the flowchart (p. 000), concerns whether the client's behavioral problems are under stimulus control.

Pavlov's (1928) finding was that dogs, after repeated exposures to a procedure in which feeding followed the striking of a tuning fork, salivated when the tuning fork was sounded without feeding. At first Pavlov called these "psychic" secretions because sensory stimuli had the effect of producing a biological response, presumably through the psyche. Pavlov then noticed that any number of arbitrarily selected stimuli could, with repeated associations, produce the response. He called the process the development of a *conditional* response. The process is now commonly referred to as *conditioning.*

Those stimuli which can elicit reflexive responses without training, as the food in the dog's mouth elicited salivation, were called the *unconditioned stimuli* or US. The salivation, or the response that follows the US without prior training, is called the *unconditioned response* or UR. Examples of US/UR relationships are the strike to the knee (US) bringing a jerking reflex (UR); the startle response that is elicited by sudden intense auditory or visual stimuli; or the withdrawal response of a limb when pricked by a pin. These responses (UR's) were not developed by repeated exposures; they occur naturally. They can, however, be conditioned to a number of neutral stimuli through contiguity with the neutral stimulus. Some reflexes are more difficult to condition than others, with the patellar reflex (knee jerk) being particularly resistant to conditioning.

It is also important to know that there are differences in the degrees of effectiveness that some stimuli have in becoming associated with a given response. So, for example, it is difficult to condition taste aversions to kinesthetic stimuli, such as shock to an animal's paw. In a series of experiments, Garcia and his students (Garcia, Ervin, & Koelling, 1966; Garcia & Koelling, 1966) found that if an animal were given shock to the paw that was associated with a novel taste, the animals did not learn the association. However, the association between a novel taste and later nausea was learned very quickly. The research on taste aversion by Garcia and his students is important in emphasizing that conditioning is not merely the pairing of any reflexive response with any specific stimulus, but that there needs to be a consideration of the sensory modality that the stimuli are on. For example, if a racoon ate a poison berry and became nauseous 8 hours later, the racoon would not avoid the place at which it became ill (as a simple classical conditioning explanation might predict), but it would associate the *taste* of the berry with getting sick and therefore avoid that specific berry. This has obvious survival value in that the animals would never learn to avoid foods that make them ill if the illness was associated with other stimuli (e.g., visual or auditory) that surrounded the nausea, rather than with specific tastes.

Nevertheless, under a wide variety of conditions, with repeated contiguous exposures, once-neutral stimuli can elicit a response similar to the UR. The previously neutral stimulus which now can elicit a response is called the *conditioned stimulus* (CS). The response elicited by the CS is called the *conditioned response* (CR).

Furthermore, stimulus generalization can occur so that stimuli similar to the original CS can elicit a CR. Tones similar to the original one that Pavlov (1928) used were able to elicit salivation. The greater the similarity of the new tones to the original CS, the greater the degree of generalization of the response. Stimulus generalization can occur over any number of sensory or cognitive modalities. Therefore, conditioning can take place if there is similarity of stimuli to the conditioned stimulus. The clinician must look for stimulus dimensions that have common features with the stimulus situation associated with the original experiences involved in the development of a conditioned emotional response.

The clinican can use the principles of classical conditioning to determine whether a response that is either disproportionate to a given stimulus or inappropriate to a given event may have developed through previous associations with a more intense US. Therefore a person who panics over being in high places may have fallen at one time and now associates height with the unpleasant experience. A person who has an intense emotional response at the sight of a dog may have had in childhood the experience of being bitten by a dog. As indicated in the flowchart, the therapist focuses assessment, in this model, to determine whether the response occurs in the presence of specific stimulus events. Classical conditioning is one of the models that must be considered under conditions of inappropriate or disproportionate emotional responses that are linked to a specific situation. In the example above, the person may have also been scratched by a cat and, because of stimulus generalization, developed an emotional response to other household pets.

THE CONDITIONED EMOTIONAL RESPONSE AND
TWO-FACTOR THEORY

Two concepts intimately involved with the application of the classical conditioning model to human functioning are those of the conditioned emotional response (CER) and two-factor theory. The CER refers to the simple classical conditioning of an emotional reaction, while two-factor theory refers to the interaction of classical conditioning with operant conditioning. The two factors of two-factor theory are: (1) a classically conditioned aversive emotion and (2) some type of operant avoidance response which removes the organism from the CS which elicits this emotion.

The fact that emotions can be classically conditioned to previously neutral stimuli is empirically well supported. Early on in the progess of behavioral psychology, CER paradigms were invoked to explain much of dysfunctional human behavior (Dollard & Miller, 1950; Miller, 1948; Watson & Rayner, 1920). In this paradigm, originally neutral stimuli were paired with fear-eliciting stimuli. The neutral stimulus becomes associated with the aversive, feared stimulus that elicits an emotional response. Watson and Rayner had an infant view a white rat. The infant did not cry at the sight of the white rat. They then paired the sight of the white rat with a loud noise. The loud noise had been previously determined to elicit a startle response and crying. According to these pioneer investigators, soon the white rat was able to elicit the infant's crying without the previous noise. The white rat became a conditioned stimulus for crying, the conditioned response. Furthermore, it was reported that other similar stimuli were able to elicit the conditioned response by the process of stimulus generalization. Not only did a rabbit elicit crying, but the white bushy beard of Santa Claus elicited crying. Although other investigators have failed to replicate Watson and Rayner's results with similar procedures (Bregman, 1934; English, 1929), the Watson and Rayner study remains a classic exemplar of the CER in humans.

Kalish (1980) reminds us that if the aversive stimulus is strong enough (too strong for ethical experimentation with humans), the CER does quickly and reliably appear. Studies employing animal subjects (e.g., Masserman, 1945; Seligman & Maier, 1967; Wolpe, 1952) have used aversive stimuli associated with a particular location in order to investigate the CER. They have found that, with repeated trials, eventually the neutral stimulus became a CS for fear. This fear state was measured by its interference with ongoing behavior, most commonly by its ability to suppress normal bar-pressing behavior in animals. When the animal returns to the cage where it was shocked, rather than getting on with its job of pressing the lever for food, the CER elicited by the stimuli of the cage interferes with functioning and the animal may just shake and defecate.

In humans, the interference of an emotional response with ongoing response is at least equally compelling. Very few individuals function effectively when they are dominated by emotions. A situation where this is often seen is in social interactions. People who have become anxious in social situations often act inappropriately. Moreover, the number of ways emotions can interfere with competent functioning is impressive. These include test anxiety, public speaking, work performance, dealing with authority figures, or just being assertive. If the individual has a history of emotional experiences associated with these situations, the principles of classical conditioning would lead to the prediction that there would be an emotional response to these conditioned stimuli, and that the emotional response would interfere with functioning. In fact, these examples are commonly seen by therapists. People will say that they knew what was expected of them, but that anxiety interfered with performance.

Much of what the clinician sees, however, is not simply the passive CR to a feared stimulus. The client is usually not passively overwhelmed by emotions brought on by a CS. Often, behaviors the person engages in to avoid or escape the emotional response become the major problem. In these cases, instrumental responses that are reinforced by fear reduction are the presenting problem. The person who is irrationally fearful of riding in airplanes, yet manages to do so when necessary, rarely comes in for treatment. Only when the instrumental avoidance responses are overpowering and restrict the person's life will the person typically seek help. Responses like a rat jumping a barrier for thousands of trials to escape a stimulus previously associated with pain, or an executive with a fear of flying taking a demotion to avoid the necessity of air travel would be explained by two-factor theorists as the interaction of classical conditioning and instrumental learning.

In the classic two-factor theory, the classical conditioning of a previously neutral stimulus to an emotional response is thought to occur first. Then the second factor, an instrumental response, is learned which functions to avoid or to terminate the classically conditioned emotional state. The avoidance or escape response is negatively reinforced by removing the person from the aversive emotional state. Thus, the person who has social anxiety may wish to be in social situations but finds that there is a reduction of anxiety each time he or she leaves such situations. The reduction of anxiety reinforces the escape behavior and makes facing social situations that much more difficult. The cumulative history of escape being reinforced makes the problem progressively more difficult for the client to overcome alone.

The senior author's wife had an incident in which she left the house with the flame of the kitchen range on and burned a pot. After that incident, through classical conditioning, she became fearful that the flame was on whenever she left the house. Frequently when she left, she would ask to return to check that the stove was off. When it was found that the stove had been turned off, she was of course relieved, and the checking response was reinforced by her reduction of fear. The checking response, as predicted by two-factor theory, became more frequent and intense. She soon asked to check the stove any time she left the house. The reinforcement of anxiety reduction took over. When we realized that two-factor theory was in operation, we had to extinquish the response of checking. She agreed, although reluctantly, to never check the stove again. We also desensitized her to the thought of the stove being on as well as to the thought of the house burning down. By using two approaches, both desensitization and extinction (and finding that the house did not, in fact, burn down), this minor obsession quickly disappeared. There were, however, some intense periods of resistance before checking the stove was no longer an issue.

Strict two-factor theory has been questioned, especially as to whether the experience of fear is necessary to the escape response (Kalish, 1981). It is clinically apparent that many people no longer feel the conditioned emotional response that initially caused them to avoid the feared situation. If they can avoid the phobic stimulus, there is no experience of fear. Thus, while the original idea of two-factor theory was that the CER "drives" the escape response, this seems to be untrue in many cases. The theory of two-factor avoidance learning which persists today does not require active fear to motivate the escape response, and is called "weak" two-factor theory (Kalish, 1981; Rachlin, 1976).

What is important to the clinician is that classical conditioning and instrumental conditioning do often interact. It is important to be aware of such interactions when assessing for operant or respondent components. If an interaction does exist, both factors may need to be addressed therapeutically. To continue the example used previously, it is doubtful that the instrumental avoidance response of the phobic wife could be modified by operant techniques alone, without addressing the classically-conditioned fear itself. Similarly in some cases, if the fear alone is treated it may not be sufficient. The client's life must once again be restructured so that new, more adaptive instrumental responses can ensue.

The Experimental Neurosis

An important concept developed by Pavlov (1928), which has therapeutic significance, is the experimental neurosis. The *experimental neurosis* is an intense emotional response that occurs when the organism is faced with prolonged difficult discriminations (Maher, 1966). It was reported by Pavlov to occur when dogs were fed when a circle was presented and not fed when an ellipse was presented. In order to make the discrimination more difficult, the experimenters made the circle more elliptical and the ellipse more circular. After the ratio was 9:8, discriminations broke down. More importantly, for our purposes, the animals responded as if they were being punished; they howled and tried to avoid the situation. Other investigators of the experimental neurosis have reported a wide variety of behavioral signs of stress (see Maher, 1966, for a review). Among the symptoms have been hyperexciteability, motor tics, defecation, and "hallucinatory" responses. What makes these results so powerful is that they have been demonstrated in the absence of aversive events. When animals are confronted with difficult discriminations and they cannot leave the field—even if the only consequence is that they either get food or they do not—the animals show these deviant behaviors. The deviant behaviors are not due to the frustration of not getting the food, but are due to the "mixed signals" that the experimentor has constructed.

Among the most intense cases of clients making difficult discriminations are cases involving "love." We have frequently seen clients who are rendered entirely nonfunctional by "love" problems. Frequently, when we analyze what the client is responding to, we find that they have a strong attraction to someone who is sending signals mixed between approval and disapproval. Sometimes this is the case of the "pursuer" and the "distancer." The *distancer* is someone who is not comfortable in a relationship that is close. That person wants the other to pursue and sends out positive responses to approaches. However, when the pursuer comes too close, the distancer moves away. We have seen pursuers who remain at home in an intensely distressed state after trying to cope with relationships with distancers.

Often, such situations can be productively conceptualized as an instance of the experimental neurosis in which the pursuer is required to make difficult and important discriminations between the approach and the distancing cues of the person with whom there is the attraction. Frequently, these discriminations are made more important because clients, interpret their personal worth depending upon how desired they are. We have seen many cases where the person "in love" is experiencing the experimental neurosis due to making difficult discriminations. These problems are often sufficiently severe to render the victim nonfunctional.

We have also seen this type of stress response among people who are in positions in which they have high levels of responsibility and who have to make difficult discriminations. The role of the therapist is to help clients elucidate what their distress is a response to. They seem to be somewhat relieved to find that there are times when it is simply part of the process of making difficult discriminations. The experimental neurosis counters the adage that, "No news is good news." Often, the ambiguity of no news is very stressful. In both the cases of "love" and of stress, the therapist can help by giving an explanation of what is going on. The clients frequently have no understanding, and feel out of control, of these very intense situations.

Assessment

Rather than conditioned physiological reflexes, the clinician is generally concerned with conditioned *emotional* responses. These are admittedly more difficult to measure but seem to fit comfortably into the respondent model. Emotional behavior has been conceptualized as largely respondent in nature (Karen, 1974). Emotional reactions, therefore, are the class of responses that the clinician should assess to determine whether the classical-conditioning model applies in a given case. The clue for the clinician as to the applicability of the classical conditioning model may be the inappropriate intensity of a particular emotional reaction. For example, being afraid of heights if one were forced to walk on the ledge of the World Trade Center is realistic, although not adaptive. However, being afraid of heights when one is asked to be in the restaurant on top of the World Trade Center is neither realistic nor adaptive.

Children who have difficulties at school often fear going to school. However, when a child becomes extremely panicked, climbs into the closet, trembles, and sucks his or her thumb at the thought of going to school, the clinician should be assessing for some classically-conditioned fears. Although an intense emotional response frequently occurs with other models (particularly the operant model if the intense response has been reinforced in the past), the classical conditioning model should be tested first. Like other models, it must be remembered that even if the response was originally acquired in some other manner, the principles of classical conditioning may be used to modify the response.

In order to assess whether a given behavioral problem fits into the respondent model, the therapist looks for specificity in terms of the stimulus condition that produced the response. The clearest example of this is the case of phobias. Although phobias may be operants which are reinforced by their consequences, those which are respondents are elicited by the specific phobic situation. One man with a fear of heights was seen by us in therapy. He could not initially specify when his fears developed. He was a steamfitter and his firm had just contracted for a job that required him to do high-beam work. He reported that he was unable to do this. Because it was during a period of large layoffs of construction workers, he would have to lose his job. His phobia also prevented him from vacationing with the family because, in order to leave his home on Long Island, he would need to cross a bridge or fly in an airplane. There was no discernible pattern of reinforcement for his behavior, so despite the absence of a reported trauma which would make respondent conditioning the clear etiological factor, we went ahead with desensitization. As he progressed in treatment, he was able to recall an incident in which he nearly fell from a high beam. He described slipping off of the beam and hanging on about 100 feet above the ground. He described how he saw small shiny hats and little people pointing up at him. He was then able to climb back on the beam and escape safely. Needless to say, this was a very powerful emotional experience for the man.

There are two interesting facts to this case. The first is that the man was initially unable to remember the traumatic event which produced the classically conditioned association between height and the response of fear. He was only able to remember it after the treatment reduced the fear so that it was not so threatening to him. His memory of the event appeared to be driven into the unconscious. This indicates that, even if the initial assessment does not give an indication of the existence of a specific model, ongoing assessment often provides a different picture of etiological events. Second, he described his bodily response to height with the typical pattern of muscular tension and increased autonomic activity with one exception; when confronted with heights, his knees sagged and became flaccid and wobbly. When we did desensitization (which we will describe later in this chapter), we worked on muscle relaxation with the exception of his knees. We instructed him to tense his knees because wobbly knees and high steel beams are incompatible. He was able to do the high steel work after 7 sessions. The careful assessment of the location and pattern of his physical fear response was absolutely essential to his treatment.

In the case of phobias, the specific eliciting conditions are usually relatively clear. However, the etiological stimuli may sometimes be more obscure. An example of this is the case of a woman who was allergic to roses. She would sneeze and become flushed when roses were in her presence. However, she was thought to be malingering when she had the same response to plastic roses. The classical conditioning model easily explains how the visual cues of roses (the CS) elicited the allergic response (the CR).

It is possible for classical conditioning to occur with temporal cues alone. For years, the senior author had found himself feeling anxious on November 22. This was finally explained by realizing that it was the date when President Kennedy had been assassinated. The trauma of that day lingered by becoming associated with the date.

One client came to our office weeping and anxious. She had been this way for days and did not understand why. First she was asked to describe her feelings. The description of tremors, sweating, and a strong feeling of impending doom were consistent with a sympathetic anxiety response typical of several models. She was unable to relate her feelings to either diet or any physical environmental event so it made a biological model less likely. There were no obvious reinforcers. She had been married for nearly a year and she described the relationship as having only the usual adjustment problems. Her history did not indicate any selective vulnerability to these usual stresses. In fact, she had worked her way through college and had been considered a strong person by her husband. The probability of an operant model was reduced by the fact that she hid her anxiety from her husband as long as possible. Although he responded to her problem by showing warm concern, the warm concern had also been demonstrated before the onset of these anxious behaviors.

After a thorough exploration of her feelings, it was determined that her emotional state was associated with her upcoming first anniversary. She had been previously married and just before her first anniversary, she returned home from a trip to find that her husband was dead from a bizarre and grotesque accident. The temporal cues of the event generalized to the timeframe of her current marriage. The respondent model was one of several which were tested in this case. Since this model is infrequently seen in cases like this, the determination was done by process of elimination. Consequences did not reinforce the woman's response and there was no immediate precipitant.

INTERVENTION

The respondent model leads directly to several strategies of intervention. These can be roughly divided into extinction procedures and counterconditioning procedures, as distinguished on the basis of whether the theoretical purpose of the procedure is to eliminate the existing stimulus/response bond or to condition a new one in its place. As shown in the flowchart (p. xii–xiii), stimulus control procedures also have a place in intervention strategies.

Extinction Procedures

Within the classical conditioning paradigm, it was early noted that when the CS was presented without the US over a number of trials, the CS lost its ability to elicit a CR. This process was called *respondent extinction*. It is important to note, for the purposes of the clinician especially, that an extinguished response will rapidly be reconditioned if the contiguity of the CS and the US is reestablished. Therefore, if a person who has been successfully desensitized to heights has an experience of falling, the anxiety will quickly be reestablished in that situation. Extinction procedures within clinical practice, then, are based on the principle of exposing the client to the CS in the absence of the US. A relatively easy way of doing this is to simply have the client describe in detail the situation that evoked anxiety. The description can serve as the CS and the absence of any cataclysmic event (US) will allow the anxiety to extinguish.

Systematic Desensitization. Joseph Wolpe (1958) made a significant breakthrough in the application of psychological principles to the practice of psychotherapy when he used the classical-conditioning model to devise a treatment for phobias. His treatment, called *systematic desensitization,* is a well-researched and extremely effective technique. Wolpe's genius was in recognizing that humans are capable of using imagery as a CS in an effective manner. Therefore, for the person who is phobic of heights, it is not necessary to have him or her actually climb to the top of tall buildings to feel the emotional reaction of fear. The person can achieve this reaction by *imagining* the CS (the feared situation). Moreover, extinguishing fear associated with fearful images effectively extinguishes fears of real-life situations from which these images were derived.

As Wolpe originally conceived it, systematic desensitization was based on the principle of inhibiting the anxiety response by introducing an incompatible competing response such as sexual arousal, assertion, or relaxation. Relaxation became the response usually employed, as it can be induced relatively easily in the therapist's office.

The procedure for implementing systematic desensitization was originally described by Wolpe (1958), and began with pretraining of the client in relaxation skills. The second step was the development, with the client, of a hierarchy of feared situations. Situations which produced fearful responses were generated by the client, then rated in terms of how fearful they were for the person. After the hierarchy was formed, the actual procedure began. The client was instructed to relax, or (preferably, according to Wolpe) was hypnotized. Then the client was asked to imagine the feared scenes while deeply relaxed. The least fear-provoking scenes were imagined first. When the client imagined slightly fear-provoking situations without anxiety, the therapist continued up the hierarchy, asking the client to imagine the more anxiety-producing items. Clients were instructed to indicate whenever they felt anxious. If they indicated that they felt anxious, usually by raising a finger, Wolpe was adamant that the imagery should be immediately terminated. This was due to his belief that the client was at risk of being "sensitized" rather than desensitized to the fear-producing images, if overly disturbing scenes were presented too early in therapy.

Wolpe also believed that hierarchies encompassing distinct "themes" were necessary for desensitization to work, since he thought anxiety was bound directly to the particular stimulus configuration which elicited the phobic behavior. An agoraphobic individual, in Wolpe's view, may require desensitization on several dimensions; for example, fear of crowds, fear of dying prematurely, fear of driving a car, and fear of open spaces.

As systematic desensitization has been researched and utilized clinically over the years, Wolpe's original theoretical assumptions (especially regarding the concept of "inhibiting" the anxiety) and his specific instructions have been challenged. Theoretically, we feel that systematic desensitization can be accurately characterized as a type of respondent extinction. During the procedure, the therapist is presenting the client with feared conditioned stimuli in a situation "safe" enough (the client is relaxed and comfortable, in a familiar place with a trusted therapist) that the client can be prevented from avoiding the CS long enough for extinction to take place.

In clinical practice, we find that systematic desensitization is a robust procedure with more room for accommodation that Wolpe originally indicated. We proceed with desensitization at a much faster pace, and we ignore many of Wolpe's procedural cautions, yet find we get faster results. The pace of desensitization, as with all therapeutic interventions, should be programmed by the client's rate of progress. If the person is good at relaxation skills (and many people, because of the increased popularity of yoga and meditation, are quite good) the clinician can spend minimal time on teaching relaxation. We first simply ask the person to become a "wet noodle" and ask if and where they experience tension. It is surprisingly difficult for most people to be able to articulate where they experience the tension. We may ask them to imagine a situation that makes them anxious in order for them to reconstruct the tension. We then probe directly to see whether the person is relaxed, by lifting an arm, leg, or moving the head to determine the level of relaxation. We use the amount of muscular resistance as an indicator of tension.

Although some therapists have reservations about physically touching clients, we feel it is extremely helpful. We tell the client what we are about to do—e.g. "I'm going to lift your arm to see how relaxed it is"— and then do it. Frequently people report being relaxed while their arms are as rigid as a steel bar. If the person is able to relax quickly, then systematic desensitization can begin. If the person is unable to relax, we specifically focus on those muscle groups that have responded by becoming tense. We need not spend time on those muscle groups that are already relaxed. A very important component of relaxation is diaphragmatic breathing. The client is taught to breath by using the diaphragm (belly breathing). There is some evidence that diaphragmatic breathing activates the parasympathetic nervous system and promotes relaxation.[1] The reader is referred to Goldfried and Davison (1976) for a thorough procedural description of relaxation and systematic desensitization.

In vivo exposure.   Actual exposure to the feared CS in the absence of the US is the therapeutic technique most clearly similar to an experimental extinction schedule. During *in vivo* exposure, the person puts him or herself in the presence of the feared stimulus, either alone or accompanied by the therapist. It is important that the client be able to remain in the feared situation long enough for extinction to take place. Primarily for this reason, *in vivo* exposures are usually introduced to the client in a graduated way, with the first exposures taking place in a situation which is only slightly fear-provoking. It must be remembered that many clients come into therapy because they find themselves engaging in behaviors designed to escape or avoid such exposures. Therefore, it is recommended that the therapist do everything possible to ensure that an *in vivo* exposure session does not become a negatively reinforced escape or avoidance trial for the fearful person. The therapist should maximize the chances that: (1) the person is actually able to complete the session without unmanageable anxiety levels; and (2) no new fear-provoking US occur to *strengthen* the conditioned fear. (For example, with a person fearful of the water, the therapist should take every precaution that the client is never actually in danger of falling in the water and being panicked).

If the stimulus chosen is too anxiety-provoking for the client at that particular time, the client may attempt to escape the situation and have the escape reinforced by the relief of being out of the terrifying state. To help the client manage the anxiety engendered by *in vivo* exposures, we have found it useful to train them in relaxation skills beforehand. Systematic desensitization can also be used as a prelude to *in vivo* exposure or as an adjunct to it. Even if a person's anxiety has been largely extinguished by systematic desensitization alone, it is helpful for the therapist to encourage *in vivo* exposures near the termination of therapy in order to aid the client in recognizing the degree of improvement that was accomplished.

For reasons not clear to us, frequently clients who have done extremely well in overcoming their phobias have not attributed their progress to the desensitization program. We have heard clients state that they improved, but that, "It did not have anything to do with the relaxation exercises." At

---

[1]Richard Friedman, personal communication.

first, we would probe to see if other factors were operating. After not finding any in several cases, and seeing a very specific and direct reduction in anxiety after desensitization (e.g., losing a long-standing fear of barbers after a haircut was desensitized), we simply smile and tell clients that we are delighted that they no longer experience anxiety in those situations.

Implosion.   Another technique within the respondent model which uses the principle of extinction is implosion. During implosion, the client is confronted with a magnification of his or her biggest fears by imagining fearful situations. In addition, the technique requires presentation of psychodynamically symbolic stimuli that are regarded as part of the internal fears of the client. Stampfl, an originator of the procedure (Stampfl & Levis, 1967) gave a demonstration of implosion that the senior author attended. The subject was a young woman who had a fear of bees. He had her begin by imagining bees flying around her. He then suggested the bees increasing in size and in number. Within a short time, the woman was asked to visualize the bees having big penises and entering every orifice of her body. The subject was in marked distress and cried violently during this presentation. At the end of the session, however, she reported that she felt more comfortable with the thought of bees than she had previously.

Stampfl and Levis (1967) explain the theoretical basis of the procedure as that of respondent extinction. They reasoned that, as the extinction of learned emotional responses in animals occurs fastest when the stimulus conditions (CS) used in extinction are as similar as possible to the original conditions (US) which caused the fear, the same principle should apply to extinction of phobias in humans. Thus, they believe that using gradual exposure to approximations of the feared stimulus (as in systematic desensitization) is unnecessary and a waste of time. Implosion, in their view, forces the completion of feared acts in imagination that are avoided in real life by the neurotic symptoms the client exhibits. The procedure of implosion, then, short-circuits the avoidance syndrome and forces extinction to occur.

Flooding is a similar procedure that exposes clients to magnifications of the feared situations, but does not have the psychoanalytic symbolism of implosion. For the person with the fear of bees, a flooding procedure would have the person imagine giant bees all over the place, probably even having them sting, but without the sexual connotations.

It is our contention that implosion therapy or flooding techniques are effective partially because they produce a contrast effect. As will be discussed more thoroughly in Chapter 6, we feel that there are important elements of the use of principles of adaptation-level theory (Helson, 1964) in flooding or implosive techniques. Exposing a person to the image of giant stinging bees provides a background comparison that diminishes, by contrast, the emotional impact of the real event of a small, generally harmless, bee.

However effective the procedure may be, there is no doubt that it is extremely distressing to clients, and may even discourage some clients from continuing therapy. It is recommended that implosion be used when other less noxious treatments have failed. Our experience has been that flooding procedures have backfired with psychotic clients. These clients, for reasons that may be related to the tendency of schizophrenics to habituate slowly (Mednick, 1970), report that they feel worse after we have used flooding procedures. It is as if they never habituate to the anxiety associated with the aversive flooding situation.

Counterconditioning Procedures

The purpose of counterconditioning procedures within the respondent model is to form new stimulus/response connections to replace the current, dysfunctional ones. Specifically, the intent is to associate the old CS with a new US. In the case of positive counterconditioning, the old CS which previously evoked fear or anxiety would be replaced, presumably, with a new connection between the old CS and a new, nonaversive US. In either case, more than simple extinction is taking place.

In the counterconditioning procedure, the point is to introduce new, positively valenced unconditioned stimuli in the presence of the stimuli which have previously been conditioned stimuli for a fear response. In one dramatic case, a 14-year-old girl witnessed her father die suddenly of a heart attack on the second floor of their home. Subsequently, she became terrified of going upstairs without being accompanied by someone. As her bedroom and the only bathroom were on the second floor, this seriously inconvenienced the rest of the family, as well as being an unhappy situation for the girl herself. One can see how the traumatic event of her father's death could be associated with the surrounding stimuli of the second floor and lead to the inappropriate emotional response. The treatment involved both operant and classical conditioning elements. The respondent portion of treatment involved redesigning the environment so as to pair new, positive unconditioned stimuli with the feared conditioned stimuli associated with the second floor. Assessment determined that the girl liked eating snacks and watching television. One of the upstairs bedrooms was converted into a den and the TV was moved there from downstairs. Snacks were served in the den. Therefore, the second floor was the

CS for the emotional response. By pairing the second floor with the positive experiences of eating and watching TV, the new CR will be a pleasant one.

On the operant side, the girl had received a great deal of attention by refusing to go upstairs herself. The attention was given by being accompanied upstairs and by having arguments about whether she should go alone. Thus, the family was advised never to argue with her, but simply to accompany her for smaller and smaller portions of the trip upstairs, and to congratulate her on her progress. She was successively reinforced for more and more independent behavior. The combination of operant and respondent approaches in this case was quite successful, and the problem was eliminated within 2 weeks.

There are other elements in the desensitization procedure that add to its effectiveness as a counterconditioning procedure in a broad sense. We instruct clients that there are feedback loops between the body and the mind and that these feedback loops are important tools for self-control. We explain the James/Lange theory of emotion (James, 1890) as an explanation as to how the response of our body can influence our emotional state. According to the James/Lange theory of emotion, a person feels a specific emotion after engaging in behaviors consistent with that emotion and observing his or her behavior. Therefore, according to this theory, we see a bear in the woods and we run. This theory holds that it is the running that makes us afraid. We then give a potent demonstration (which the reader may wish to try) and ask the client to, "Smile and think a hostile thought." We then ask the client to "Smile and think a warm loving thought." Next we counterbalance and ask the client to clench a fist, the jaw, and lower the eyebrows and repeat the procedure. The overwhelming number of clients have reported that smiling facilitates warm thoughts and inhibits angry thoughts, while clenching facilitates angry thoughts and inhibits warm thoughts.

There are two explanations of this phenomenon; one is that we have countless experiences of smiling while being happy and classical conditioning has occurred. Because of the countless number of times that we smiled and felt warm, smiling has been associated with warm thoughts. Smiling has become the CS for warm thoughts, the UR. The other theory is that there are innate neurological feedback loops that create the effect (e.g., Brown and Schwartz, 1980; Vaughn and Lanzetta, 1980). We use an extension of the James/Lange theory to teach the use of the body as a therapeutic intervention in many cases. We have used this principle very effectively in dealing with unwanted emotional expressions in autistic and retarded individuals. For instance, one teenage retarded girl in a residential care facility frequently cried because she missed her parents. If allowed to "get going" on a crying jag, the episode typically lasted 1 to 2 hours, increasing all the while in intensity until she fell asleep or became physically exhausted. It was hypothesized that her crying became a cue (CS) for her further upset. The intervention was to get the girl moving in a way associated with happy emotions. Thus, whenever she began to whimper, her counselor was instructed to begin to dance with her. The somatic feedback of dancing stopped the tears immediately, and frequently the client would be smiling and dancing vigorously, with the tears still wet on her cheeks. A Skinnerian therapist might never try this intervention because the dancing, being done contingently upon the client's weeping, would be expected to reinforce the crying, and thereby increase its frequency. This assumption only holds true if the model operating is the operant model, discussed fully in chapter 5. There were clues that this problem did not fit the operant model. This girl did not stop her crying in response to other events which she normally liked more than dancing (e.g., attention from the counselor, hugging, or snacks). Therefore, the crying did not appear to be an operant. When the intervention was evaluated several weeks after it was initiated, the overall frequency of crying had not increased, while the duration of crying spells had decreased considerably. This confirmed our conceptualization of the problem as respondent rather than operant.

We had a 40-year-old woman come to therapy with an extreme phobia of cats. Her phobia was so intense that she panicked in a department store when she saw a porcelain figure of a cat. As a way of habituating her anxious response to cats, we asked her to talk about cats. She was reluctant to even discuss them but did so with an expression of disgust. Her lips were tightly curled, her nose was wrinkled, and her eyes were tight. We required her to change her expression to a calm one as she continued the conversation about cats. She was asked to relax her facial muscles and even try to smile when she spoke about cats. At first she was resistent, but we explained the reason why her expressions amplified her feelings. We all laughed at the humor of her facial expressions and that encouraged her to try smiling while talking about cats. She reported that her feelings of disgust decreased as she replaced her expression of disgust with a calm one. We also conducted a desensitization program. The effect was rapid and positive.

Coping Model of Systematic Desensitization.   It is certainly debatable whether the extinction procedures do not also contain elements of counterconditioning. However, it was felt that the major component of these procedures was extinction, since new responses were not overtly conditioned to the old CS.

Systematic desensitization, as usually practiced, was included in that category. Goldfried (1971) presented a new conceptualization of systematic desensitization and suggested some procedural changes which make the procedure one more accurately described as a counterconditioning technique. Goldfried reconceptualized the process of systematic desensitization (SD) as the acquisition of a general anxiety-reducing skill by the client, rather than the passive extinction of conditioned fear. He saw SD as teaching the client to cope with proprioceptive anxiety responses. Thus, he changed the conceptualization of SD from a passive respondent extinction paradigm to the active learning of a connection between the old, fear-provoking CS and the positively valenced state of relaxation (a US).

Following from his conceptual change, Goldfried (1971) suggested procedural changes. First, that it is unnecessary to desensitize to distinct "themes" since it is the person's own bodily tension responses that she or he is being desensitized to. Rather than terminating the imagery when it became anxiety provoking as was stressed by Wolpe (1958), the client should maintain the image while attempting to relax away the tension is evoked. In this way, the connection between the imagined conditioned stimuli and the US of relaxation can be conditioned. Although Goldfried described the new conceptualization as "self-control," it fits well into a counterconditioning paradigm.

In many respects, there is a direct teaching element to desensitization; clients are taught a response incompatible with the anxiety response. They are taught how to relax when in the presence of stimuli that once evoked anxiety. Replacing problematic responses by teaching more appropriate responses is an important ingredient to successful therapy.

There are times when habituation procedures can be used effectively. These procedures require that the client have repeated exposures to a situation so that any emotional component of that situation no longer occurs; it habituates. In perhaps the most dramatic case treated by the authors, a habituation procedure was used. The senior author was supervising a second-year graduate student who reported that her client, a very bright attractive 20-year-old student, claimed to have a 19-year-old daughter. Our first response was that this was a reporter for the student newspaper who was trying to do an exposé on the student clinic. When we sat in on a therapy session and asked the client to describe her daughter, we thought that a "plant" would break down and be unable to describe details. However, ample detail was given, down to the length of the fingernails and the eye color. We then directly asked the client, in a menacing tone, how a 20-year-old woman could have a 19-year-old daughter. The response was quite casual: "I must have been one year old." The response was the classic *la belle indifférence* seen in hysterical disorders.

We quickly realized the seriousness of the symptom and were utterly confused. Within weeks changes occurred. The daughter became able to take over the body of the "mother" and did so at inopportune times. The client's boyfriend (who had originally insisted on her entering therapy) came in. He was alarmed because the daughter took over while he was making love to his girlfriend. He reported a distinctively different response pattern. The client was able to report other times when the "daughter" took control. One was while driving when the daughter took control of the car and drove the car into a ditch in an attempt to hurt or kill her mother.

The relevent background of the client was that she was an extremely competent 20-year-old woman who was able to both maintain a full course load with a near "A" average and was able to work 40 hours per week as an executive. She was from a religious Catholic background where premarital sex was strongly frowned upon. She had had an abortion 6 months previous to the emergence of her "daughter."

We were absolutely confused on how to intervene. We rejected any aversive conditioning approach for reasons discussed in the next section, and we rejected an operant approach as being too removed from the situation. It seemed that if we presented aversive stimuli to her concurrent with her reporting her "daughter," she might simply find therapy aversive. Remember, she was not sure she had a problem and she was sure she had a daughter. If we differentially reinforced her for statements other than those of her daughter, we would barely scratch the surface of the available reinforcers in her life.

We consulted a colleague, Marvin Levine, who was not associated with the behavioral tradition. Seeing that the client had guilt over the abortion and had wanted to have the child, he recommended that we habituate the guilt. He felt that the woman's belief that she had a daughter was a way of resolving an unconscious conflict. Because of the client's strong Catholic background, she was guilt-ridden over the abortion, and for perhaps the same reasons, she also wanted to have the child. By "having" the "daughter," the client could resolve these intense conflicts. That the daughter started to harm the client was consistent with the Freudian explanation that there was a great deal of guilt involved.

We had the client repeat the details of the abortion many times until she could do so with no emotional expression. The experience was tedious for both the client and for us. We continued this for 6 weeks. The client then reported that her boyfriend told her that she really did not have a daughter. The client agreed and acted somewhat confused about how she could believe that she had a 19-year-old daughter.

The next semester the client did an independent academic study with us. She reported no recurrance of the "daughter." If anything, she was incredulous that she could have ever believed that she had a 19-year-old daughter. However, when we discussed that period of her life, it seemed as if she rarely thought about it.

Aversive conditioning.   A response sequence may be stopped by pairing the stimuli associated with the unwanted response with a noxious stimulus. So, for example, a person who wants to stop smoking may enter a program in which smoking is paired with electric shock, with the intent that smoking acquires the aversive characteristics associated with shock. Aversion therapy has been used to discourage "deviant" sexual practices (e.g., MacCulloch, Feldman, & Pinschof, 1965; Marks and Gelder, 1967), as treatment for alcoholism (e.g., MacCulloch, Feldman, Orford & Mac-Culloch, 1966), drug addiction (e.g., Wolpe, 1965) and overeating (e.g., Meyer & Crisp, 1964).

However, the results of aversive conditioning have been equivocal (Rachman & Teasdale, 1969). There are several theoretical problems with aversive conditioning as usually practiced. As pointed out by Rescorla (1967, 1968), it is the *correlation* of the CS and the US, rather than simply the number of pairings of CS and US, that lead to classical conditioning. Every occurrence of the CS in the absence of the US reduces the effect of the conditioning. Rachman and Teasdale acknowledge that extremely rapid extinction usually occurs once the person is outside the lab where the aversive conditioning took place. Each time the person engages in the unwanted behavior (cigarette smoking, homosexual acts, etc.) without receiving a noxious stimulus, he or she is undergoing an extinction trial, and the conditioned aversion to the behavior is weakened. The association that is perhaps best learned in aversive conditioning is that between the shock apparatus and the shock; that association is contiguous and correlative. With the use of this procedure, it should be expected that the person will avoid the shock apparatus and not the cigarette.

In a series of brilliant experiments which led him to earn the Distinguished Scientist Award of the American Psychological Association, John Garcia and his associates (Garcia, Ervin, & Koelling, 1966; Garcia & Koelling, 1966) demonstrated that there are biologically determined limits on which configurations of stimuli can be associated through classical conditioning. For example, in the case of rats (the experimental animal used by Garcia et al., 1966), it was found that the CS of taste could be associated with the US of sickness, but controlled stimuli in other modalities (visual and auditory) were very difficult to condition to the US of sickness. Conversely, visual and auditory stimuli could be successfully associated with the US of electric shock, whereas taste stimuli could not.These biologically determined associations differ from species to species. The implications of these findings for aversive conditioning with humans is that, for the procedure to be effective, it may be necessary that the US and the CS be chosen for their "associability." It seems unlikely that electric shock would be, for humans, particularly associable with eating or smoking.

There are some aversive treatments that do make use of US/CS pairs that, on an intuitive level at least, seem more associable. The senior author smoked 3 packs of cigarettes a day at one point in his life, and immediately prior to quitting the habit, increased his intake to 6 packs a day. After 2 days of this, smoking became aversive, and after 3 days, it was painful. When the last cigarette was crushed, smoking cigarettes was clearly associated with pains in the chest. The impulse to smoke was accompanied by a definite association with intense chest pain. This association lasted for about 6 months, by which time the habit of smoking had been replaced by other activities. That was 19 years ago and there seems to be little chance of relapse. Two recent reviews of behavioral treatments to end smoking concluded that the technique of rapid smoking, in which the client puffs rapidly until unable to continue, is the most effective behavioral technique currently available (Bernstein & McAlister, 1976; Lichtenstein & Danaher, 1976). Rapid smoking utilizes a CS/US pair from the same sensory modality. It should be pointed out, however, that this technique is potentially physically harmful for some people.

Aversive procedures certainly have the potential for misuse. In an analysis of aversion therapy, Rachman and Teasdale (1969) state their belief that aversive procedures should only be used when other procedures have been tried first and when the client gives permission for their use. We would add to these constraints the consideration of the harm of the habit relative to the pain of the procedure. For theoretical reasons, we feel aversive conditioning should be used only when it can be effectively correlated with *all* occurrences of the response, and when the CS/US pair are selected from the same sensory modality. These conditions do not occur often in clinical practice. Therefore, aversive procedures are of very limited clinical use.

Contingent Negative Practice.   An approach to the treatment of involuntary motor responses was based upon, among other things, principles of the specificity of punishment. The treatment is called *contingent negative practice* and it has been used successfully in the treatment of tics (Levine & Sheff, 1979) and in the treatment of stuttering (Levine, Sandeen & Ramirez, 1981; Levine & Ramirez, 1985). Negative practice has been used by Dunlap (1932) for controlling bad habits and had been used, with some reported success, by Yates (1958).

The treatment requires that the client repeat the involuntary response *contingent* upon its occurence for a prescribed period. In the case of tics, the client is asked to, during a limited period of the day, repeat the tic each time it occurs for a period of 30 seconds. In the case of stuttering, the client is asked to repeat the stutter 10 times after each occurrence, generally during a 15-minute period of reading. In both cases, the contingent negative practice is to be administered only in those times that there would not be any social stigma; i.e., times when the family is alone or times that the individual will not be embarrassed. This program has both respondent and operant elements.

The point to be considered here is that the punishment is precisely in the area that the response is to be inhibited and that the punishment is relatively contiguous with the unwanted response. Clients report that it becomes quite aversive to repeat a tic for 30 seconds, especially when the tic is a very high-frequency occurence. In some subjects, the frequency of tics decreased from as many as 600 per hour to zero in 3 weeks. In some subjects the decrease in tics could be seen within the session, while others did not respond for as long as 2 months. Over 90% of the research subjects did improve. All of these tics were of long standing and had resisted other forms of treatment.

Spontaneous Recovery.   Whenever a classical conditioning procedure is used, the client should be made aware of the likelihood of spontaneous recovery of the response. Spontaneous recovery refers to the process by which an extinguished response tends to strengthen without reinforced trials. For example, desensitization may well remove a fear of heights. After the client has mastered heights for some time, the fear response may spontaneously reccur. It is important that the client be made aware of this, so that the client does not panic and feel that the gains made were lost. For example, one 20-year-old woman who had responded quite well to contingent negative practice for her stuttering felt she could now talk fluently. She then had 2 days that were almost as bad for her as before treatment. Although she had fears that the treatment "failed," these fears were greatly reduced by warning her that spontaneous recovery was a possibility. After the troublesome period, she recovered her previous gains. It is important to alert clients to spontaneous recovery in order to avoid their feeling of failure when and if this predictable phenomenon occurs.

Stimulus Control Procedures.   Responses that occur in contiguity with a stimulus become, over trials, under control of that stimulus. The stimulus, simply by being present whenever a response is made and absent when the response is not made, eventually comes to have the power to elicit that response. The concept of stimulus control can be used by the clinician to increase or decrease the frequency of a target response.

In the case of overeating, for example, the environments in which eating occurs are numerous, and include "hidden" places where food can be gorged in private. Once, while explaining stimulus control procedures to lecturers in a weight loss program, all of whom had once been obese, we gave the example of how people rarely get hungry in the bathroom because they never eat there. Well over half the people in the room immediately responded with surprise; they had often eaten in the bathroom. Obese people frequently eat while in front of the TV, in the bedroom, or in the car, as well as in the kitchen or dining room, and all of these locations can become conditioned stimuli for eating. It is therefore necessary to decrease the frequency of eating by narrowing the range of stimuli in the presence which it occurs. Ferster, Nurnberger, and Levitt (1962) were the first to suggest stimulus-control procedures designed to control eating. They suggested that overweight people eat only in the presence of a very discrete set of stimuli: at one place in the dining room. Localizing eating will, over time, limit the eliciting cues.

An ingenious plan to put studying under stimulus control was proposed by Goldiamond (1965). He advised a student, who was having trouble studying, to design her study area so that it was comfortable and free from distractions. The student was advised to do homework *only* at this desk, rather than at any other location. She was also asked to do only *homework* at this desk, i.e., not to daydream, doodle, or do anything else. It is important to note that daydreaming and doodling were not forbidden, they were only prohibited at the desk. If the student felt like daydreaming, she was required to get up and daydream elsewhere and return to the desk when the daydream passed. In this way, studying was coming under the control of the stimuli surrounding the desk. It is also important to note that no quota on the amount of time spent was applied; she was only asked to follow the rules of studying only at the desk and doing nothing but studying at the desk. The procedure was reported as quite effective for Goldiamond, and we have used this approach frequently with good results. It also helps to incorporate the principles of operant psychology in the treatment of such a problem, and suggest that the student can watch TV or perform some other desirable activity only after the homework is finished.

Goldiamond (1965) also reported the use of stimulus control procedures to control the obsessive jealousy felt by a man after he had discovered that his wife had had an affair. Goldiamond suggested he go sit on a "sulking stool" in the garage whenever he felt jealous thoughts and sulky mood coming on. For a combination of respondent and operant reasons (it was undoubtedly unpleasant and ineffective to sit alone in the garage), the man's jealousy decreased.

Bootzin (1972) described a stimulus control treatment for insomnia.

Although he conceptualized it as an operant procedure, we think it is more accurately viewed as emerging from a respondent analysis. Since an insomniac has many trials of pairing the bed with tossing and turning, eventually the stimulus of the bed itself comes to control the response of restlessness. Bootzin suggested that the client get out of bed and do something else as soon as he felt he was unable to sleep. This reduces the contiguity between being in bed and being restless. The client was instructed to return to bed only when he felt sleepy, and to repeat the procedure as many times as necessary. Bootzin reported good results with this treatment. It is important to keep in mind that needs for sleep change over the life cycle, and frequently people force habits of sleep on themselves which are no longer functional. Attempting to get more sleep than one needs may lead to the false belief that one is an insomniac.

If the therapist has adequate control over the client's environment, stimuli can be regulated to either increase or decrease the frequency of responses. All that is required is knowledge of the stimuli associated with a given event and knowledge of the resources available to change the contiguity of the response with those stimuli. Stimulus control procedures also have utility with populations that engage in self-stimulation behaviors. We have consulted with a school for youngsters having multiple disabilities and some of them would talk to themselves or just grin and wave their hands. When we completed a functional analysis, we could not see any pattern of reinforcement for these behaviors other than the reinforcement inherent in the self-stimulation. We placed small mats in the classroom and required that these youngsters stay there whenever they could not control themselves. They were allowed back into classroom activities only when they stopped the self-stimulation behaviors. The mats then functioned as discriminative stimuli for the self-stimulation, limiting the performance of the behavior to times when the children were sitting on them. There was also an operant component to this intervention, in that children were removed from the classroom activity contingent upon self-stimulation. While several youngsters showed significant clinical improvement under these conditions, one became worse. We judged that it was reinforcing for him to become more isolated and we changed the procedure.

In an article published in a popular magazine, F. M. Levine (1982) recommended stimulus-control procedures that could be used to increase intimacy in the family. The development of intimacy is not automatic; it requires communication of feelings, experiences, fears, and weaknesses; it also requires that we offer support for each other's faults and failings. In addition, the development of intimacy also requires that we experience conflict in order to be able to learn how to resolve inevitable conflicts that develop when people live together.

Television frequently inhibits the experiences necessary for the development of intimacy in families. Because the average American spends approximately 30 hours a week watching television, it becomes a major, if not the major, source of social interactions within the family. Approximately 50% of American families own more than one set, and 14% have more than two televisions. Because of this, we see many families in therapy who simply do not have opportunities to communicate. Many with multiple sets avoid conflict about programs by going off to their own room whenever there are disagreements regarding which programs to watch. These family members are being deprived of opportunities to communicate and basic training in conflict resolution.

We often see couples or families in therapy who fit this pattern. We use stimulus control principles to create conditions that can increase the opportunities for the development of intimacy. First, we strongly urge that couples remove the television from areas that are conducive to dialogue. Many couples, for example, eat dinner with the television set on and therefore never have a dialogue. We have them place the TV in a den or living room. Our goal is to have the dining place become the discriminative stimulus for dialogue.

Next we urge them to get rid of all TVs except one. They are encouraged to learn how to make and abide by rules when differences arise, or to learn how to handle the inevitable frustration of not getting one's way.

Most families report that they have initial periods of silence when the set is not at the table. Soon, however, they report that they start speaking to each other. Several have reported that after they no longer watch television at dinner, they are able to continue discussions with each other throughout the evening. We cannot *require* that people speak to one another, but we can use stimulus control principles to design an environment that is conducive to the development of intimacy.

PROBLEMS ADDRESSED BY THE RESPONDENT MODEL

In addition to the problems of fears, phobias, and difficulties with stimulus control which have already been discussed, two other common dysfunctions often fit into the respondent model. These are the problems of anger control and sexual dysfunction. It should be emphasized that these problems do not necessarily fit into a respondent model (that would be determined by the facts of the particular case), but they frequently do so. It is therefore imperative to investigate whether a respondent conceptualization fits when such problems are presented. However, the therapist must be assured that other models are ruled out. Ruling out rival models is always an important part of the assessment procedure.

Anger Control

Just as fear can become a classically conditioned response in the presence of certain conditioned stimuli, so can anger. There are times when a person has had a history of getting angry in the presence of specific stimulus conditions and then these conditions either elicit anger themselves or lower the threshold for anger to occur. Most of us have some people with whom we have a history of dispute. One family we saw in therapy came in because of extreme difficulties with a teenage daughter. The girl had, at the age of 16, already run away three times. Since the age of 10 she had been using drugs and since 12 she had been sexually promiscuous. While the mother and daughter got along relatively well, the father was unable to tolerate his daughter's behavior and was at the point where he never spoke to her in a rational tone of voice. Her presence was literally a discriminative stimulus for him to get angry. She responded the same way to him for the same reasons. The first few sessions were therefore marked by one or the other leaving in a rage.

Although there were certainly other dynamics present in this case, it was felt that it was essential to extinguish the automatic anger responses of father and daughter to each other, before any other intervention could be attempted. We focused on the father, since, as we told him, he was the adult and had to take more responsibility in changing the situation. We suggested that he make every effort to be positive or at least neutral when he was with his daughter for the following week. Although this was extremely difficult for him, he was able to comply. The following week we asked him to plan several pleasant interactions with his daughter. Although these were not significant by most people's standards (they included kissing her goodnight and getting her a snack while they watched TV), they made an impact. Father and daughter were at least able to tolerate each other's presence without leaving the room, and therapy could continue. Other explanations could be invoked for the change (the father was expressing love, making his daughter feel more secure, etc.), but a respondent model fit the data and guided the intervention effectively. The point in this case was to extinguish the anger response by reducing the likelihood that the father be argumentative, and to create new competing associations by asking the father to act nicely toward his daughter. Her positive (or at least less negative) reactions to his efforts also changed his associations between her and anger.

More practically, however, the client can be taught how to better handle situations which evoke anger. Novaco (1975) has developed a nine-pronged treatment program for anger control which deals with all of the different dynamics which can result in anger-control problems. The treatment component most directly related to the respondent model is that of relaxation training. In this case, the relaxation is a competing response that is incompatible with anger. Systematic desensitization has been tried with anger-control problems and has been successful (Rimm, DeGroot, Boord, Reiman, & Dillow, 1971).

In our clinical experience, we once had a group of parents of hyperactive children who were being taught operant reinforcement procedures for managing their children. The entire group reported no change in two sessions. When this was investigated further, the members of the group reported that there were times when they were simply too angry at their youngster's provocations to carry out the reinforcement procedures they had been taught. The children were therefore on an intermittant schedule of reinforcement, with their disruptive behavior sometimes reinforced and other times ignored. We shifted the emphasis of treatment and conducted desensitization of the parent group to the provocative behaviors of their children. We constructed a hierarchy with items of varying degrees of provocation to anger. In the final item, the parents were asked to remain relaxed while their child bit their leg as they served coffee to the local minister or priest. Once the parents were able to control their anger, they were able to implement the procedures consistently and effectively.

Sexual Dysfunction

Classical conditioning may be responsible for *some* sexual problems. If a man experiences erectile problems when nervous or intoxicated, the sexual cues may become associated with anxiety. This anxiety inhibits subsequent performance. Orgasmic dysfunction among women may be similarly conditioned, with each failure at achieving orgasm further reinforcing the association of sexual stimuli with anxiety and frustration. The basic approach of Masters and Johnson (1966) can be seen as an extinction procedure. Intercourse is initially forbidden, and couples are instructed to concentrate only on giving and receiving pleasure from nongenital areas of the body. When they are comfortable with this stage, they move on to genital stimulation, with intercourse still prohibited. An anxiety conditioned to sexual stimuli diminished, the couple can begin to enjoy intercourse again.

In general, the classical conditioning model should be examined thoroughly in cases which show excessive or troublesome emotional responses, or when problematic behavior is elicited by specific preceding events. The treatment procedures which flow from the respondent model are among the most robust and best-researched tools we have, and when appropriately applied are of great help in the therapeutic process.

5 The Operant Model

The basic concepts of the operant model are reinforcement and punishment: the consequences of a response determine the probability of the future occurrence of that response. As shown in the flowchart (p. 000), the basic assessment question is: Are the consequences of the problem behaviors initiating or maintaining those behaviors? Those consequences that increase the probability of a response are called *positive reinforcers,* and those that decrease the probability of a response are called *punishers.* To employ the operant model means to be selectively attuned to the consequences of the behavior of interest.

For the operant model to be of any use, reinforcement must be defined empirically for each person. For example, if being scolded by a parent has the effect of increasing a child's temper tantrums, then the scolding is a positive reinforcer. If the scolding decreases the tantrums, it is a punisher. (For an overview of the theoretical intricacies of operant theory see Reynolds, 1975, or Rachlin, 1976). It is important to keep the empirical definition of these principles in mind: An event is reinforcing or punishing, not because of our own responses to it, but because of the client's responses. Events that punish most of us may reinforce others. Masochistic homosexual prisoners, for instance, may prefer prison life to community life because the ordinary system of reinforcements and punishments is at least partially reversed for them. The concepts of reinforcement and punishment would be completely circular were it not for the fact that events that reinforce (or punish) one activity are also likely to reinforce (or punish) other activities. In other words, reinforcers and punishers are consistent from activity to activity and from time to time (if not from person to person). Identification of those consistencies is the job of *functional analysis.*

THE FUNCTIONAL ANALYSIS

The operant model is basic to our technology of both assessment and therapy. The model has led to many of the techniques of traditional "behavior therapy" (e.g., token economies, contingency contracting, child-management strategies). However, while it can prove valuable in therapy (as will be elaborated on in this chapter), the operant model, by means of the functional analysis that it dictates, it also an important component of assessment.

As indicated in the flowchart (p. xii–xiii), when consequences seem to be involved in maintaining the behavior, a functional analysis is required to specify the reinforcing conditions. The functional analysis springs directly from the operant approach. Its purpose is to determine reinforcement and punishment relationships surrounding the problem behavior of interest. In order to do this, information must be collected carefully. The client is asked to describe (or the therapist may directly observe) events antecedent to, concurrent with, and consequent to the problem behavior. Systematic patterns among these events may then be discovered and the contingencies maintaining a troublesome pattern may be rearranged. For instance, an event that has been reinforcing a given problem response may be made contingent upon a more appropriate response. If the initial relationships were correctly observed, the pattern of behavior should then change. In a way, therefore, the rearranging of contingencies represents an experimental tests of the operant hypothesis. If the hypothesis that the response fits into the operant model is correct, and the therapist has correctly identified the reinforcer, behavior should change in the predicted direction. If the behavior does not change, the therapist is obliged within this model to change the hypothesis about what is reinforcing it, or to consider that the behavior of interest is not an operant but fits into a different model.

It is often possible to find dysfunctional patterns and to intervene therapeutically by rearranging contingencies. Equally often, however, a functional analysis will help us by serving as a springboard from which to find which of the various other models fits in a particular situation. A functional analysis is very useful in this way because it delineates, makes concrete, and gives temporal sequence to the behavioral occurrences. If, after completing a functional analysis of a problem, the operant model does not "fit" the data, another model can be superimposed on the behavior pattern to see if that "fits." For example, if a person's temper outbursts follow a temporal pattern during the day, occurring at 11 AM and 4 PM, and no external reinforcers seem to occur at those times, a biological rather than an operant model might be applicable.

Let us say that the functional analysis has shown us that the person's outbursts do not seem to be elicited by an identifiable external stimulus, and that the consequences of these outbursts appear to be negative or neutral for the person. In the absence of any established relationship between the outbursts and environmental events, we would search for biological factors that may be involved. We know that there could be several: metabolic disturbances previously mentioned such as hypoglycemia or diabetes; central factors like a tumor of epilepsy; or biological irritants such as hunger or allergies may be involved. We have seen cases of each of these categories. Thus, performing a functional analysis of a presenting problem is helpful, even when problem dynamics do not turn out to fit within the operant model. It is suggested that a good functional analysis be conducted as an assessment device, with the knowledge that the information gained from it may well fit better into a nonoperant model than it fits into the operant model.

In principle, other models could serve just as well as starting points in the assessment process. We feel, however, that the functional analysis can be the framework which produces the richest information about a problem of interest. This is because the type of information sought in a functional analysis need not be restricted. Employing the behavioral framework of antecedent, concurrent, and consequent events, we can expand the type of information asked for in each of these categories to include much more than current, overt behavioral events. We can (and should) include cognitive, somatic, and emotional events on a broad timeframe in the analysis, thereby providing us with a wealth of information from which to proceed in fitting a particular case into a model.

Assessing the Applicability of the Operant Model

The important point in conducting a functional analysis when assessing for operant dynamics is to look for types of consequences which increase the occurrence of a particular behavior. We are not interested in the "purity" of the analysis (in the sense of eliminating "mentalistic" events), but rather in whether we can usefully classify the consequences so as to make therapeutic sense. For example, the clinical psychology graduate students who snarl at their advisors, who miss class, who are late for therapy appointments, and who perform poorly in research and academics may very well be demonstrating that they do not get reinforcement out of psychology. Though Skinnerians may be reluctant to abstract at that motivational level, those abstractions are clinically very useful.

The functional analysis is concerned with the question of what maintains the behavior, or: "What's the payoff for this person?" The analysis looks for patterns of events which surround deviant behavior. The analysis is not necessarily concerned with the etiology of the behavior, but rather is concerned with the current maintaining events.

Often, behaviors without an operant etiology develop operant components over time. For example, a child with asthma may initially wheeze only when having an attack (i.e., the wheezing is caused by internal events). Later, after obtaining special attention from parents when wheezing occurs, the child may begin to control wheezing at least occasionally to gain attention or to avoid unpleasant tasks. This may, in fact, occur without the child's "awareness" or "intention." The psychotherapist's task here is to rearrange the contingencies in this child's life so he or she finds reinforcement in "healthy" behavior. In other words, the therapist need only (and *can* only, in this case) deal with the maintaining variables. The etiological variable, the asthma itself, need not be addressed to make an impact on the secondary operant components of the problem. These secondary components can often be more disturbing than the primary disorder itself.

Freud (1960) talked about the operant components of a problem as "secondary gains." The primary gain of a neurotic disorder was thought to be its use as a defense against anxiety, usually caused by conflict over unacceptable impulses. So, for example, a hysterical glove paralysis which leaves the hand immobile may be caused by unconscious guilt over masturbatory impulses. However, the maintenance of this psychodynamic disorder could be conceptualized within the operant model. If this hysterical paralysis leads to a disability pension, the pension and the escape from work may maintain the behavior.

When assessing for operant dynamics, it is imperative to determine exactly when reinforcement occurs, because different patterns of reinforcement would indicate very different interventions (not all of them operant). For example, a frequently heard complaint of parents is that their youngster does not study. The consequences for not doing homework may be that: (1) the work is inappropriate for this youngster in that it is either above or below grade level and is therefore punishing. Thus, avoiding homework is negatively reinforcing for the child; (2) the youngster is angry at his or her parents and is reinforced by their getting upset when homework isn't completed; (3) the youngster wants to retaliate for some "slight" of the teacher. Not doing homework is a way of showing that the teacher does not have control over him or her. The list of possible reinforcements for any one behavior can be expanded indefinitely. Each pattern of reinforcement requires a different intervention. Without a functional analysis, a therapist might simply institute a reinforcement system by which the child is rewarded with tokens for doing homework. Even when such treatment is initially successful, the problem behavior often reappears when the tokens are withdrawn (F. M. Levine & Fasnacht, 1974).

In the situation presented above, for example, the functional analysis might show that a child's refusal to study was followed by, say, the parents becoming upset and angry. We have frequently found that certain family patterns occur in which the child feels overcontrolled and fights back by doing whatever annoys the parents. The child cannot fight back directly since the child is so weak compared to the parents, so anger is expressed indirectly, by not doing homework or by otherwise acting out. The parents' angry "punishment" is reinforcing to the child. The intervention, of course, becomes considerably different when the analysis indicates this pattern of reinforcement as opposed to others. Parents are instructed to limit punishment, to find positive activities that the family can enjoy together, and to give the child some control over those activities. The goal is to decrease the youngster's anger at the parents while increasing the child's control over the environment, so that upsetting the parents is not his or her only means of controlling their behavior.

After the pattern of reinforcement is determined, the work of the therapist really begins. Once the therapist conceptualizes the behavior of the youngster not doing homework as an attempt to make the parents angry, the therapist must analyze the situation to determine why the angry response of the parent is reinforcing to that child. In most cases we would conceptualize the child's noncompliance as being an angry response. In many cases that we have seen, the parents were often highly critical of the youngster and did not allow for alternative expressions of anger. The youngster would express the anger by not doing homework. It is now up to the therapist to try to alter the seeds of the anger so the child need not retaliate in a destructive fashion. It may help these parents if they understand the reasons behind their frustrations with the youngster, so that they can develop less reactive ways of dealing with their frustration than by being critical.

The Matching Law

In adult cases, a functional analysis may reveal that the client's goals as expressed behaviorally are considerably different from what is verbally expressed. Baum and Rachlin (1969) give an important conceptualization of behavior in their temporal version of Herrnstein's (1970, 1974) matching law. Simply stated, the matching law says that organisms match the proportion of time they spend performing a certain response (relative to the time they spend performing other responses) to the reinforcing value of the consequences of that response (relative to the reinforcing value of the consequences of the other respones). As an example, a patient may say that he or she loves family life. However, inspection of this patient's behavioral patterns reveals that the patient lives on Long Island, while working 2 hours away in New York City, and also is active away from the family on weekends, playing golf. This person is "saying" behaviorally that he or she dislikes the family and finds it more reinforcing to be away from them. The clinical analysis also must then determine what it is about the family that the patient dislikes in order to intervene effectively.

The matching law is a powerful assessment and treatment heuristic. It allows therapists to evaluate the time that the client spends on activities as a measure of the reinforcement value of these activities. It adds a specifically behavioral dimension to assessment. Not only do therapists evaluate the verbal reports of the client, but they observe the behaviors of the client as an important source of input about the reinforcement patterns for the client.

Often people will present themselves in therapy by talking about interpersonal problems which prevent them from getting close to others and developing intimacy. Sometimes these problems arise out of social-skill deficits, but a functional analysis may alert the clinician to the fact that the person engages in behaviors which are obviously chasing others away. The therapeutic question which arises is whether the absence of other people is more valuable to this person than their presence. "What is the payoff for avoiding intimacy?" is the question to be asked here.

THERAPEUTIC USES OF THE OPERANT MODEL

Direct contingency management is not possible with the great majority of adult clients seen in therapy. It is a feasible strategy only when the therapist can control important aspects of a person's environment. This is usually the case with children, with institutionalized populations, or when the therapist has access to the significant others in an adult's life (when conducting family or couple's therapy, for example). A good review of the state of the art in operant behavior-change techniques has been done by Kazdin (1978b).

When a functional analysis indicates that an environmental consequence is maintaining a problem behavior of an individual adult client, the intervention of choice is often simply telling the client what the contingencies are. This is often sufficient to bring about change in a motivated client. For example, an adult client came in complaining of her spouse's hypochrondriasis and overdependence. After an assessment of the case dynamics, the therapist pointed out that the client was actually reinforcing her husband's hypochondriasis by giving him a disproportionate amount of attention and affection on those occasions on which he complained of feeling ill. Since the client really did dislike her husband's complaints and dependency, she made efforts to change those contingencies. The therapist must be aware that all disorders occur in a social context and that, to continue the example, the hypochondriasis may be reinforcing to the wife. A wife's sympathetic response to imagined ills may be the best available method for her to become a vital part of her husband's life. She will, in that case, resist changing the contingencies of her husband's hypochondriasis unless her own needs are addressed in some other fashion.

There are also occasions on which clients may be unaware of contingencies acting *upon* them. A woman may find herself having an inordinate amount of trouble becoming more assertive. A functional analysis might reveal that her boss is giving her reinforcement in terms of attention and praise only when she behaves unassertively. If the therapist informs the client of these contingencies, the woman may then be able to be assertive (if it is important enough to her) *even though* her boss will not reinforce her for it (that is, her own knowledge that she is acting assertively must be more reinforcing to her than her boss's reactions). Alternatively, the new information supplied by the therapist can aid the woman in discriminating between the reinforcement contingencies of the office and elsewhere, and she may decide to maximize her reinforcement by acting less assertive in the office than in environments where assertion is reinforced.

Sometimes an adult client's behavior can be modified by changing the reinforcing value of a particular reinforcer through information. In the previous example, the woman may have, at one time, found the reinforcing value of a male authority figure's praise so great that she would have worked hard to gain it in any way she could. Information, in the form of feminist analyses of male/female power relationships, may have changed the reinforcing value of a male boss's praise. It became less important to her than being able to express herself.

Often, the values of reinforcements are modified by giving the client information about the consequences of the behavior. Most often this is done by pointing out that the long-range consequences of a behavior may outweigh the value of the short-term gains. For millions of people, the reinforcement value of smoking was changed by the information about its relationship to health. For the worker who preferred being a commuter on the Long Island Railroad to being with his or her family, the relative value of escape may be modified by information that this pattern of time allocation may lead to a divorce. Quite frequently, people are not aware that their behavior may be leading to a different outcome from the one they articulate.

We have seen parents within blended families (i.e., families to which both the husband and the wife bring children from previous marriages) provoke their spouses' children into acting out. Functional analyses revealed that the parents' behaviors had the effect of chasing the other spouse's children away. The information about the behaviors may change the reinforcement values. The assessment must yield insights about why the client desires to "chase the child away." This may mean that past experiences are reviewed and reanalyzed (The role of information will be further explored in Chapter 6). It is important for the therapist to be aware that information can be a powerful tool in changing the reinforcement value of a response pattern. It is, of course, the function of the therapist to evaluate the impact of the current behaviors and help the client develop a repertoire of responses which are more effective in promoting the client's goals by use of a wide range of interventions. The cognitive model and the operant model are hardly mutually exclusive.

In the application of operant procedures, two critical principles are important. The first is that the goal of the procedure is to replace rather than remove the problematic behavior. The "symptom" behavior exists because it is functional for the person. The symptom is supported by reinforcement. When reinforcement is removed and behavior is extinguished or punished, all animals (human and otherwise) tend to increase the variability and intensity of their behavior. Therefore, if a problem behavior were simply punished or extinguished (by ignoring it), the person might escalate inappropriate behaviors. For example, a depressed person whose crying was ignored might, in order to get attention, attempt suicide or assaultive behaviors. Such behaviors compel attention. The notion of "always playing to strength" is one to keep in mind when employing an operant intervention. This means simply that the goal of an operant approach is to *replace* the problematic behavior with more appropriate behaviors through selective reinforcement. Problematic behaviors that are reinforced need to be extinguished, but, simultaneously, appropriate incompatible behaviors should be reinforced. If a client is already exhibiting some desirable behaviors, the therapist should "play to strength" and reinforce these while extinguishing the undesirable behavior(s).

The matching law of Herrnstein (1970, 1974) and of Baum and Rachlin (1969) has a good deal to say about the necessity of replacement. The matching law mandates that reinforcement be evaluated not only in terms of the immediate consequences of a response/reinforcement relationship, but that the total environmental context of reinforcement be evaluated. McDowell (1982) gives specific rules for the utility of the matching law for behaviorally oriented clinicians. The matching law emphasizes that a major point of intervention is often increasing reinforcement in the environmental field. As an example, Ames (1976) used three techniques to control temper tantrums in children; time-out (punishment by social isolation), time-out and reinforcement of appropriate requests, and just reinforcing appropriate request. Just reinforcing the appropriate requests was as effective in reducing the temper tantrums as the other approaches, and in a follow-up of family relations, yielded slightly higher scores of family "happiness."

As pointed out by McDowell (1982), the matching law also explains why, although many of us receive sympathy and affection when we are ill, we do not all become hypochondriacs. Most of us have alternative, preferred sources of sympathy and affection, and we spend proportionately more time performing acts which will provide us with those reinforcers (e.g., interacting with members of the opposite sex). Persons who come into therapy, however, may have impoverished sources of reinforcement. Their "dysfunctional" behavior may therefore be functional for them, considering they do not have alternative methods of obtaining rewarding results. By receiving attention and "positive regard" in therapy, those clients gain an alternative source of reinforcement, and should not need to act as inappropriately to receive attention in other situations. The matching law explains why replacement of unwanted behaviors with behaviors that can gain the person positive reinforcement is an essential part of an operant intervention.

Frequently, when extinction procedures are used, the client will respond with an extinction burst, or an increase in the intensity and frequency of the behavior. The extinction burst seems as if it were a way to test the resolve of the person who changes the contingencies. For example, one youngster who was told that his mother would never give in to any demand made by a temper tantrum, no matter how reasonable the request (and also, of course, that appropriate requests would be responded to) engaged in a series of temper tantrums that tested the mother's resolve. He threw things and screamed so loudly that his mother closed the window so the neighbors would not be disturbed (or accuse her of child abuse). The temper tantrums were essentially over that day. The people applying extinction procedures should be absolutely prepared by the therapist for a response that will test their resolve. Clients should be warned, emphatically, that things usually will get worse before they get better.

Resistance to extinction is increased by intermittant schedules. If reinforcement is given sometimes and withheld on other occasions, it is much more difficult to eliminate the response by extinction than if reinforcement were initially given each and every time a response occurred and then was withheld. Because of this, the people who provide the reinforcements must be clearly apprised that not matter what, they cannot give in to temptations to yield to the demands for reinforcers. We advise them that it would be preferable that they not begin an extinction procedure if they think they will give in. Even though there is room for accommodation for an occasional reinforcer, just like there is room for a little cheating in diets, it is better that people be prepared for a high standard of performance. Otherwise they may interpret the room for accommodation too broadly, and unwittingly maintain a problem behavior through intermittant reinforcement of it.

One case tested the resolve of both the parents and us in not yielding to high demands for reinforcement. A 10-year-old youngster was referred to us for a school phobia. First we analyzed the school situation to discover whether there was something going on in school that led him to be phobic (e.g., being bullied, teachers assigning work that was too demanding for him), and found that he was generally well-liked by his peers and was normally intelligent. Then we discovered that he had a history of being reinforced by becoming "sick." He avoided situations that he found difficult by having stomach aches and being nauseous. His family had recently moved to the area and it was simply difficult for him to try the new school. The combination of his reinforcement history and his current stressor led us to conceptualize the case in terms of operant dynamics. We then negotiated a date with the youngster when he would be able to return to school. It is important that there be an alliance with the client in setting and implementation of goals.

However, it was more important that the avoidance behavior be extinguished. The parents were told that the youngster would do whatever he could to resist going to school. They were advised that he would become very sick, he would yell and scream, and accuse them of not loving him. They were also strongly advised about how difficult it would be for them, that their stomachs would be sick, and that they would be convinced that he would do better by not going to school. (We specifically amplify negative expectations to produce a contrast effect; this will be discussed more fully in Chapter 6.) They were told that if they could not handle the predicted stress of the extinction burst, that we would not attempt the treatment. It was emphasized that they could not show any signs of weakened determination to bring the youngster to school, even if they had to do so physically. The parents grimly agreed.

On the day designated for him to return to school, in addition to the above predictions, the youngster also ran 101 degree temperature. He threw up, complained of stomach cramps, and actually had a fever. The mother called up and asked for our advice. This was a rough test of our confidence in the model; we did not anticipate the fever. Because we had confidence in the model (all the predictions except the fever were borne out), we felt that it was better for him to go to school sick than be on an intermittent reinforcement schedule. If we gave in, we felt that there would be more occurrances of these behaviors because of increased resistance to extinction. The mother promised not to display the slightest doubts about her resolve and the youngster went to school. He was less sick the next day, and even less the following day. The school phobia had not reoccurred 2 years later.

In this case, two alternative interventions were used to replace the phobic response. The immediate was that the boy was taught relaxation as an alternative to his stomach aches. More important, an alternative reinforcer to avoiding school was that he made friends very quickly in school. Without these, our technique might not have worked, and we would have had to try to provide some other reinforcement. If we had not known the boy possessed social and relaxation skills, we would have needed to work on these before applying the drastic technique that we did.

A second critical principle in the application of operant procedures is the concept of shaping. Shaping involves reinforcement of behaviors which are steps toward the final goal. For example, in helping a child overcome his terror of the dark, a parent should at first praise the child for sleeping through the night with the door to the lighted hallways open only a foot. Praise should be delivered as the door progressively closes. Later, praise should be given only for sleeping with the door open a crack and still later, praise should be given for sleeping with the door shut in a dark room. If the reinforcement were programmed so that praise was initially to be given only if the child could sleep with the door completely shut, the child probably would not be able to do so. Consideration must be given to the response repertoire of the person at a given time. Shaping proceeds in steps toward the goal with the rate of movement programmed by the rate of responsiveness of the client.

Self-control. Another way operant techniques can be useful with adult clients is in the area of self-control. Self-control procedures are usually applied to behaviors which have both aversive and positive consequences for an individual. Rachlin and Green (1972) conceptualize self-control as choice guided by larger long-term consequences rather than by smaller, more immediate consequences. For instance, a choice we call a matter of self-control is one between a small or nonexistent positive event now followed by a small or nonexistent negative event later, and a large positive event now followed by a very large negative event in the future. An obvious example of this would be the dilemma of overeating. The person is confronted with a choice between eating a delicious piece of cake now and weighing more in the future, or denying themselves the cake now in order to weigh less in the future. Few overweight people would choose the piece of cake if it were an *immediate* choice between the cake and the new figure. The problem enters because weight loss is a diffuse event removed in time from the present situation.

When considering whether to initiate self-control procedures in a given case, the clinician should be alert to several things. First, the therapist must determine whether the behavior in question is a problem because of the lack of immediate positive consequences in the environment, or whether it is problematic because of skill deficits, excessive anxiety, or some other reason (Rimm & Masters, 1979). Self-control procedures are most effective in increasing the salience contingencies which are weak in the natural environment. As Rimm and Masters point out, it would be naive to institute an elaborate self-control program for a behavior that will be reinforced naturally once it is emitted. They give the example of a socially anxious male. Once the therapist can help him to initiate competent social interactions, positive consequences can be plentiful and immediate. There is no need for self-control procedures. As always, the clinician must be tuned in to the dynamics of the particular case. Although self-control techniques may be effective in many cases of overeating, for example, they may not be appropriate when the overeating occurs for reasons other than lack of environmental consequences. Overeating and being fat can be products of many different models. For example, obesity can effectively distance a person sexually from an unloved spouse. If this is the case, self-control procedures may initially be neither appropriate nor effective.

A second consideration in instituting self-control techniques is that, because the client is to a large degree his or her own therapist while implementing the procedures, some degree of comprehension of the basic concepts of self-control is necessary on the part of the client. This may be beyond the capacities of some clinical populations, e.g., young children, mentally retarded, or psychotic populations.

Throughout this chapter, it has been stressed that no behavior should be eliminated without substituting another behavior in its stead. This holds true for behavior change accomplished by means of self-control procedures as well. If a bad habit is being suppressed, an alternative behavior should be shaped to take its place in the behavioral sequence. For example, we have seen several self-injurious children. A recent autistic client who scratched her gums and pulled off her toenails was given a small rubber ball to squeeze when she went to bed. Squeezing the ball replaced the self-mutilation.

Self-observation is usually considered to be an essential first step in a program of self-control. It is used to gather baseline data to which treatment results can be compared, but the reactive effects of self-monitoring are well known. Self-observation alone alters behavior (Kazdin, 1974). In fact, Rachlin (1976) sees self-observation, through its function of providing feedback on the problem behavior, as an essential component of self-control.

When observing problematic behaviors, clients should be instructed to not only record the occurrence or nonoccurrence of a behavior, but also to notice the events antecedent and consequent to the problem. In the case of overeating, clients should be asked to monitor their mood, physical and social environments, and time of day during which problem eating occurs, to get a picture of the typical behavioral chain which leads to overeating. Once the chain is perceived, the client and therapist can agree to intervene at any point along the chain which they feel will be effective. In general, the earlier in the chain change is instituted, the more effective it is at altering the target behavior. In the example of overeating, it would be better to change the severe hunger that leads to a 4 PM binge by eating more for lunch, than to use rational-emotive techniques when confronted with a kitchen full of food after work (e.g., "I really don't *need* that piece of cake"). Another way to view this is in terms of modifying the "forbidden" event. In the case of a client who wants to avoid drinking too much at a party, it may be helpful for the person to fill up with water before going to the party. Eliminating thirst may lead to less drinking of alcoholic beverages at the party.

Goal-setting is another necessary component of self-control procedures. Goals should take the principle of shaping into consideration, and should therefore increase gradually in difficulty. The first goal for a student with a problem studying may be 5 minutes of concentration. Later, the goals could be set in more molar units, as in projects completed over longer time periods.

Clients may also want to rearrange contingencies for problem behaviors. They may make contracts with the therapist or others in their environment so that, contingent on their success or failure at reaching certain goals, they receive a reward or punishment. This "commitment strategy" (Rachlin, 1976) is a most useful way for clients to use contingencies surrounding problem behaviors to change the frequency of the problem.

Examples

The prime reason for completing a functional analysis is to look for points of intervention, or points in the process where clinical intervention will be the most effective in changing the specific problem that the client presents. For example, a client with a severe obsession in which she imagined herself killing babies had compulsive rituals which she developed to avoid any possibility that a baby would be killed. She would not drive for fear of running over a baby; she could not close a door for fear of squashing a baby; she could not throw the garbage out for fear that a baby would be thrown out; she would not light the stove or flush the toilet because of similar fears. Unquestionably the etiology of these bizzare compulsions was complex and included psychotic elements as well as the conflict between her desire to have a baby and strong irrational needs for independence. As shown by a functional analysis, however, these symptoms also had the consequence of keeping her husband close to home. He usually travelled during the day and would often be out at night. Because of her need to present herself as being entirely self-reliant, she could not directly confront her husband with her dependency needs. The compulsive behaviors compelled him to hover over her without a direct request for him to do so. We discussed this openly and worked out ways by which alternative autonomous behaviors could result in attention from her husband and replace these bizarre and upsetting compulsions.

We worked out a program where they would go out together only when she drove the car. This was difficult at first and the trips were initially of very short duration. The driving behavior was continued to meeting her husband at further distances. They did not leave the house until she closed the door behind her. He would give a great deal of support to these activities. The husband was also advised to pay no attention whatsoever to the compulsive behaviors. For example, he simply took the garbage out rather than argue with her about why she should do this. After an immediate period of rapid improvement, these compulsive behaviors slowly disappeared. It must be pointed out that there was still a great deal of pathology that led to a subsequent course of psychiatric hospitalization, but there were improvements in level of functioning which still persist. The functional analysis revealed that the bizarre behaviors were reinforced by virtue of their consequences in getting the husband's attention. Neither party was aware of the contingencies. The analysis gave a very specific point of intervention.

Another case illustrates the potential for operant methods in creating change. A 72-year-old single woman started to become extremely regressed. She cried to her inlaws and friends about how she wanted her mother (who was long dead) and she demanded to be treated like an infant. The functional analysis revealed that a reinforcer for these behaviors was the attention and help that they elicited. In both this case and the one mentioned above, helplessness became a rather effective way of coping with the demands of life. The reinforcement was receiving attention and having people do many of the things that this woman would rather not do. The family and friends of the elderly woman were instructed to walk out or hang up the telephone when she wept like an infant and tell her, "I can't deal with you when you are in this mood. I'll be back later when we can discuss things more rationally." They were advised to apply the basic operant law of intervention; to play to strength; i.e., reinforce appropriate behaviors which are incompatible with the problematic behavior. Relatives were advised to help when she was realistic and coping and not reinforce pathological behavior. Relatives and friends visited and assisted only while this woman was calm and rational. These behaviors were therefore reinforced. This woman remained independent without a similar incident until her death 15 years later.

Systems

To complicate interpretations of operant analysis even further, another question must be asked before intervening: "What is the function of the pathology in the system?" We have often seen an individual in a family reach the articulated goal only to see other members of the family fall apart. One example was the case of an angry and punitive father of four. His demands on his children were beyond their capacity. He required them to sit and eat quietly. Since two of the children were hyperactive, this demand was not realistic. He then would yell and threaten and occasionally use corporal punishment. This characterized his interactions with his children. His wife, on the other hand, existed to provide succor for the children. Not only would she go from doctor to doctor, but she would give a great deal of emotional support to them, often revolving around the father's abuse.

The wife, husband, and therapist set out on the goal of teaching him how to control anger and express warmth. He did extremely well and the children gravitated to him. As they did, the wife became somewhat isolated. She withdrew from the family at a pace parallel to the husband's advance into the family. Because these problems were neither anticipated nor dealt with in therapy, and since the problem was incorrectly viewed as only the father's, the problem re-emerged in almost the same form. When the couple came back into therapy, we explored the idea that part of the problem was functional in the sense that it increased the "status" of the mother, and that she may have shaped the father's behavior to be belligerent to the children as a way of maintaining family equilibrium. The mother resisted treatment and there were no gains. This case would be handled considerably differently now with recognition that "symptoms" may not be directly functional for the individual, but are frequently functional for the unit, usually the family, within which the symptom develops. In other words, what is asked here is not only "What reinforces the problematic behavior?," but "What does the problematic behavior reinforce?"

The same recognition that the symptom may be reinforced by the family as a way of maintaining the family has been extensively dealt with by those working in the field of family therapy. Their contention is that the individual's problem must be treated within a social context (Bowen, 1978; Minuchin, 1974). The social context they study intensively is the family. The family is seen as a unit, with complex interdependencies and a self-perpetuating character. Family therapists see the etiology of most personal problems as lying within dysfunctional family dynamics. Therefore, therapy is aimed at reorganizing the family interactions. Haley and Hoffman (1967) state their view that family therapy is not a new treatment but rather is a new way of *conceptualizing* the etiology and treatment of psychological problems. From an operant perspective, the family therapists can be seen as taking a broad view when they do their functional analyses of what is causing and maintaining a problem behavior. They investigate the contingencies provided by various family members for a particular pattern, and thus can avoid the mistake of concentrating on an individual's internal dynamics, while ignoring the person's interaction with the social environment.

Punishment

Punishment is defined as an event which, when contingent on a response, decreases the probability of that response. Within the behavioral literature there is a great deal of research demonstrating the effectiveness of some forms of punishment. Punishment has been used effectively in suppressing self-destructive behavior in retarded and psychotic children (e.g., Lovaas & Simmons, 1969; Merbaum, 1973). In these studies and other similar ones, shock was applied contingently upon occurrence of self-destructive behavior (head-banging, hand-biting, etc.). It was found that the self-destructive behavior was immediately suppressed following introduction of shock, and that prosocial behaviors like eye contact and body contact with the experimenter increased concurrently.

A problem with the procedure was that children could learn to discriminate situations in which shock was never given and people who never used shock, from situations and people associated with shock. Self-destructive behavior was maintained in the latter situation. However, if generalization was programmed by implementing the procedure with many people in many situations, the children's behavior remained consistently much improved. Other therapeutic procedures employing aversive stimuli have been tried with overeating, smoking, alcoholism, unwanted sexual orientation, phobias, and compulsions. These treatments generally follow a counterconditioning paradigm, and are thus more appropriately discussed in Chapter 4. For a general discussion of the theoretical and practical aspects of punishment and aversive conditioning, we refer the reader to Walters and Grusec (1977), Rachman and Teasdale (1969), or Azrin and Holz (1966).

Azrin and Holz (1966) make general points on the use of punishment which they have gleaned from the experimental literature. To maximize its effectiveness, the punishment should be strong enough to be definitely aversive to the person, and it should follow the undesirable behavior consistently. For children younger than seven, it should follow the undesirable behavior closely in time. For persons older than seven, punishment need not follow immediately to be effective. Azrin and Holz point out that the punishment should not be followed by a subsequent reward. Often, for example, parents hit their children and then, out of guilt, are very affectionate and generous for a few hours after that. That may well be a counterproductive strategy. Azrin and Holz also stress a point we have stressed throughout this chapter; that an alternative behavior should be reinforced to take the place of the punished one. The misuse or overuse of punishment can lead to many problems. The therapist should therefore be aware of the effects of the misuse of punishment. Following are some further guidelines for its proper use, as well as cues to signal the therapist to its misuse.

Let the Punishment Fit the Crime.   Both the intensity and the modality of the punishment should be designed to relate the crime to the consequences so that the behavior is inhibited.

Punishment, when used appropriately, is an effective method for changing behavior. It has been shown with retarded and normal children that verbal punishment ("no," "wrong") was more effective in changing their behavior than was verbal reinforcement (Lee, 1976; Paris & Cairns, 1969). These authors suggest that the negative response is more effective in changing behavior because it carries greater information value than does the positive response. The negative response is more specific to the paticular action of the child, whereas positive responses are typically given independently of any one specific action.

Just as the verbal punishment is effective because of its information value to the person, the intensity of the punishment should convey information about the intensity of the misdeed which brought about the punishment This concept is central to our penal system, in which the severity of prison sentences for various crimes generally reflects social values regarding the seriousness of those misdeeds. Similarly, children are frequently sent to their room for infractions of manners, such as consistently interrupting. However, the "crime" of impulsively running into the street requires, because of the dangers involved, a more intense punishment. The intensity of the punishment has information value and it is therefore imperative that punishment not be used in a stereotypic manner for a variety of offenses. For the individual, usually the child, to learn the seriousness of a given violation, the child must be exposed to a range of punishments. This range is within those given by authority, usually the parent. For some parents, a disapproving frown is the extreme and will strike terror in the heart of a child, while for others corporal punishment is reserved for serious infractions. However, the impact of the punishment is relative. The frown is often as effective as hitting. The effectiveness of punishment seems to be related to the range of the scale of punishment characteristically used by the punisher.

Whatever the range, the effect of punishment quickly habituates with repeated exposures. If the parent frowns too often, the frown ceases to strike terror. All too dramatically corporal punishment also habituates and it takes an ever-increasing intensity to make an impact. People can habituate to intense physical punishment, as do boxers who do not flinch when they are hit very hard. Because of this habituation, punishment can escalate to dangerous proportions, as it does in some cases of child abuse, without having an effect (Sheff & Levine, 1981). Therefore, punishment should be kept to a low point for the usual offenses of violations of manners and routines. Discussions in the behavior modification literature, concerning what length of time-out is most effective, have not addressed the ideal relationship of the intensity of the violation which led to the punishment to the intensity of the punishment itself.

For punishment of an angry child, a period of time-out could be used to both teach the child the behavior was inappropriate and to give the parent and the youngster a cooling off period. In one case, a 12-year-old youngster was hostile, especially to her siblings. If time-out were imposed in an authoritarian manner, it was our feeling that she would have been even nastier. It was explained to her that her nastiness was causing her difficulties and that she needed help in controlling her attacks. She agreed, and we worked out a program where she also agreed to go into her room when her mother saw her being nasty. She was free to leave her room whenever she felt in better control of her feelings. The youngster was also told that if she agreed to this program, she could not decide to stop after it had begun. It was our feeling that forcing her into her room without her consent would have escalated her hostility. The punishment decreased her hostile attacks because of her feeling of having some control over it.

Time-out or, more correctly, social isolation, is an effective period of cooling off. Often youngsters will go to their room (or chair, couch, or corner) with apparent indifference, if not cockiness. If the frequency of the offensive behavior decreases, however, time-out is a punishment whether or not it seems to be aversive.

Punishment must also fit the crime in that the type of punishment has to be related to the modality of the crime. For example, children who are angry should not be given a punishment which increases their already high arousal level. A child who has been fighting will not calm down if he or she is either hit or screamed at. Hitting as punishment in that case, not only will increase the youngster's anger, but would provide a model for physical relating. The youngster who cries excessively is not helped when the parent states, with a menacing gesture, "I'll give you something to cry about!" These youngsters need a period of time when they can calm down. Sending them to their room in a calm but firm manner will facilitate teaching them that the behaviors are not acceptable, that the behaviors have negative consequences, and that time for the child (and often the parent) to calm down is required.

Modality of Punishment.   The use of punishment should be minimized because of its reactive effects. Since punishment is often, though not necessarily, aversive, it carries excess baggage in its consequences. Although it may suppress the punished behavior, punishment often leads to an emotional response that is frequently counterproductive. Punishment is frequently a frustrating experience. The frustration/aggression hypothesis (Dollard, Miller, Doob, Mowrer, & Sears, 1939; Miller, 1948) would predict that a likely consequence of frustration is some form of aggression. It follows, then, that a likely consequence of punishment is aggressive behavior. Given that aggressive behaviors are rarely desirable, the use of punishment may actually lead to increases in other undesirable behavior. The child who is spanked for fighting may become even angrier at what he or she regards as inequity (Adams, 1965), and become even angrier at both the person fought with and the punisher. These children need to be calmed down.

Often the emotional response is related to disapproval. Punishment necessarily connotes disapproval of behavior, but it frequently contains elements of disapproval of the person. Sometimes these elements dominate the punishment: "You are a bad person!" or "I hate you!" The disapproval part of punishment can be detrimental to the individual's feelings of self-worth, especially when it becomes the major way of relating to significant people in the environment. A goal of therapy is to teach people to like themselves, to be comfortable with themselves. Punishment must be used with care to make sure that it is not counterproductive.

Punishment should be separated from retribution or retaliation. The goal of punishment is to teach self-control and to teach what are unacceptable behaviors. Since retaliation and retribution are often the motive for punishment, the therapist must teach parent or other punishers how to use punishment effectively. Frequently the anger and outrage of the punisher prevents punishment from being used effectively. Distressed marital couples frequently use punishment in a way that violates all of the preceding cautions. The distressed spouses's use of punishment frequently leads to an emotional response of anger, brings out feelings of inequity, and makes the recipient feel uncared for, all of which undercut dramatically the stability of the relationship. One wife punished her husband's lateness by destroying his 10-year collection of rare plants. He never forgave her for this and he eventually left the marriage.

Married couples sometimes punish with refusal to perform chores, with accusations, with silence, or by other means, all of which add to marital tension. Telling these couples, or parents, of the counterproductive nature of punishment often has little impact because of how angry and desirous of retribution they are when they feel violated. It becomes the therapist's function to teach the punisher anger control so that their capacities for effective interaction become increased. Often, the punished behavior is misinterpreted as being directed at the individual. The punisher will be known to say, "Look what he (she) is doing to me!" This type of misinterpretation will be elaborated upon more in Chapter 6.

The operant model is extremely useful both in the conceptualization of problematic behaviors and in intervention for these problems. Since reinforcement is a powerful method of shaping behavior, this model can also be used when the problem is not operant in nature. The use of operant interventions requires that the therapist have influence over the client's environment. There are times when the behavior may begin because of a biological etiology. In our work on a rehabilitation unit we frequently see impulse control problems associated with central brain damage. These control problems are usually anger control but are sometimes sexual impulses. In many of these cases, we have worked with a cooperative nursing and rehabilitation staff and that allows us to use reinforcers. Rewards and punishments have helped patients develop impulse control. If the therapist is in control over the environment, such operant interventions can prove extremely effective.

Generally, interventions within the operant model occur through cooperation with others. We have worked with teachers, parents, and spouses, and with other professionals in developing operant-based programs. In the usual one-to-one situation of office therapy, we rarely have control over the environment. Because of that, it is often difficult to rearrange reinforcers. In those cases, the operant model is most useful for assessment. The functional analysis is invaluable at leading to points and types of intervention.

6 The Cognitive Model

There are certain assumptions about the psychological domain that, if accepted, can greatly facilitate the development of a psychological system. These assumptions should be treated as axioms and regarded as true until disproved. Just as it is axiomatic within Euclidian geometry that a straight line is the shortest distance between 2 points, it can be useful for psychologists to treat as axiomatic the assumptions that people think and that what people think can determine their behavior. Without these assumptions, a great deal of justification is required that can impede the development of our field. Although axioms, by definition, cannot be proven, it would cause a great deal of mischief not to consider them to be true. It should be remembered, however, that the Euclidian axiom that a straight line is the shortest distance between 2 points was, in fact, eventually replaced by Einstein's notion of curved space. Similarly, when the cognitive axioms are refuted, we should not delay abandoning them. However, at this point in time, so much of our language and, we dare say, our thinking, is based on these axioms that we should simply assume they are true.

As cognition has become a respected area of psychological research in recent years, psychotherapeutic interventions based on cognitive-change processes have flourished. It has been said that the conditioning model, which dominated psychology and behavioral psychotherapy for many years, is being replaced by an information-processing model (Murray & Jacobson, 1978). Although we believe that the usefulness of the cognitive model does not diminish the usefulness of other data-based models, it is certainly the case that most psychologists today accept the basic premises (axioms) of cognitive psychology: Our beliefs and perceptions affect the way we feel and behave; our reactions are not totally "determined" by environmental stimuli; and emotional and behavioral change can be effected via cognitive change (Beck, Rush, Shaw, & Emery, 1979; Kazdin, 1978a; Mahoney & Arnkoff, 1978).

Whereas traditional psychotherapy has always been cognitive in the sense that behavioral or emotional change has been viewed as a product of intellectual insight and understanding, direct evaluation and manipulation of cognitions was uncommon (Wachtel, 1977). Carl Rogers (in Evans,

1975) stated some of his goals for a psychotherapeutic endeavor as: development of insights by the patient; the fostering of better communication abilities; and the offering of feedback to the patient from the therapist. All of these goals can be seen as processes of cognitive change. Similarly, Singer (1974) describes a successful outcome of psychoanalysis as one in which the analysand is alert to his or her current feelings, and hence more relaxed and better functioning. These are processes closely akin to those of a successful course of cognitively oriented therapy.

Although traditional therapies have shared a "quasicognitive" orientation (Mahoney & Arnkoff, 1978), behavior therapy originally echoed the trend of American academic psychology in its reluctant acceptance of cognition. The early behaviorists, most notably John Watson, rejected the concept of internal events as appropriate targets of study. Although Hull, Mowrer, and Tolman, among others, introduced mediational or cognitive concepts into the Stimulus-Response dominated zeitgeist of the 30s and 40s, cognitive concepts were not translated into the practice of therapy until much later (Kazdin, 1978a).

Some of the earliest attempts at modifying cognitions were conducted by researchers attempting to directly apply operant-conditioning principles to internal, mental events. This *covert conditioning* made the assumption that stimuli presented in the imagination have the same relationships to covert and overt behavior as do externally presented stimuli (Cautela, 1971). Cautela dscribes the processes of covert conditioning as covert reinforcement (in which a desirable behavior and its positive consequences are imagined) and covert sensitization (in which an undesirable behavior is paired with extremely noxious consequences in imagination). Although the covert-conditioning model of mental events has not proven to be empirically strong (Mahoney & Arnkoff, 1978), it did open up the area of cognition to the behavior therapists who had previously shunned internal events altogether. Bandura (1969, 1977) has been instrumental to the "cognitive movement" as a theorist in ushering in the next stage of cognitive influence, that of recognition of the importance of expectancies and cognitions in the behavior-change process.

In the decade of the 70s, behavioral/cognitive techniques thrived. Many new procedures were introduced, and older approaches, predating the "cognitive revolution" (Mahoney, 1977a), gained in acceptance and popularity. The current behavioral/cognitive approaches will be reviewed briefly. First, however, we will review some outstanding findings gleaned from the cognitive psychology literature which, although not originally intended for direct application in psychotherapy, we feel have a great deal of relevance for the behavior-change process.

THEORIES OF COGNITIVE PSYCHOLOGY

Blank Trials Law

Marvin Levine, in a series of experiments in problem solving, found that, in the absence of feedback, people act as if their hypothesized solution to a problem is correct. People will persist with an incorrect response unless they are given specific feedback on its inappropriateness. Levine called this the "Blank Trials Law" (M. Levine, Leitenberg & Richter, 1964; M. Levine, 1966, 1971). This finding has major implications for psychotherapy. In a society which values politeness and avoidance of confrontation, specific, direct, negative feedback about a person's behavior is rarely given. Therefore, people may develop hypotheses of what constitutes a good solution to a social problem, and although the solution may not be functional, will persist with this behavior in the absence of feedback. Thus, the job of the therapist often is to give direct, unambiguous feedback about the appropriateness of the person's behavior.

During the heyday of student protests, one young woman entered therapy who was unable to hold a job. She could not understand why she was typically fired from any new job in a brief time, as she was reliable and did her work well. When the factors surrounding her work situation were discussed, among the behaviors she reported was that she felt compelled to lecture her bosses on the evils of capitalism in an effort at enlightening them. She did this on frequent occasions. Since her employers never gave her direct feedback that they regarded her as obnoxious, she acted as if she were being effective in a noble effort to improve the lot of the working class. This same client also could not understand why people were unfriendly to her. Her social situation at work was quite grim. People were reported as avoiding her or as being quite unfriendly to her. When we asked her to give a detailed description of her behaviors at work, it was clear that she did nothing that could be regarded as cheerful; she never smiled and she never asked her coworkers questions about their lives.

The client was a victim of the Blank Trials Law. The job of the therapist was, of course, to give her feedback about the consequences of her behavior. After we told her that it was quite likely that she was perceived as a "pill" because of her unfriendly behavior, we asked her to smile and to ask her colleagues questions about their lives. She reported that, to her amazement, they were friendlier to her when she did this. Regarding her interactions with her supervisors, she actually had a hard time understanding that her employers did not yearn for enlightenment and that her evangelical style was only self-destructive. She was told directly that work was not a podium for social change, unless she was prepared to be fired. Other opportunities for her to express her social values were also pointed out to her. She became aware of the consequences of her behavior with the feedback and was able to hold a job.

Although this case was extreme, the Blank Trials Law is operating to some degree in much of the neurotic behavior the therapist sees. In this case it would have been easy to hypothesize about the woman's passive/aggressive style and its origins. However, we think change would have been produced much more slowly by delving into the intrapsychic "reasons" for her behavior. This case demonstrates how simple feedback from a credible source can lead to major changes. It should also be noted that while the source of the problem (the functional model) was informational and therefore cognitive, the intervention was both cognitive (information-giving) and operant (suggesting new behaviors which would lead to happier outcomes for the client).

Marital relationships are also common victims of the Blank Trials Law. Frequently, when couples are angry at each other for violations of territory or protocol, they simply hide their anger. In the absence of feedback, each partner continues the behavior that angered the other in the first place. Instead of feedback leading to changed behavior or compromise, supressed anger leads to no change in the original behavior, and to growing dissatisfaction with the marriage. One woman complained about how hurt she was that her husband flirted with other women whenever they went to parties. She felt humiliated that her husband would be so insensitive to her feelings. When we asked her whether she had ever expressed her feelings of being hurt to her husband, she seemed somewhat surprised and answered in the negative. With a great deal of righteous indignation, she explained that her husband should be sufficiently sensitive to her feelings to know how hurt she was. We agreed that perhaps he should be, but pointed out that such "should" statements were luxuries which did not help solve the problem she had. After she had the Blank Trial Law explained to her, she was able to tell her husband that she wished he would not flirt during parties because she felt hurt. Although he did not stop altogether, she reported that he decreased most of the obvious flirting as a result of her feedback.

The sexual area is full of sensitivities and is therefore even more vulnerable to problems stemming from inadequate feedback between partners. People are rarely taught how to discuss personal sexual issues and simply avoid doing so. It is common to see couples in therapy for whom sex is mutually unsatisfactory yet never discussed. A woman in therapy discussed her lack of enthusiasm for sex with her husband. She related to us that her husband did not engage in foreplay with her, and that she found the whole act frustrating. Although she complained to us, her husband had no inkling that he was not satisfying her. In fact, the available evidence was that he was an adequate lover, as she not only never discussed her dissatisfaction, but she feigned orgasm. In the absence of valid feedback, he assumed his behavior was correct.

For the clinician, as well as to the wife in this situation, it is important to provide feedback in a way that can be accepted by the other person. It is of no use to tell someone that she or he is wrong in a way that will provoke hurt and denial. The skill of the clinician is the ability to tell people they are wrong in a manner that they will find acceptable. To this end, we owe a debt to the Rogerians who emphasized how important it is that there be no hint of personal evaluation in therapy in order for change to occur. Although we do not feel obliged to be nondirective, evaluations can be counterproductive. If the wife presented the feedback about her husband's bedroom performance in a critical tone, he would most likely be wounded and withdraw from her even more. It is therefore apparent that couples be taught communication skills to avoid this trap. Gottman, Notarius, Gonso, and Markman (1976) list several valuable communication skills that can be used in teaching couples. These skills emphasize communication of feelings in an honest, direct, yet nonhurtful manner. Their recommendations can increase the effectiveness of the Blank Trials Law by specifying ways that the patient can more effectively communicate with others, to bring about desired changes. We frequently tell people who try to convince us of the correctness of their position that they may be correct, but that being right is easy; the real skill is in being *effective*.

In the same manner, it is important that the therapist be free to provide feedback in a direct and nonambiguous way, without giving the slightest hint of evaluation of the client's worth. It is the nonevaluative aspect of the therapeutic climate which makes it a safe haven. Clients are more likely to relate problems when they feel that they are accepted as people of worth, than if they feel that they are going to be judged. In an article on social-skills training in children, Ladd & Mize (1982), while admitting there are few data on what they regard as an important topic, state:

> The instructor-child relationship may well influence every aspect of the skill-training process. Children may pay closer attention and learn more quickly when skill information is presented by a trusted and well-liked adult; a warm and supportive adult may be more effective in building children's self-confidence and allaying their anxieties; and children may accept and implement performance standards and feedback more quickly when they are administered by an instructor who conveys interest and acceptance [pp. 153–54].

We feel that these rules about the teaching of social skills apply equally to adults. It also appears that by directly stating the feedback, the therapist *decreases* the evaluative component of the message. If the therapist is hesitant about telling the client that the client behaved in an erroneous way, the therapist is transmitting the message that the content is too horrible to talk about openly and the person's error is somehow shameful.

Giving direct and unambiguous feedback has been a tradition in therapy. Sullivan, in his *Psychiatric Interview* (1954), speaks about the interpretation of the transference relationship in the same manner in which we are discussing the use of feedback. Transference, to Sullivan, consisted of the client relating to the therapist in a neurotic manner. For example, a client may be overly dependent on the therapist. Sullivan would regard this dependency as a neurotic trait which is probably typical of the client's day-to-day relationships as well as the therapeutic relationship. The therapist's job is then to interpret (that is, notice and comment upon) the client's distorted manner of relating to the therapist. This is directly analogous to what we are referring to as the use of feedback.

After the cognitive portion of the intervention—the feedback—the client is usually in need of some specific behavioral alternatives for the previous, unsatisfactory behavior. It is important for the therapist not only to give feedback, but to help clients develop positive alternatives for their nonfunctional behavior. For example, in the case of poor sexual communication, after the husband has been told that there are more satisfying ways of making love, he may also need direction as to what to do. His wife should be teaching him, in very specific terms, how she likes to be touched or kissed. The therapist can also be of service at this point in teaching alternative actions. Simply telling the husband that his wife is not satisfied sexually is a small service, unless his behavior is replaced by more appropriate behaviors. Helping clients develop alternative behaviors is a vital function of the therapist. Often direct suggestions are sufficient.

Adaptation-level Theory

Helson's adaptation-level theory (1964, 1971) is a perceptual theory with relevance to a wide variety of human problems. Simply stated, Helson's theory says that judgments are made on the basis of comparisons between the object or event to be judged and some standard. Within adaptation-level theory, the standard is hypothesized to be the pooled/weighted geometric mean of all relevant stimuli impinging upon an organism. In other words, the person's past and current experience is pooled together to form a standard against which new experiences are judged. This judgment may also have a strong affective component. Central to this perceptual theory, then, is the tenet that perceptions are not direct representations of external "reality," but are dependent upon the expectations and internal norms of the person perceiving. This is a concept shared in common with many other cognitive theories.

For example, on Long Island, a 50°F day in July would be perceived as quite cold, whereas the same temperature would feel absolutely hot in February. The perception, and accompanying emotional reaction, are dependent not upon the mercury reading, but upon subjective expectations constructed from past experience. Similarly, most of us have had the experience of having a friend rave about a movie, which almost inevitably leads to disappointment when we actually see the film. The friend's raves, according to adaptation-level theory, raise the level of expectations to such a magnitude that the odds of disappointment are greatly increased. Adaptation-level theory would maintain that a *contrast effect* occurs whenever one's judgment is shifted in the direction opposite to the background, as a result of a background change. Thus, when expectations develop which are considerably higher or lower than the actual experience, the experience is likely to be judged even more dissimilar in terms of the expectations than it actually is. The friend's raves about the movie set the standard so high that when we later see the movie, we judge it as even worse (further away from the standard) than it objectively is.

In a classic study, Tinklepaugh (1928), while investigating the delayed response in monkeys, reinforced correct discriminations. If the monkeys were able to delay the response and make the correct discrimination, they were rewarded with either lettuce or a banana chip. They learned the response for either of these reinforcers, and seemed pleased with each. However, Tinklepaugh tried to trick the monkeys. He had the monkeys watch him place a banana chip under the card but when they later made the discrimination, he replaced the banana chip with lettuce. These monkeys shrieked, threw the lettuce, and were generally furious. When these monkeys expected banana chips and "only" received lettuce, they were angry. Remember, when they expected lettuce and they received lettuce they had no negative emotional response. It is important for the therapist to be aware that there are many situations in life where the client expects "banana chips." Our job often is to see that these clients learn to accept those inevitable situations in life when "lettuce" is received instead.

The contrast effect applies to many areas in which clinicians are involved. Research has indicated that patients facing surgery do better if they have realistic expectations about the difficulty of recovery. Janis (1974) found that men who had very low preoperation fear became angry and hard to manage after the operation. Although Janis explains this effect as a result of the facilitative effects of anticipatory anxiety on coping, the data were also in line with an adaptation-level interpretation; realistic expectations of pain and discomfort shift the standard so that subsequent discomfort does not produce a contrast effect. Similar results have been shown in pain tolerance (Staub & Kellet, 1972; Staub, Tursky, & Schwartz, 1971) and to the response to a noxious medical examination (Johnson & Leventhal, 1974).

In an experiment in which expectations shifted the way a feared stimulus was perceived, Burkart and Levine (1982) found evidence for both the contrast effect and the assimilation effect. An *assimilation effect* is when the judgment is shifted towards the standard. Assimilation occurs when there is a small difference between the standard and the event, while contrast occurs when the difference is large. Subjects who rated themselves as having a high level of fear of rats were given different expectations about how closely they would be required to approach a rat. Although all subjects were required to do the same task—touch a rat— they were told in one contrast expectation that they would be required to pick up the rat and in another contrast condition that they would just look at the rat. On behavioral, psychophysiological, and rating measures, the group that was told they would have to pick up the rat had *lower* levels of fear than the group that expected to just look at the rat. It was as if they were relieved that they did not have to pick up the rat, but merely had to touch it. In this experiment, an assimilation effect was also found. Those subjects that expected to grasp the rat had higher levels of fear than those who were told they would be required to place their hand near the rat.

The direct implications of these data for clinical practice are significant. When clients are given assignments, it is important that the assignments be presented in a way that does not give the client the false expectation that doing the assigned task will be easy. If the difficulty of the task is understated, when the client actually performs the assignment and finds it somewhat difficult and/or annoying, the contrast effect will be counter-therapeutic. The client will perceive the task as "too difficult" or "a pain," and may not complete it. The contrast effect can also be used to enhance compliance with assignments. For example, we are currently researching contingent negative practice as a treatment for stuttering. Performing contingent negative practice (i.e., the repetition of a stuttered word 10 times after each occurrence during 15–25 minute trials) is simply not fun; youngsters dislike doing it intensely. We try to use contrast to facilitate our program. When introducing youngsters to the treatment program, we instruct them that completing the assigned contingent negative practice homework is extremely difficult, and that they will hate doing it and probably hate us for assigning it, but that we believe it will help their problem and is therefore worth doing. By describing the task as more difficult than it actually is, we are building in a contrast effect. We have had a dropout rate of under 5% with this procedure, which is quite low.

Adaptation-level theory also has implications concerning the distribution of reinforcers. F. M. Levine, Broderick, and Burkart (1983) investigated the relationship between reinforcing events, to determine if a contrast effect could occur by which a reward could undermine the reinforcing value of a given response. For example, could giving a youngster a bicycle for getting good grades undermine the reward of just getting good grades? There may be a contrast between the reinforcing value of the bicycle and the reinforcing value of doing well in school. Levine et al. asked youngsters to rate how much they would like various situations; they found that a highly rated situation did produce contrast, and led to the less highly rated situation being lowered by contrast. These authors caution against giving reinforcers without reviewing possible contrast effects. In other words, if the reward were too great for the task, the reward can reduce the intrinsic value of the task by contrast.

F. M. Levine et al. (1983) note that adaptation-level theory predicts situations where a reward will enhance the reinforcement value of an event. An assimilation effect will occur, according to adaptation-level theory, when the two events to be judged are close to each other. One judgment, in this situation, will be the anchor for the other and draw the judgment closer. Therefore, if the same friend gave a rave about a movie you loved, your judgment of the movie would be shifted towards his rave. This shift is in the opposite direction of the contrast effect and only occurs when the two situations to be judged are similar. Therefore, giving mild rewards for school performance, such as praise or a gold star, should enhance the reward value of the mildly rewarded task. Remember, the assimilation effect occurs when the anchor and the event are close together, and the contrast effect occurs when they are distant.

The concept of *hedonic relativism* is a direct extrapolation of adaptation-level theory to affective behavior (Brickman & Campbell, 1971). These theorists explicitly state that our subjective experiences are not a function of what we have (money, status, love) in some objective sense, but are a function of the difference between current hedonic levels and past levels. This concept goes a long way toward explaining the experience of people who are remarkably successful from most objective points of view yet who express a profound sense of discontent. This phenomenon has been referred to as the "Scarsdale Neurosis." Brickman and Campbell point out that we quickly adapt to new levels of achievement and reward, after which the same levels are no longer rewarding. To optimize the subjective feeling of happiness, a person should experience a series of discrete but small increases in possessions and accomplishments over a lifetime.

The alternative mode of achieving satisfaction is, as Brickman and Campbell (1971) state, to get off of the "hedonic treadmill" entirely. This can be done by a major shift in expectations. Many persons suffering from the Scarsdale Neurosis have an unstated assumption, promoted by the popular media, that human beings have a "right" to happiness. It is helpful to contrast this Western ideal with the Buddhist notion of suffering as an essential condition of life. Buddha claimed that we are born in pain, we die in pain, those we love die in pain, and we are often shackled to someone we do not love or who does not love us. Acceptance of the Buddhist philosophy, then, sets a very different standard against which to judge the events of life than does the Western expectation. Whether the Buddhist outlook is "correct" or not is of less interest to us than that it sets a standard that allows for positive contrast. By having a background standard of suffering, the normal problems in living do not look so terrible. This strategy of changing assumptions, whether they are spoken or unspoken, and lowering expectations is central to cognitive restructuring approaches, most notably Ellis's Rational Emotive Therapy (RET), which will be reviewed under "Misinformed Belief Structures."

The therapist can help the person suffering from the effects of negative contrast by aiding the person in rearranging his or her life experiences so as to renew a sense of increasing accomplishment (starting a new, challenging occupation or avocation, for example) or by challenging the assumptions that lead to the "hedonic treadmill." When life has, indeed, dealt the person severe blows, challenging the assumptions of a person's "right" to happiness is probably the more productive route, at least during the crisis period when the client typically has little energy for development of new sources of achievement and self-esteem.

This approach was taken with one female client whose life circumstances were unusually severe. Within a relatively short period of time before she came into therapy, she had suffered more stresses than many people cope with in a lifetime. Her daughter had been diagnosed schizophrenic (incorrectly, as it turned out), the client was in an auto accident and developed nerve damage that ultimately deafened her, she had a precancerous kidney problem that defied diagnosis and was often painful, and she was in a second auto accident in which she broke her arm. The broken arm leached calcium from her leg and delayed recovery. Her mother then had a series of small strokes and had to live with her while close to senescence. In addition, not only was her husband having an affair during this period, but he married his mistress in a bigamous marriage. Certainly, the expectation of happiness was hardly fulfilled in this case. At first, the client frequently said "Why me?" We talked at great length about the fact that suffering is part of life, and that the reality is that life is not fair, while emphasizing that she could still be effective in many areas.

We worked on distinguishing between effective and ineffective action, and the client was ultimately able to come to some level of acceptance of the "givens" in her life, while changing what she could. We emphasized that, although she experienced extremely difficult events, these events were not under her control and could not be changed. The therapy had, then, focused on giving her new standards ("life is suffering," etc.) by which to judge her situation. The woman was quite depressed and suicidal at the beginning of treatment, constantly carrying with her a vial of medicine with which to overdose. We heard from her recently. Her life has not improved (in fact, the precancerous condition developed into an inoperable tumor), but she is the pillar of strength in her family and her mood is positive. She is also a wonderful woman with a marvelous sense of humor, especially in the face of adversity, and despite the "bad karma" or conditions beyond her control, she is extremely well adjusted. She wrote us and attributed her handling her condition so well to therapy. We interpreted her letter as a farewell note, because of her advanced cancer.

According to adaptation-level theory, it is not the absolute state of life that determines one's reactions to events; rather, it is the relative position of the current state to one's expectations and one's standards. This theory maintains that we can adapt to wide ranges of levels of life; it is the relative shifts from these levels of adaptation that determine how we judge a new situation. This theory can explain why people can have happy moments in situations that many of us would find difficult, e.g., poverty, prison, or even during battle. People adapt to a great range of life experiences. We are all going to die, and if this is the acceptable background for judgments, other problems in life become, by contrast, diminished. Furthermore, this client, like millions of others, has learned to accept the reality of death. It can be done.

Although adaptation-level theory does not have a rich research tradition behind it in terms of clinical utility, it is a well-established perceptual theory that we feel has important implications for the development of cognitive points of intervention for the therapist. The function of the therapist is to change the level of expectations of the client and give standards that do not lead to an unnecessarily negative judgment. For example, we saw a 35-year-old man who had advanced multiple sclerosis. His multiple sclerosis led to an inability to walk, double vision, memory loss, loss of sexual functioning, and will, most likely, lead to his death. We tried to talk openly and candidly about death so that he slowly adapts and becomes more able to accept this reality. It is important that his standard judgment about death changes from being intensely negative to being acceptable. The point to be made is that people can adapt and accept the reality of death. If they are able to accept death, they are certainly able to accept other "tragedies" of life.

Reactance Theory

A cognitive theory of motivation which has implications for a number of interventions, and especially family functioning, is reactance theory, proposed by J. Brehm (1966). An exposition of the clinical utility of the theory was later performed by S. Brehm (1976). The essence of the theory is that when people perceive their freedom to be threatened, they are motivated to reestablish that free choice. Within families, youngsters' reactance motivation is often aroused by what the child perceives to be unreasonable restrictions of freedom made by parents. For example, a child who is told that she must be in at 9 PM, while all her peers can stay out until 11 PM, will perceive that her freedom is being threatened by her parents. To restore that freedom, she may act directly and simply stay out later, or she may choose another act which symbolically establishes her freedom. Keeping her room messy, failing at school, or using drugs may be methods by which a youngster in such a situation can demonstrate her capacity for free behavior.

The reactance of children against their parents' restrictions has long been shared wisdom and has become the subject of many literary endeavors. Romeo and Juliet's romance was doubtless, at least partially fueled by their families disapproval of the relationship. In a modern story, *The Fantasticks,* two neighbors want their children to marry, so they build a wall between their properties and forbid the children to see one another. Their understanding of reactance principles is displayed in a song they sing about their children's motivation, "Never Say 'No.'"

Within families, lack of understanding of reactance principles often leads to a spiraling escalation of hostilities between parents and children. Parents impose restrictions, children respond with reactance and more acting out, and parents fear they are losing control and thus tighten restrictions even further. Often when restrictions are somewhat relaxed, acting out behavior will decrease because its function of reestablishing freedom is no longer needed.

We saw a 7-year-old youngster and his parents in therapy. Among other presenting problems, the child was encopretic (i.e., had bowel movements in his pants). Although the encopresis was not addressed directly in therapy, after the issue of control was addressed and the parents were able to give their child more choices, the encropresis decreased spontaneously. We have seen many cases where encopresis was an act of defiance from a child who felt overcontrolled. This would be predicted from reactance theory.

J. Brehm (1966) also presents guidelines for reducing reactance. Reactance is reduced when the infringement on freedom is justified and legitimized. Thus, telling a child that he or she cannot have a cookie because "Mommy says so" is a weak justification, but explaining that the cookie can be eaten after dinner because it may otherwise ruin the child's appetite should reduce reactance. Giving choices wherever possible is also helpful in reducing reactance. Thus a forced choice between two elements which are determined by the parents, while actually not allowing much real freedom, still enhances perception of freedom (e.g., "Would you like to brush your teeth or take your bath first?").

Additionally, Brehm states that reactance is only aroused when there exists a perception of freedom initially. Therefore, if there are areas of behavior in which parents decide they will not tolerate deviation (e.g., no hitting, no running in the street, no playing with fire), they should be very consistent in their reaction to such behavior. Consistent restriction in one area contributes to the cognition that no freedom exists in that area. Further restriction of a child's freedom to hit, for example, will not then be responded to with reactance. If the youngster is allowed to hit at some times but not at others, the youngster may perceive that hitting is a free behavior and may hit more when restricted. Many parents come into therapy reluctant to set reasonable, consistent restrictions on their children, and thus unwittingly create conditions conducive to reactance. The children in such situations perceive virtually all of their behavior as being "free," and hence resist all control.

ASSESSMENT

Problems with a cognitive origin spread across all diagnostic categories and problem types. As shown in the flowchart (p. xii–xiii), we ask whether there is specific evidence of cognitions being involved in the development or the maintenance of the presenting problem. Rather than using a cognitive intervention based on diagnosis, we would first assess the *type* of cognitive problem (if any) that is behind a particular presenting problem. Following are two basic categories of cognitive dysfunctions which can contribute to psychological difficulties: problems of misinformation and problems of deficient cognitive skills. These areas should be investigated when assessing the presence of the cognitive model.

Misinformation

We see misinformation (broadly defined) as the most common cognitive problem which clients present. We define *misinformation* as any set of ideas or beliefs which are factually false or are dysfunctional for their owners. Misinformation can occur on several levels. We will discuss misinformation about facts, about appropriate internal standards for behavior, and about patterns of cognitive inferences.

Factual Misinformation.   Very often people enter therapy with incorrect or incomplete information about themselves or about their environment. Since people tend to work with the information that they have in the absence of feedback (recall M. Levine's (1966, 1971) Blank Trials Law), the incorrect information tends to persist and interferes with functioning. It is common for graduate students to report the feeling that a particular professor is "out to get them," as a result of an isolated negative or ambiguous interaction with the professor. Such a student also reports feeling anxious in the professor's company, and often acting "stupid" as a result of that anxiety. When a "friendly" professor reports that the "enemy" professor has been supportive of the student in faculty meetings, the behavior of the student often changes. The new information challenges the old hypothesis that the professor is an "enemy."

One example of incorrect information affecting behavior was seen in the case of a 26-year-old man from the Bahamas who had travelled all over the world for the treatment of his "premature ejaculation." He had been told by his beer-drinking cronies that a man had to last at least half an hour in intercourse before ejaculating. This man was able to sustain intercourse for only 5 minutes before ejaculation ensued. After travelling to England and the Continent for help, he finally went to Harvard Medical School for treatment. Although his misinformation was not immediately apparent, it became clear with further assessment. When he was shown the Kinsey report's findings (Kinsey, Pomeroy & Martin, 1948) on actual duration of intercourse, he was greatly relieved to find that he was "normal." Much of current sex therapy centers on eliminating dysfunction-producing myths of sexual functioning and replacing them with more realistic standards. Although this man was college educated and quite bright, he relied upon an invalid source of information that led to negative results.

Some men and women attempt to have an orgasm by effort. A role of the therapist in many of these cases it to teach the clients that increasing effort in an attempt to achieve orgasm can contribute to orgasmic difficulties. These people often also believe that it is terrible to not have orgasm. In therapy, they should be encouraged to enjoy sexual experiences for their own sensual value. In many other cases, couples may learn that they simply do not need therapy. They may find that what they regarded as symptoms of sexual malfunctioning may be perfectly normal behavior. Some couples are relieved to find out that it is not abnormal to have intercourse fewer than three times a week, for example. This information alone can be all the therapy some couples need (although, as more sexual information is available through the popular media, the clinician sees fewer of these types of cases).

Many family problems stem from parents' misinformation about reasonable standards of conduct for their children. Frequently the clinician sees parents who are furious at their children for acting like children. The misinformed standard that these parents carry is that children are little adults and should act like adults. For example, a mother may expect her young children to wait quietly for an hour in a doctor's waiting room. This is simply beyond the capacities of most children under the age of 10. Many times, children's natural egocentrism is labeled by the parents as evidence of "selfishness" or "irresponsibility." Children frequently have problems seeing their own role in the provocation of unpleasant incidents. They see themselves as being in the right in every instance, even when the parent can see who threw the first punch or hurled the first insult. This can greatly anger the parents.

Often, parents complain about the irresponsibility of their children when it comes to performing chores or doing other "thoughtful" tasks around the home. Parents usually fail to view the chores from the child's perspective. When they are aided in doing so, it becomes apparent that from a child's view, taking out the garbage is very low on the priority list. Children are usually unimpressed with the reasons their parents give for them to do the task, especially when there are other more enjoyable things to do. Although parents must still be firm in requesting the child to do some things that he or she does not want to do, understanding the child's point of view eliminates parental judgments of the child as "bad" or "sloppy".

Parents often need to be educated about the basics of a child's cognitive development. Piaget and others have demonstrated the systematic development of self-control and the decrease of egocentrism throughout childhood (Flavell, 1977). *Egocentrism,* the inability to distinguish between one's own perspective and that of someone else, is prevalent in early childhood (2–6 years of age) and declines thereafter (although Flavell points out that even as adults we are always "at risk" of slipping back into seeing our viewpoint to the exclusion of others'). A child's egocentrism makes it difficult for the child to have empathy for another's position and to act on that empathy. Thus, it is unreasonable of parents to expect their children to see the "reasonableness" of emptying the garbage daily. It doesn't seem reasonable to a child, and it is certain that they won't have empathy with the parents' reasons for wanting it done. Similarly, the ability to control one's own behavior is age-related, with impulse control increasing over childhood. Although young children do show some self-control, it tends to be sporadic and situation-specific, according to Flavell. When they lack correct information about normal child behavior, parents can become unnecessarily angry at or worried about their children. They may think they have "bad" or "abnormal" children when they actually have children who act age-appropriately.

The clinician should be alert for statements of misinformation on the part of the client. More importantly, the clinician should be attentive to behavior which may reflect misinformed assumptions. Of course, it is also imperative that the therapist have correct information concerning human functioning by which to evaluate the faulty assumptions carried by the client. Misinformation about standards can be behind many sorts of clinical problems. In various circumstances, misinformation could lead to low self-esteem and depression (as in the graduate-student example), and poor interpersonal or family relationships. Additionally, misinformation may be a component of the problem in situations which fit into another model of dysfunction.

Misinformed Belief Structures.   Ellis (1962, 1977b) developed an influential cognitive theory of human psychological dysfunction and therapy which is also based on a type of misinformation model. Ellis stated that when a person is psychologically distressed, it is a result of a faulty or misinformed belief structure. He set forth a set of commonly held beliefs which he labeled *irrational* because they are not rationally supported by empirically gathered evidence. Such beliefs include: the belief that one must be loved by virtually everyone; the belief that one must be totally adequate in all circumstances in order to consider oneself worthwhile; the belief that some persons are "bad" and should be severely punished; the belief that it is terrible when things do not happen as one would like them to happen; the belief that human unhappiness is externally caused and that people are helpless to control their unhappiness. Holding on to these or other similar beliefs, Ellis reasoned, causes persons to label their situation in ways that cause them unnecessary unhappiness and distress.

For example, a woman who held the irrational belief that she must be loved and approved of by everyone she knew, was emotionally crushed when she overheard a slightly catty conversation about her at an office party. It was not because of the true impact of such conversation upon her life that she became upset; rather, her assumptions about the necessity of universal love inflated the event to an emotional importance of great dimensions. Although we do not share Ellis' (1962) enthusiasm for the universality of irrational beliefs as causal factors in human dysfunction, we have seen clients whose idiosyncratic and unchallenged beliefs about how the world *should* work played a major role in their psychological problems. Ellis (1977b) stated that the therapist should assess for the presence of a faulty belief structure by being tuned in to the patient's use of "should," "must," or unempirical, unchallenged assumptions. We agree with this method of assessment, and add that "irrational beliefs" do not consist only of the group outlined by Ellis, but may well be idiosyncratically generated by particular patients (Goldfried & Davison, 1976). In other words, the list that Ellis used was certainly not exhaustive; there are ample numbers of alternative irrational beliefs that clients bring into therapy.

Many of the cognitive interventions used by Ellis can be viewed from the perspective of adaptation-level theory. Often Ellis changes standards and expectations when he changes "irrational" beliefs. As an example, when Ellis tells people that they are irrational if they believe that they are going to be loved and approved by everyone, he is shifting the standard of what constitutes appropriate levels of social acceptance. He is avoiding a contrast effect. If we expect to be loved and approved of by everyone, then receiving mild disapproval from someone becomes a major emotional event because of the contrast from our expectation. If, however, we "rationally" recognize that some people will approve and others will not, the contrast effect is nullified and disapproval is not enlarged.

Virtually every one of Ellis's irrational beliefs provide an extreme standard that lends itself to events being judged as catastrophic because real situations are far below the extreme standard. Ellis is quite right when he teaches clients that it is not necessary to be the best in everything one does. When one has that expectation, and inevitably discovers someone better, the result is frustration and unhappiness. If this "irrational" expectation is replaced by one that allows room for the strengths of others, the experience of being less-than-best is not threatening. Ellis's system cognitively alters extreme and problem-producing expectations. He shifts the standards of judging oneself so that contrast effects are reduced.

Patterns of cognitive errors.   By *patterns of cognitive errors,* we are referring to overlearned cognitive habits of making assumptions and inferences which are dysfunctional for the client. Patterns of cognitive errors have been investigated most throughly in their relationship to depression.

Beck (1976; Beck & Rush, 1978; Beck, Rush, Shaw, & Emery, 1979) has been a proponent of a cognitive model of depression. He and his associates have described a pattern of cognitive errors which they believe lead to a subjective feeling and clinical syndrome of depression. First, Beck claims that depressives experience what he calls the "cognitive triad": a negative view of the self; a tendency to interpret experiences in a negative manner; and a pessimistic view of the future. (See Beck & Rush, 1978, for a review of empirical work supporting the existence of the cognitive triad in depressives.) Additionally, Beck proposes that depressives have faulty schemata, or stable cognitive patterns, which cause them to organize their experience in ways conducive to becoming depressed.

Although there are outcome data showing the effecitveness of cognitive therapy for depression, there is still some question as to the universality of faulty cognitive schemata as the causal factor in depression. As acknowledged by Beck et al. (1979), there may be other "kinds [p. 26]" of depression for which their cognitive model does not fit. From our own clinical experiences, there have been instances of persons with symptoms of depression who did not display systematic cognitive errors of the type listed above. As we have stated in other chapters, there may be biological, operant, social learning, or even classical conditioning dynamics behind any particular display of depressive symptomatology. These may occur instead of, or in addition to, cognitive dynamics (Beach, Abramson, Levine, 1981).

The literature on learned helplessness and its relationship to depression describes another line of reasoning which places cognitive errors at the heart of the syndrome of depression. Maier and Seligman (1976) summarized the animal research on the effects of inescapable trauma on producing the effects called learned helplessness. Maier and Seligman concluded that the perception of uncontrollability led to three classes of effects in animals: (1) motivational effects—motivation to learn new responses decreased; (2) cognitive effects—the ability to perceive contingency relationships was decreased; and (3) emotional effects—the uncontrollability of the aversive events produced great emotional upset in the animal subjects.

Abramson, Seligman, and Teasdale (1978) reformulated the learned-helplessness hypothesis in terms of human functioning. They stated that depression consists of four classes of deficits: emotional, cognitive, and motivational (as in Maier & Seligman, 1976), as well as self-esteem. It is a cognitive, attributional model, in that Abramson et al. state that those people who tend to attribute failure experiences to external, unstable, and global causes are "at risk" for depression, as compared with individuals who attribute failure to external, unstable, or specific causes (see Abramson et al., 1978, for a full exposition of the attributional framework). Further research has generally supported the reformulated hypothesis (e.g., Golin, Sweeney, & Shaeffer, 1981; Matalsky, Abramson, Seligman, Semmel, & Peterson, 1982; Seligman, Abramson, Semmel, & von Baeyer, 1979).

However, the research on this subject is still young, with few studies so far employing a prospective design to investigate the directionality of attributional styles and depressive affect (e.g., Metalsky et al., 1982), and most of the work using nonclinical populations. Additionally, the original reformulation itself stated that expectations of helplessness (and the subsequent emotional, motivational, cognitive, and self-esteem deficits predicted by the helplessness model) are sufficient, but not necessary, conditions of depression. Thus, the advocates of the learned-helplessness model acknowledge the possibility of other causes of depression. Evaluation of a client's attributional style can be conducted informally, by inquiring about attributions made for salient negative and positive events, or by means of an attributional style questionnaire used for research purposes (e.g., Peterson, Semmel, von Baeyer, Abramson, Metalsky, & Seligman, 1982).

Abramson et al. (1978) were particularly articulate in differentiating depression which occurs with self-esteem deficits and depression without such deficits. They claim that self-esteem deficits will only occur if the person is making internal attributions for failure. Thus, if two persons are both turned down by all the graduate schools to which they applied, they may both feel depressed, and suffer cognitive and motivational deficits associated with depression. However, if one attributes the failure to internal qualities (e.g., stupidity) while the other attributes the failure to external qualities (e.g., arbitrary standards of the schools), only the internalizer will suffer self-esteem deficits. Thus, it may be worthwhile to assess for attributional style even in the absence of overt depressive symptomatology (as attributional styles are assumed to precede depressive incidents) if a client has problems of low self-esteem.

When clients are resistant to therapy.   Misinformation should always be assessed for when clients are resistant or noncompliant with therapy. Too frequently, behavior therapists have ignored the very common problem of noncompliance with treatment goals or homework assignments (Wachtel, 1977). Often, when a client is noncompliant with homework or other aspects of therapy, it is because the therapist has failed to fully investigate the *meaning* of a particular intervention for an individual.

Although keeping diaries of many kinds of behavior is a common behavioral technique, we once assigned this type of task to a schizophrenic client with very poor results. The client simply did not show up for the next session. When finally contacted, he was able to voice strong objections to the assignment, stating that if the therapist thought he was a 5-year-old child, he might as well act like one. Obviously, the assignment aroused very strong feelings in this individual, and meant something very different to him than it did to the therapist who assigned it. Many behavioral techniques, because of their concreteness and simplicity, have the potential to arouse similar reactions from clients if the meaning of the task to that person is not fully explored. Alternatively, clients may be resistant because the subject matter at a particular juncture is too upsetting or threatening. In either case, the meaning of the resistance must be explored with the client. In some cases, this may constitute the bulk of therapy, as when a fearful, passive/aggressive individual enters therapy and immediately begins to refuse all strategies offered. For this individual, an exploration of his or her typical mode of action in the world (extreme passivity) *is* highly therapeutic, for it is this very "resistance" which has caused the client's life problems.

Deficits in Cognitive Skills

It is often the case that despite correct information about what they should do cognitively, clients are in therapy because they have not yet acquired the *skill* to use that information effectively. This is the major problem with pop psychology and self-help approaches to psychological problems. Although such programs may dispense accurate information, without practice in applying it the information is useless to the individual. Therefore, along with assessing for misinformation on the part of the client, the therapist must also assess whether the client has acquired the skill of using correct or adaptive information.

Practice of New Cognitive Information. The importance of practice within the cognitive model is frequently underestimated, especially among new therapists (as well as among clients). We have heard graduate students state that they have tried cognitive approaches to therapy and that they do not work. These students maintain, sometimes arduously, that they have met the exact requirements of the model, and that it was not effective. Although there certainly are cases where, even with a good conceptual analysis, the intervention is not sufficient to produce change, more often the student does not appreciate the practice necessary for cognitive change. These students know about shaping and learning curves when the operant or classical-conditioning model is applied, but they do not understand that the same principles are pertinent to learning new cognitive skills.

Anderson (1982), in an important paper on the acquisition of cognitive skills, claims that, "It requires at least 100 hours of learning and practice to acquire any significant cognitive skill to a reasonable degree of proficiency [p. 369]." Often change is rapid within the cognitive model, especially when the patient suffers from essentially a misinformation problem. However, time and practice are necessary when new cognitive skills are being acquired. Anderson states that the first stage in the acquisition of cognitive skills is the declarative stage. During this stage the individual learns the facts involved. For example, the client may rehearse, "I am upset because Joe criticized me. I must learn that I cannot get the approval of everyone for everything I do." The declarative information itself would not be sufficient to decrease the response to criticism. The neophyte therapist may say that the client tried Rational Emotive Therapy (RET) but it did not work. However, the development of this cognitive skill requires a good many trials before it is utilized.

The declarative knowledge must, according to Anderson (1982), become interpreted into procedural form. The procedural knowledge is learning the rules by which the declarative knowledge can be applied. The therapist must chip away at the client's bad habits by repeated exposures of the specifics of how to apply the information. For example, it is often not sufficient for the clients to know that they are being "irrational," but we recommend reviewing how that knowledge could be applied. "Right," we would say to these clients, "You were upset because you believed that you should be approved of all the time. Now what else could you have told yourself?" According to Anderson, repetition should lead to this process increasing in efficiency and even becoming automatic. We would repeat this procedure many times in order to help the client.

Parenthetically, we feel that Anderson's (1982) paper also explains another phenomenon: the time it takes to learn the task of therapy. Frequently we see graduate students, who do very well on exams about therapy (the declarative stage), flounder when they see clients. They often will sound very good when they talk about the therapeutic process but their sessions are still weak. These students have mastered the declarative stage of therapy (the learning of the verbal knowledge), but it simply takes time and experience to be able to put this knowledge into effective action.

Deficits in Cognitive Control.   When clients display problems in constructing and organizing their lives, or in controlling themselves, they may be suffering from deficits in cognitive control of these functions. The whole self-control literature has shown many attempts at reinstituting personal control by teaching techniques to sharpen the use of logical thought and self-statements (e.g. D'Zurilla & Goldfried, 1971; Mahoney, 1977b; Meichenbaum, Gilmore, & Fedoravivius, 1971; Meichenbaum & Goodman, 1971). Therefore, problems with facing and solving life problems, difficulties controlling one's anger, fear, or other emotions, and impulse-control problems may have a cognitive root. The therapist should evaluate the client for the presence of current cognitive-control techniques, however informal. Many people, without the aid of therapists, have found that talking to themselves, thinking through the pros and cons of a dilemma, or setting goals for themselves are useful techniques. Clients who present self-control problems, however, are frequently deficient in such spontaneously occurring strategies.

INTERVENTION

Within the models approach the etiology and intervention procedures of a particular individual's problem do not necessarily fall within the same model. A person may have a severe anger control problem because of a history of being operantly reinforced for such behavior, yet we may elect to treat the current problem using a cognitive approach due to the relative awkwardness of rearranging the reinforcement contingencies operating in that person's environment. Following are some common treatment approaches which utilize a cognitive approach. One need not necessarily believe that a problem has a cognitive etiology to employ these intervention procedures, although in some cases, the intervention and etiological factors may, logically, both fall within the same model (e.g., the presence of misinformation will be treated by the presentation of correct information). Essentially, all of the interventions, as indicated in the flowchart (p. 000), are ways to change cognitive patterns, through information-giving and practice in acquiring cognitive skills.

Attribution Therapy

Kopel and Arkowitz (1975) set forth guidelines drawn from attribution research with which to enhance maintenance and generalization of therapeutic gains. The recommendations of these authors are congruent with both client-centered or insight-oriented therapeutic approaches. They emphasize that clients should take an active role in deciding on goals and assignments in order to maximize the self-attribution of change gained thereby. This recommendation also decreases reactance motivation by keeping goal achievement as the clients' free behavior. They also encourage therapists to use the least powerful reward or punishment during therapy in order to increase the patient's self-attribution. Kopel and Arkowitz note that the impact of external aids (such as drugs) should be minimized to give the client internal attributions for change. Davison and Valins (1969) found that there was less maintenance when change was attributed to external forces than when it was self-attributed. Finally, in accordance with Bem's (1967) self-perception theory, Kopel and Arkowitz emphasize that the salience of the client's perception of his or her changed behavior should be increased through feedback from the therapist and self-monitoring.

Abramson et al. (1978) propose four therapeutic strategies to combat the four cases under which (according to their model) depression is most far-reaching. The four aspects are (1) when the estimated probability of a desired outcome is low or when the perceived probability of an undesired outcome is high; (2) when the outcome itself is *highly* desirable or undesirable; (3) when the outcome is perceived to be uncontrollable; and (4) when the attribution for this uncontrolled outcome is to an internal, global, and stable cause. The four strategies emerge directly from these four aspects which predispose to depression: You must (1) change the estimated probability of the desired or the undesired event's occurrence. By this is meant active intervention in the environment such that a very desirable event (e.g., getting a job) becomes more probable, or that a very undesirable event (e.g., losing one's home) decreases in probability. (2) Make the highly preferred outcomes less preferred. This can be done by either aiding the client in relabeling and accepting the "very undesirable" outcomes as "okay" or "pretty good," or by relabeling the "very desirable" outcomes as unrealistic (when they are). (3) Change the expectation from one of uncontrollability to controllability. This is central to the learned-helplessness model. This can be achieved by training the person in skills to control the outcome of their responses (e.g., child-management skills). If the person already has the relevant skills, the expectation of controllability can be aided by the introduction of success experiences via graded tasks and role play. Alternatively, clients could be aided in attributing failure to inadequate effort, thus increasing the likelihood of improved performance after failure (Diener & Dweck, 1978). (4) Change attributions for failure to external, unstable, and specific causes while changing attributions for success to internal, stable, global factors. This would presumably occur through the therapist relabeling and reattributing success and failure to new causes, and hoping the client comes to agree.

Cognitive Restructuring

A more far-reaching method of cognitive intervention is cognitive restructuring, which is applied to change the basic cognitive style and structure of a person. Rational emotive therapy (RET), developed by Albert Ellis (1962, 1970; Ellis & Grieger, 1977a) is a system of changing a person's "irrational beliefs" (partially listed earlier in this chapter). Ellis accepts the true cognitive model of psychological dysfunction, by which it is the *belief* about any event, not the event itself, which causes emotional upset and psychological problems. Ellis described the method of RET as a logico-empirical method including scientific questioning, challenging, and debating between the therapist and the client (Ellis, 1977).

Typically, RET is a process of the therapist trying to expose the client's irrational, maladaptive beliefs (e.g., "If I fail at giving this speech, it will be horrible. No one will respect me and I couldn't live with that.") The irrationality of the client's beliefs is then analyzed, using questioning and challenging by the therapist. The therapist may use role reversal, and attempt to get the client to tell why a particular belief is irrational. When the client recognizes the irrationality of these beliefs, then he or she is taught to use emotional upset (anxiety, anger, etc.) as a cue to look for an irrational thought. The client is then taught to replace the thought with a more rational, adaptive one. The end result of a treatment with RET, according to Ellis (1977b), is a new philosophy, or way of looking at and reacting to the world. As pointed out previously, we view Ellis' approach as being an extremely useful application of adaptation-level theory.

Beck's (1972, 1976) cognitive therapy for depression is another type of cognitive restructuring. Beck and his associates (Beck et al., 1979) have developed a comprehensive method for teaching and evaluating therapists, and conducting the therapy itself. Beck's therapy focuses heavily on teaching the client to recognize, evaluate, and test his or her depressogenic cognitions. This is done largely through the homework assignments which are frequently designed as "experiments" to test cognitions that the client believes to be absolutely true. For example, if a depressed housewife concluded that there was absolutely no way she could get a part-time job because no one would hire her, she might be instructed to test such an assumption.

The process of Beck's (1972, 1976; Beck et al., 1979) therapy consists of learning the connection between one's cognitive errors and one's emotional state, via self-monitoring and discussion with the therapist. Beck advocates behavioral as well as cognitive techniques when the depression is severe, and uses a variety of cognitive techniques within the total system of therapy (e.g., reattribution, cognitive relabeling, reality testing of cognitions, information-giving). Thus, his system actually works well within the models approach, which emphasizes treating on a case-by-case basis as called for by the particular dynamics of a situation rather than treating by diagnosis. (See Beck et al., 1979 for a fine exposition of this method of cognitive therapy.)

Coping-skills Training

Coping-skills-training procedures bring together a fairly divergent group of cognitive techniques, the main shared feature of which is their emphasis on teaching the client *skills* which will aid adaptive behavior in many different settings (Mahoney & Arnkoff, 1978).

Meichenbaum & Cameron (1977) describe a "stress-inoculation" procedure. They speculate that it may not be the incidence of "irrational" thoughts which distinguishes functional from poorly functioning persons, but the manner in which such cognitions are coped with by the person. Thus, they developed a stress-inoculation procedure through which they present stressors (either through imagination or in vivo) and develop and rehearse internal dialogues which the clients can then use to cope with the stressful event. This internal dialogue consists of self-statements *preparing* one for the stressor ("Here it comes. What shall my plan be?"), *handling* the stressor by giving self-instructions ("Just keep calm and concentrate on the task at hand"), *coping* with overwhelming feelings ("I can handle this, it will be over soon"), and *reinforcing* oneself for coping ("I really handled that much better"). After these skills are mastered in one problem setting, they are transferred to other areas. Meichenbaum and Cameron point out that such a procedure is more helpful to retarded, psychotic, or child populations than a cognitive-restructuring approach, because the stress-inoculation procedure is much more concrete and lends itself easily to imagery. (They suggest using images like, "I won't go any faster than a slow turtle" for children with impulse problems, for example.)

Systematic-desensitization procedures have been re-evaluated and re-formulated as cognitive-coping procedures with some success. As mentioned in Chapter 4, Goldfried (1971) altered the traditional method of performing systematic desensitization so that the client, rather than being passively conditioned, is taught to actively cope with anxiety. Whereas in the traditional method of systematic desensitization clients were told to switch from the anxiety-producing scene when it became uncomfortable, Goldfried advocates urging the client to "stay with it" and cope with the physical and emotional feelings produced by the anxiety. This is done via relaxation and cognitive relabeling.

Meichenbaum et al. (1971) compared desensitization to "insight" therapy for speech anxiety. The "insight" treatment actually focused on how maladaptive self-talk produced anxiety, and how to monitor and replace that self-talk with incompatible self-instruction and behavior. They found that the "insight" treatment was equal, in general, to the desensitization treatment in relieving the anxiety, but that the focus on cognition was especially effective for those subjects who had high social distress in many situations.

Problem-solving techniques teach skills that are applicable in a wide range of life situations. People who will most benefit from such training tend to be those displaying great amounts of ineffectiveness in their life (not secondary to another major problem; one would not do problem-solving training with a person incapacitated by severe depression), or those who are frequently labeled "dependent personalities" (D'Zurilla & Goldfried, 1971). Problem-solving training is the delineation of rules which competent problem-solvers use naturally, but which may be deficient in certain individuals.

We counseled a 30-year-old man who was unemployed and depressed. He had worked in a variety of production positions in the entertainment business, but was unemployed when his last firm failed. He spent 6 months waiting to be called to another job. In the first session, we went over a variety of employment alternatives for him. Since job openings in the entertainment business are mainly found through individual contacts rather than by following advertisements, he was advised to contact every employed person he knew to generate leads. We spent that session and most of the next on generating alternatives. His mood was improved for the next session even though he did not have anything concrete, because he felt less helpless. This man then had several interviews before finding a job that was significantly better than the one he lost. Obviously, his depression went down once he saw he was not helpless and certainly improved after finding employment. More important than the results of these particular interviews was that the client was able to expand his response repertoire to include active problem-solving skills. He is aware that, even if the employment market is poor in the entertainment field, he would still have to generate alternatives. He no longer thinks in terms of solving problems, but he thinks in terms of generating alternatives and choosing from the available ones. It is often a destructive luxury to think in terms of solutions to problems; clients have to learn to recognize that there are rarely solutions to problems, just selections of alternatives.

Another type of problem-solving technique has been developed by Mahoney (1977b). He states that the purpose of teaching such a skill is to enable clients to become their own agent of self-control. Mahoney's technique is called "Personal Science," and he views it as a method of using general problem-solving with personal problems. It is more heavily "scientific" than what is proposed by D'Zurilla and Goldfried (1971) because it emphasizes generating hypotheses, gathering data, and evaluating the data. Although both of these problem-solving techniques depend heavily on behavioral trials to verify the worth of the problem-solving plan, they are heavily cognitive in that they are designed to aid clients in the cognitive steps necessary for successful problem-solving.

Problems of impulsiveness may in certain cases be problems of deficient cognitive control. Meichenbaum and Goodman (1971) reported on a training procedure they developed for use with impulsive children. Impulsive children have a great deal of trouble in school because of their inability to focus long enough on academic tasks in order to complete them to the best of their ability. Meichenbaum and Goodman's procedure consists of a 5-step program. First, the child observes an adult model performing the task at hand while talking to himself aloud, giving self-instructions. Then the child performs the same task with overt verbal instructions from the model. The child then performs the task while instructing him or herself out loud. In the final stages, the child fades the self-instruction to a whisper, and then performs the task with silent self-instructions. Meichenbaum and Goodman found that impulsive kids were able to stay on-task with this procedure, and retained these gains at one month follow-up.

Novaco (1975) has developed a multicomponent treatment program for people with anger problems. He uses role-playing, systematic desensitization to anger-provoking stimuli, relaxation training, the use of incompatible behaviors in anger situations, and replacing maladaptive self-statements with helpful ones. He has found the cognitive component of the program to be highly effective. The self-statements aided the client in changing perceptions of the provocation (instead of "This guy's just out to get me," they would substitute "He looks tired—maybe he's having a bad day"). From the clients' point of view, the most helpful result of self-statements was an increase in ability to attend to the task at hand ("Just ignore that guy's comment and go on with your presentation.") Thus, we see that the principle of cognitive intervention can be used with a wide variety of clinical problems.

Although human beings are creatures of thought, it does not follow that the cognitive model will always be employed in therapy. Frequently, although irrational cognitions are present, another model may fit the facts of a case more parsimoniously and intervention should therefore initially center on that model. Irrational cognitions may well be secondary to some behavioral problems, and the therapist would do better to first intervene in the model of best fit before using cognitive techniques.

7 The Social-Context Model

When confronted with a client who is suffering from subjective psychological distress, it is often tempting for the therapist to investigate the person's individual functioning in detail while neglecting to look outside the individual for explanatory factors. It is always important, since we are social creatures, for a therapist to examine the social context of any psychological disturbance. The basic premise behind this chapter is that individual dysfunction and pain can emerge, not from a "flaw" in the individual, but from pressures exerted by social institutions of the family, community, and society at large (cf. Kazdin, 1978a). Although social behavior usually helps an individual function well in the environment, when social or personal norms are in a state of flux, individuals often feel distress because they are subject to incompatible social demands.

Choosing to explain individual problems in terms of social forces does present some problems. First, why should this level of analysis be employed at all? After all, clinicians from backgrounds as disparate as traditional psychoanalysis and radical behaviorism have traditionally focused on the individual. It is true that problems we will discuss in this chapter can be analyzed using models of individual dysfunction (e.g., the depression that occurs in middle-aged housewives who have lost their role as mother might be analyzed in terms of cognitive or operant factors). Using the social context, however, provides us with a wealth of information from which we can determine points of intervention.

When a social-context model fits the data of the case, it will be a more parsimonious explanation of the facts than would other models. Thus, a female graduate student's anxiety at taking exams may be due to her family background in which it was considered wrong for women to enter the professional world. This explanation can be more parsimonious than explaining each symptom individually via its biological, operant, respondent, or cognitive components. The role-conflict explanation also provides us with an additional point of intervention over what would be provided by focusing only upon individual analyses. In addition to interventions suggested by a respondent model, the social-context model provides us with intervention strategies such as changing the social pressures or changing the *relation* between the individuals and other individuals or groups. It should be noted that the presence of the social-context model does not preclude the usefulness of other models. Therefore, although we may be aware that the client is in a dilemma related to a social conflict, we may use relaxation training as our intervention if we felt this would help the client handle the stresses of the conflict.

When discussing the example of the female graduate student, it becomes clear how pervasive and important roles are. Both of the descriptive terms "female" and "graduate student" have role connotations that we automatically process just by thinking of the terms. When we use a relatively simple term such as "mother," we are immediately implying a social role which demands conformity to a broad set of expectations and responsibilities. The demands placed on women who are not mothers are significantly different from those who are. For example, if we state that the female graduate student rarely came home in the evenings because she had a great deal of work to do, it would be responded to quite differently than if we said the same statement about the mother. Roles are powerful determinants of behavior and expectations and their power must be evaluated when dealing with clients.

An advantage of the social model is that it makes use of the knowledge of fields other than traditional individual psychotherapy. That is, if a social analysis of psychological problems is taken to its logical endpoint, one could argue that more than individual psychotherapy is required when the real problem lies in society, not in the individual (Archibald, 1978; Ryan, 1971). We feel that awareness of social forces is often of use in therapy and that other professionals (e.g., social workers, social psychologists, or sociologists) should also examine the impact of society on the individual. Intervention can be accomplished in larger social arenas, from the family to the national level. When one looks at the legislative changes of the past century which affect the daily lives of minorities and women, conceptualizing change at larger social levels is not grandiose.

As with all models, the fact that the social model fits the facts of a case does not mean that only social interventions will be of use. The model provides one with a schema for conceptualization and clues about points of intervention; it does not dictate that the intervention must directly address the dynamics of that model in order to be effective.

In order to give theoretical "meat" to the social model, we explore two theories about the acquisition and maintenance of social behavior, social-learning theory and role theory. We suggest some instances in which socially-learned behaviors and roles become problematic for individuals, which may bring them into therapy.

SOCIAL-LEARNING THEORIES

As Cairns (1979) points out, there is no one "social-learning theory." Rather, there are several theories of the acquisition of social behavior which share the assumption that *learning* is central to the process. Although the roots of modern social learning theory come from Dollard and Miller's (1950) translation of learning theory into psychoanalytic terms, in addition to B. F. Skinner's (1974) radical operant conditioning view, Bandura and Walters (1963) ushered in what Cairns calls the "second generation" of social-learning theory. It is their fundamental ideas which form the basis of current conceptualizations of social-learning theory.

As explained in Bandura and Walters (1963) and Bandura (1977), social-learning theory holds that social behavior is acquired through two types of learning: observational learning and reinforced learning. While reinforced learning was a concept "handed down" by previous theorists, the concept of observational learning (and the related concept of modeling) were the innovations of Bandura and Walters.

Observational learning is that learning which can take place merely by watching a model perform some new response (the process of a model displaying behavior which is then observed and learned by someone else is called "modeling.") Thus, a child need not be reinforced (by either social or primary reinforcement) to imitate his or her parents in order for this to occur. This principle represented a major divergence from the "old" social-learning theories which held that new responses were acquired through a process of shaping; first a new subresponse must occur spontaneously, then it could be reinforced and gradually more and more adaptive responses would occur. However, as Bandura and Walters (1963) point out, "it is doubtful . . . if many of the responses that almost all members of our society exhibit would ever be acquired if social training proceeded solely by the method of successive approximations [shaping] [p. 3]." Although many social behaviors could be acquired (theoretically) through reinforcement alone, modeling was posited as a quick and efficient way for new behavior to be acquired. The most rapid acquisition of a behavior, in this view, is thought to occur via the combination of modeling influences with differential reinforcement of desired responses.

Social-learning theory differentiates between the learning of a response and the performance of that learning. This enables social-learning theorists to elaborate on the role of modeling influences apart from their use in the acquisition of new behavior. Modeling also affects the performance of previously learned responses through its *disinhibitory* or *cueing* effects. Disinhibition occurs when a previously learned (but rarely or never performed) response takes place in the presence of a model who is performing the previously inhibited ("taboo") response. The taboo response may be defined by society (e.g., murder) or it may be taboo only in a particular individual's view (e.g., being assertive). In either case, performance of the inhibited response is facilitated by the modeling of that response.

Modeling can also serve an eliciting cue function. The presence of a model performing a particular socially acceptable behavior can elicit that behavior in another person. Thus, if one person in a group stops before dinner to wash hands, he or she may elicit similar behavior in others.

Whether or not a modeled response will be performed depends on a complex array of factors. Among these are the consequences of the behavior for the model. Do the model's actions lead to rewards or punishment, or do they obtain no environmental consequence? Observers tend to inhibit responses which they see punished in others, while they are more likely to perform responses for which the model goes unpunished or rewarded. This process of observing the consequences of behavior for a model and acting according to those consequences is called *vicarious punishment* and *vicarious reinforcement*. Obviously, this type of reinforcement and punishment is a long way from the events called reinforcement and punishment which influence animals' behavior. Cognition must be inferred when a person observes a behavior and its consequences, and is guided by those "unfelt" consequences in the future performance of that behavior.

After Bandura and Walter's (1963) initial work, the role of cognition in social-learning theory was emphasized. Bandura (1969) discusses "higher-order modeling." This occurs when information is abstracted from modeled behaviors so that the observer need not perform the exact behavior he or she has seen performed in order for modeling effects to have taken place. The *information value* of the modeling influences is assumed to be the most important function of observational learning (Bandura, 1971). Bandura writes: ". . . observers acquire mainly symbolic representations of modeled events, rather than specific stimulus-response associations [p. 16]."

In sum, modern social-learning theories stress the role of observational learning and differential reinforcement in providing the learner with information about what is acceptable and remunerative in the environment. Thus, we can view social-learning theories as learning-based models of how social values and roles are acquired by the individual. This gives us a theoretical structure from which to view difficulties caused for individuals by their socially acquired behavior and values.

ROLE THEORY AND ROLE CONFLICT

Role theory goes a step further than social-learning theory in explaining social behavior. Role theory emphasizes socialization occurring in adulthood, and neglects the precise mechanisms of acquisition of behavior on which social-learning theories focus. A *role* is defined as a pattern of behavior which is characteristic of persons within certain contexts (Biddle, 1979) and which is the fulfillment of their set of socially-defined expectations (Sarbin, 1954). Role theory is based on several assumptions, according to Biddle: (1) roles are often associated with groups of people who share a common identity; (2) persons are aware of their role expectations, and these expectations act to delineate roles; (3) roles persist (if they do) because of their usefulness and because they are integrated into the structure of society; (4) persons must be socialized into their roles, and these roles may be sources of satisfaction or frustration.

Role conflict occurs when the individual, his or her close associates, or society at large hold conflicting expectations about the individual's role (Shaw & Costanzo, 1970). The role conflict may take the form of interrole conflict or intrarole conflict. Interrole conflict occurs when a person holds several different roles, each of which makes incompatible demands. For example, a graduate student who has a husband and several children may find herself hard-pressed to fulfill the role of mother, wife, and provider while simultaneously fulfilling her role as dedicated scholar. She, her husband, and her professor may hold incompatible expectations for her. Intrarole conflict occurs when there is a lack of clarity about the expectations surrounding a single role. Thus, a secretary who works for two different bosses may find himself subject to the conflicting expectations by each that he should spend 90% of his time on each bosses' assignments. Biddle (1979) points out that role conflict is associated in the workplace with loss of morale and lowered productivity.

Biddle (1979) also discusses *normative role conflict*. This occurs when persons are caught between changing societal standards for behavior. This may happen in persons who, like many Catholics today, were raised with a set of rules for conduct which are no longer considered necessary even by the Church. Finally, Biddle mentions *role overload*—the situation in which a role set is too complex for an individual to handle and leads to great stress. If the family and professors of the graduate student all agreed on their role expectations for her, although she would be free of interrole conflict, she might still suffer from role overload simply due to the many demanding roles she must fulfill.

Many clients who enter therapy are caught in role conflicts that are not only intense, but which produce a wide variety of symptoms. Frequently, these clients see themselves as depressed or anxious, and inadequate to handle significant problems in their lives. In other words, they see their problems as being intrapersonal rather than interpersonal. This model applies in many situations where there are intense and conflicting demands placed upon the individual with no readily available escape. Unfortunately, the effect of social influences upon individual functioning has been discussed infrequently in the psychotherapy literature.

These people rarely see themselves as being in the middle of an intense social conflict. Instead, they frequently exhibit depression, relationship problems, anxiety, and low self-esteem. Because the client is unable to perceive the situational determinants accurately, the "solution" that the client employs often is not directed at reducing the conflict, but may instead take forms that can increase the problem. As an example, a client who is caught in a situation where he or she resents the demands placed upon him or her by aging parents may act towards these parents in a way that suggests rejection and may make the parents feel more desperate and even more demanding. The function of the therapist in this situation is to try to delineate the nature of conflicts and attempt to provide conditions which maximize the client's ability to approach the problems in a "rational" manner.

The groups we have seen most often displaying the effects of dysfunctional socialization or role conflict are women, people undergoing role changes which occur throughout the life cycle (especially role reversals which take place between parent and children as the parents age), and persons of low social or economic status. We explore their potential psychological differences from the rest of society with a social-learning and role-theory analysis in mind. We emphasize, however, the danger inherent in viewing disadvantaged groups as homogeneous entities deficient in some constellation of middle-class attributes. Valentine (1968) has given an excellent review of the problems with such a viewpoint, and emphasizes the adaptive nature of the behavior of many individuals in disadvantaged situations.

WOMEN

The role of social learning in producing sex-stereotyped behavior (which some argue to be detrimental to women's psychological well-being) has been a subject of investigation in recent years. In a thorough review and evaluation of the literature on this topic, Maccoby and Jacklin (1974) conclude that, while it is undeniable that boys and girls are thoroughly sex-typed by the age of 4 years (choosing toys, activities, and playmates in a sex-typed manner), this does not appear to be a function of modeling. That is, studies investigating the correlation between the sex-stereotyped femininity of mothers and the femininity of their daughters have found no significant results (e.g., Fling & Manosevitz, 1972; Hetherington, 1965). While modeling does appear to be important in the acquisition of many behaviors, it does not appear to be a factor in sex stereotyping (both "feminine" and "masculine" behaviors are learned by both sexes through modeling).

There is some evidence that girls and boys undergo differential socialization experiences. Mischel (1966) states that sex-typed behaviors are those that are differentially reinforced depending on the sex of the subject. Indeed, Maccoby and Jacklin (1974) do conclude that, while the majority of their socialization is "remarkably similar [p. 342]," boys and girls are treated differently in some behaviors on the basis of their sex. Boys are strongly discouraged from sex-inappropriate behavior (e.g., wearing girl's clothes or playing with dolls), while this sanction is not so strong for girls. Girls are treated as more fragile and fathers are instrumental in encouraging "feminine" behavior in their small daughters. In general, Maccoby and Jacklin conclude that boys have a more intense socialization experience, receiving more of both positive and negative feedback than do girls. "Adults respond as if they find boys more interesting and more attention-provoking than girls [p. 348]."

Dweck and her associates (Dweck, 1975; Dweck, Davidson, Nelson, & Enna, 1978; Dweck, Goetz, & Strauss, 1980) have produced research on learned-helplessness phenomena in children which supports Maccoby and Jacklin's (1974) point of view. Dweck and her associates have shown that girls attribute failure to lack of ability, whereas boys tend to attribute failure to lack of effort or bias of the evaluator (Dweck & Bush, 1976; Dweck et al., 1978; Dweck et al., 1980). Additionally, girls show the performance deficits after failure which would be expected under the learned-helplessness formulation (Abramson, Seligman, & Teasdale, 1978). Dweck has shown that teachers give feedback differently to girls and boys. For boys, negative feedback is often directed to nonability factors (e.g., "Don't write on the back of your paper"), whereas positive feedback is largely directed at ability factors. The opposite pattern is true for girls. Thus, girls receive a pattern of feedback which is positive for ability-irrelevant factors ("Good try"), while being largely negative for ability. Dweck et al. (1978) reversed the contingencies and found that boys, on a "girl" contingency (negative feedback for ability, positive feedback for ability-irrelevant factors) showed the same learned-helplessness deficits that girls usually show. The researchers conclude, "it is possible that these differences, although agent specific and manipulable at grade school age, may become more generalized and stable in later years [p. 275]."

Stockard and Johnson (1980) postulate that, although modeling does not seem to be a potent factor in the acquisition of sex-stereotyped behavior in children, perhaps older children acquire more complex sex-typed behavior by learning a generalized sex role rather than specific behaviors. The potent factor to come out of differential socialization of boys and girls may not so much be differences in specific behaviors as differences in *expectations* concerning their own abilities and their roles in life. Stockard and Johnson report that by high-school age, girls perceive marriage and family matters as central to their lives, whereas boys see their future careers as central to their identity.

While it is certainly true that men and women need not have identical roles, the roles women have traditionally held have been somewhat limited, and attempts to expand their roles have put women in conflict situations. Broverman, Broverman, Clarkson, Rosenkrantz, & Vogel (1970) in a remarkable study, asked mental-health professionals to describe a healthy man, a healthy woman, and a healthy adult (sex unspecified). While the standards for "healthy man" were the same as those for "healthy adult," a healthy woman was supposed to be more submissive, less independent, less adventurous, less objective, more easily influenced, more emotional, more conceited, less competent, and more easily hurt than a man. This highlights the social conflict inherent for women—to be a healthy person and a healthy woman concurrently has been difficult. The difficulty is present because of changing social norms; women have conflicting expectations placed on them whereby some people expect them to be "women" and some expect them to be "people."

Many women are currently embroiled in what Biddle (1979) called normative role conflict: the shift in values over time. We have seen a large number of women clients present with "low self-esteem" problems or symptoms of anxiety or depression who are placed in situations in which there are incompatible demands. The last decade or so has seen large shifts in the defined roles of women that have led to many women being in positions of confusion or conflict. One need only examine many book stores to find evidence for this conflict; there are frequently whole sections of books about "women's issues," while there are not comparable sections on men. Many of these books are about the new roles of women.

One of the most common conflicts that women experience relates to the change in values and goals that has been taking place since the beginning of the century. Many women were married and raised children at a time when the primary responsibility and role of women was to be a wife and a mother. Recently one woman described how determined she was to become the best possible wife and mother that she could be when she was first married. She came from an old-world European family and those values became hers. She was quite successful at her vocation of being a wife and mother, raising four children and watching her husband develop a prosperous and prestigious medical practice. Now, however, the children were grown and the husband spent a great deal of time on professional affairs and she felt inadequate and mildly depressed. Although she was active in running the house and in helping her aging mother (which was another social-role conflict), she felt dissatisfied with her life. She knew that the model of wife and mother that she had been brought up with was not meeting her needs, but she did not know the intensity of the problem. She described how she dreaded being asked what she did when she was at parties and even fantasized about telling people that she was a nuclear physicist. Those statements reveal how the social status of being a mother and a housewife has eroded and was not satisfying to this bright woman in her mid-40s.

She had moments when she blamed her children for her feeling of being neglected, and she had prolonged periods of blaming her husband for spending too much time at his practice. However, when we raised the subject of role conflicts and pointed out how the model of wife and mother did not meet her current needs or values as well as it did when she was first married, she was able to look into her situation and consider making changes in her life. It was important for her to realize that the problem was not based on being either inadequate or unloved, but was related to changes in social goals of women. We are now trying to change her activities so that she can find both aggravation and satisfaction in additional activities. She rejected the idea of holding a job because of the time restrictions that it would entail, but we are working towards other satisfying activities. It is generally important that these activities also have the potential to cause aggravation; otherwise they may not have enough intensity to be effective in helping the woman shape her redefinition of herself.

The therapist must be very cautious in this type of case to see that other parts of the family are not disrupted by changes in the role definitions of one of the members. As this woman redefines her roles, there will be major effects on other members of the family. If there is no forethought about the implications of her changes, it can lead to considerable changes in her relationships with other members of the family, especially her husband. In this case, the woman had been married for 25 years and she described the relationship in generally positive terms. We were prudent in discussing possible effects of her changes upon her relationships. If we had just assumed that we were dealing with the individual alone and we did not have a picture of the social matrix, the changes that occurred in this woman could disrupt the entire family's equilibrium and cause more problems than the woman initially had. The client discussed the fact that she was looking for more independent sources of satisfaction with her husband, and the fact that she would not simply be available, as she had before, for his support. With forewarning and with justification as to why this was important to her, the husband was supportive.

The therapist must realize that clients are not separate from the complicated social networks that are often involved in producing the problems of social-role conflicts. Because of this, it is frequently optimal to see the entire family or spouse of clients who are having role-conflict problems.

We stress the therapist's duty to look for *points of intervention*—those points in the situation which, if manipulated, will produce therapeutic change and which the therapist has a realistic possibility of changing. Frequently, family members and marital partners do not want to come into therapy, and the therapist must work with an individual client. The therapist can always attempt to keep the social context in mind while doing this.

Role conflict also displays itself as overt marital conflict. Williamson (1970) believes that role conflict makes up a large part of general marital dissatisfaction. Role conflict appears to be destructive to relationships both when it is covert and when it is openly acknowledged. Miller and Mothner (1981) describe the "covert conflict of unequal marriages," in which dissatisfaction over the roles they lead causes the marriage partners to try to harm each other psychologically without ever acknowledging that there is a real conflict. These authors attribute the dominant mother/ineffectual father scenario to the unacknowledged unhappiness caused by role dissatisfaction. They describe a situation in which the mother never overtly steps out of her role, but her resentment is unleashed on her husband, emasculating him and further destroying the possibility of working within the old role system. Steinmann (1974) states that both men and women, as a result of cultural changes, suffer from ambiguity about their sex roles. This instability and lack of clearly defined expectations increases the likelihood of relationship problems. It should be noted that sex-typing per se is not necessarily detrimental to people psychologically, as highly traditional communities are highly sex-typed but are freer from mental disorders than the surrounding society which is in a state of flux in its values (Weissman & Klerman, 1981).

Whether because of early socialization pressures, later role requirements, or biological reasons, women are overrepresented in the numbers of those diagnosed and treated as mentally ill, especially for depression (Chesler, 1973; Weissman & Klerman, 1981). These authors point to role requirements as at least partially responsible for this overrepresentation. They cite data which show that while marriage has a protective effect from mental illness for men, being married increases the likelihood that a woman will be psychologically disturbed. Chesler and Weissman and Klerman both blame the limited, boring, isolated, low-status role of housewife as being responsible for this trend. Weissman and Klerman reported that, for women, work had a protective effect from depression by decreasing boredom while increasing self-esteem, social contacts, and economic conditions.

More women than men are overweight by mid- to late adulthood (Stuart & Davis, 1972) and many more women than men suffer from anorexia or bulimia (Bruch, 1973). Orbach (1978) views these abnormal responses to food as indicative of maladaptive responses to the strictures of the female role. Bart (1972) found that middle-aged women who identified greatly with their mother and housewife role were more likely to become depressed when their children left the house; they experienced what Bart calls "maternal role loss." This depression was more likely to occur when the women lacked other roles besides mother. Stockard and Johnson (1980) point out that the maternal role loss is often accompanied by decreased status.

MINORITY AND LOW SOCIOECONOMIC STATUS CLIENTS

Due to past and present social pressures, minority and low socioeconomic status (SES) clients may present problems specific to their social context. Although it is true that not all "minorities" are also low in SES level (some, such as the Japanese-Americans and the Jews, enjoy higher SES levels than the rest of the country, Sowell, 1981), there is considerable overlap, with the highly visible minority groups of black and Hispanic Americans being lower in overall SES level than the average American. Additionally, nonminority poor and minority middle- or upper-class members face unique conflicts. However, these are statistics based on group averages, and we are well aware that therapeutic decisions cannot be made simply based on the demographic facts about an individual. The intent of this section is to enumerate conflicts and problems which *may* beset minority or low SES individuals because of the social pressures on them. We are certainly not concluding that these are the only problems that a minority or low SES person could present.

Therapists often have problems dealing with minority or low SES clients. Middle-class therapists tend to assign more derogatory labels to lower-class clients, and to reject them from therapy more often than they do middle-class clients (Goldstein, 1973). Settin and Bramel (1981) found that client class and gender interacted to determine therapist's perceptions of clients presented in a case history. They found that therapists viewed male clients more positively the higher their social class, while female clients were viewed more positively the lower their class status. The authors explain this interaction by positing that expectations of economic success differ for men and women. Men are expected to "provide," and are judged accordingly. Women, on the other hand, are not held accountable for their economic position, and if anything, a lower-class woman is seen as somewhat heroic for her central place in the lower class family (as both homemaker and provider). We believe that at least part of the problem of therapist prejudice against lower-class clients (apart from difficulties stemming from low therapist/client similarity and identification) emerges from attempts to view these clients' problems from an inappropriate perspective. Frequently a social perspective must be employed when the "presenting problems" are largely a function of social pressures.

There are several psychological effects of poverty which have been documented. Miskimins and Baker (1973), in a study of 660 urban adult poor, concluded that the poor suffered from a general increase in relationship problems and individual maladjustment relative to the nonpoor (this is consistent with the general tendency of mental illness to be overrepresented among low SES groups; Brenner, 1973; Dunham, 1980). Additionally, they found that the poor suffered from self-concept problems, with women having low self-esteem and men having "exaggerated self-esteem." Increased education and nonminority status were found to have a protective effect on self-concept problems among the poor.

Bee (1978) concludes that by far the most clearcut psychological effect of poverty is a lowering of measured IQ. She points out that this effect is specific to poverty, not to ethnic groups, as there are distinct social-class differences in IQ *within* various ethnic groups. Thus, middle-class blacks have higher measured IQs than lower-class blacks; middle-class Polish-Americans have higher IQs than lower-class Polish-Americans, and so on. These IQ differences are matched by differences in school performance and other tests of cognitive function.

Other psychological effects of poverty are less consistently documented than IQ differences. These include lower achievement motivation, increased sensitivity to both approval and disapproval, and the presence of an external locus of control (Bee, 1978). In general, these differences point to a decreased sense of personal efficacy and an increased sense of being controlled from without: a learned-helplessness phenomenon (Abramson et al., 1978). This is consistent with a social situation in which lack of economic resources does, indeed, decrease one's ability to determine one's own achievements and makes one more dependent upon outside agencies.

The socialization experiences of low SES individuals may account for some of these differences (Bee, 1978; Goldstein, 1973; Sears, Maccoby, & Levin, 1957). Lower-class mothers have been found to be more punitive and more status and rule-oriented in their discipline techniques, which may be associated with increased orientation toward externally-imposed standards (Goldstein, 1973), and may be less conducive to cognitive development than the "rational" or "socioemotional" methods typically employed by middle-class mothers (Bee, 1978; Sears et al., 1957).

Modeling effects within low SES subgroups may lead to patterns of behavior that are considered dysfunctional or antisocial in the society at large, but which are highly valued within the subculture. Quay (1964, 1972) did factor-analytic work dividing delinquent behavior into several subtypes, one of which was labeled "socialized delinquency." Thus, gang behavior labeled sociopathic may be more accurately viewed as a successful modeling of high-status behavior by inner-city youths. In order for this behavior to be modified, the gang members' models and reinforcers for this style of behavior must all be changed first (Bandura, 1973). Other examples of this "social learning of antisocial behavior" would be the machismo of Mexican youths which leads to dare-devil driving and a very high level of automobile accidents (Sowell, 1981), or the black male "hustler" who has very high status on the street but whose behavior is problematic in the home setting (Sager, Brayboy, & Waxenburg, 1970).

Because economic pressures impinge more saliently on poor persons, there is even less distinction between the psychic and the socioeconomic realms than there is for other people (Sager et al., 1970). Brenner (1973) has presented a convincing analysis of psychiatric hospital admissions in relation to economic trends, and has concluded that "instabilities in the national economy are the single most important source of fluctuations in admission rates [to psychiatric institutions]." [pp. ix]. Thus, the therapist should not underestimate the power of a change in economic status to affect the psychological well-being of the client. Miskimins and Baker (1973) showed that, while successful job experiences had positive effects on the individual's self-concept, failure in a work experience has negative self-concept effects which are worse than the self-concept deficits of those who failed to obtain employment at all. This is consistent with decrements in performance after failure experiences that would be predicted by the learned-helplessness reformulation.

In a society with racism and discrimination, the minority member will experience both helplessness and some paranoia. As in the experimental neurosis paradigm of Pavlov (1928), difficult discriminations lead to increased psychological distress. Simply knowing that hostility exists toward one because of one's race or sex can cause minority members to become suspicious of nonminority members' intentions. Many blacks and other minority groups experience an environment replete with racism; however, this racism is now rarely expressed overtly. We were once involved in a local political attempt to legislate an ordinance forbidding discrimination on the basis of race for the rental and sales of property. A great many people in the community supported this ordinance, while many were intensely against it. We canvassed the community with the leader of the movement to support the ordinance, who was black, and virtually everyone was cordial to him. Many of those same people later expressed contempt towards him to us in his absence. It was clear to us that his direct perceptions, at least based on this small sample, indicated that racism did not exist in this community. However, because of the opposition to the fair-housing ordinance, he was amply aware of the omnipresence of the problem. This man was placed in an uncomfortable position of having to be suspicious of everyone's honesty in relating to him, since he knew he could not trust their behavior as an indication of their feeling toward him.

These subtle discriminations may also play a role in the therapeutic relationship. While our clinical experience of dealing with minority groups has not shown racial issues to have a profound effect upon the therapeutic relationship, there were several cases in which the minority client sent out a "probe" to determine the feelings of the therapist. One client related early in our first session how one of his drunk customers referred to him as a nigger to his wife. When asked how he felt, he replied that it did not bother him because the man was drunk. Therapy progressed rapidly after we told him how angry we would have been at the comment. The nonminority therapist should be aware that past histories of discrimination and racism can influence the therapeutic relationship.

While many problems plague the minority poor, minority members who attempt to increase their social status are confronted with a new set of problems which can be examined from the point of view of role conflicts. As minority members assimilate and accomodate themselves more to the larger society's norms and values, they may find that, while they gain in money and status, they lose their former roles in their family and/or community. This can be a very painful transition, with both normative and interrole conflicts occuring. In other words, the person may be in conflict over which set of roles to adopt: the old ethnic ways or the new American ways. Additionally, members of the person's two reference groups may have different and contradictory expectations of him.

For example, Rodriguez (1982) recounts the struggle he experienced within himself over whether to write and publish his personal memories of growing up in a Spanish-speaking household and gradually becoming a member of middle-class American (English-speaking) society while growing away from his family. While Rodriguez felt the personal and professional desire to write about his family, his parents pleaded with him not to "dishonor" them by writing about their personal lives. Such disclosure, while commonplace in mainstream American society, is unusual and disreputable within Mexican standards. In the book, Rodriguez writes movingly of the pain he experienced in moving away from his origins toward a place in the mainstream of society: "After English became my primary language, I no longer knew what words to use in addressing my parents. The old Spanish words . . . I had used earlier—mama' and papa'—I couldn't use anymore. They would have been too painful reminders of how much had changed in my life [pp. 23–24]." A Newsweek article on blacks in corporate America (1983) emphasized the social isolation they experienced. One woman said that, in achieving a higher level of success than any of her family or friends, she found herself with no one who could understand her experience. She felt isolated both from her coworkers, who could not understand her background, and from her family and friends, who could not understand her current work situation.

ROLE CONFLICT THROUGH THE LIFE CYCLE

As people age, they take on new roles and discard others in a continuous socialization process. Each time a role change occurs, the potential exists for role strain or conflict.

The increasingly common conflict situation of career women between their career commitment and the desire to have children, has been labeled "a developmental crisis" (Stockard & Johnson, 1980). The intensity of this conflict is great, and increases as the demands of a professional career and the biological limits on safe pregnancy both peak in the mid-to-late 30s. Women are caught in this dilemma because they typically commit to a professional life at a very early age, when the ideas of marriage and child-bearing are remote. Additionally, there are few role models or societal accomodations for women who wish to excel in their field and also have children.

When the children of a family enter adolescence, many role changes occur. It is frequently a time of conflict within the family. The adolescents themselves must change roles from children to young adults, and this entails many changes in social, sexual, and familial relating. The parents must undergo a more subtle role change, that of transition from parents of children to parents of adults. Different behaviors and skills are required in the role of parents of adults, and tenacity to "old" parenting roles (those that were appropriate with children) can cause difficulties. The role relationship between parent and child connotes a dominance order. However, when children reach or approximate adulthood the child role vis-a-vis the parents may be in conflict with any number of other adult roles. It appears to be ubiquitous that parents will still relate to their children as subdominant even if their child is president of a major corporation.

Adolescents see themselves as adults and their parents frequently see them as children. Intense conflicts are frequent during this period. McGoldrick and Carter (1982) state that, while many changes over the life span are incremental, changes necessitated by children becoming adolescents are qualitative as well as quantitative. Adolescent children in a family call for completely new role definitions. For instance, the adolescent child must not only be seen as a "child," but also as a young adult, a sexual being, and a wage-earner. Unless these types of role changes occur, conflicting roles can cause tensions and anger if the individuals involved do not see the social determinism of these roles and instead blame each other.

Middle-aged people typically are overcommitted, with work, family, and community obligations peaking during the middle years (Hess & Waring, 1978). This overcommitment may lead to role strain. A new phenomenon, probably due to difficult financial times and high costs of housing, is the increasing tendency of grown children to return to the family home after a social or financial setback. Thus, it is increasingly common for a divorced daughter to return to her parents' home with her children until she gets "back on her feet." We have seen several middle-aged persons who feel overwhelmed by the enormous responsibilities that they must shoulder at this time in their life.

One responsibility that occurs often is the care of aging parents. It is always a possibility that role reversal will occur in this situation as the aging process leads to reduced sensory, intellectual, and physical capacities in the parents. Role reversal, in which the child fulfills the role of the parent or vice versa, is painful and unsettling for both parties. Parents dislike the loss of autonomy and self-esteem that comes with a decrement in status, and children are uncomfortable seeing their models for old age (their parents) reverting to a childlike role (Hess & Waring, 1978).

Clients in this situation rarely see their difficulty from a social perspective. Rather, they may only be aware of the feeling that their parents are placing unreasonable demands upon them. Additionally, the parent is only the parent of one member of the middle-aged couple. Resentments from this, or from a past history of grudges, may further complicate this problem. If the middle-aged child expresses his or her resentment, or reacts by withdrawing from the parent, the parent may feel even more threatened and become anxious. We have seen cases in which the parents have threatened suicide or have become hypochondriacal in order to maintain the attention of their children. Although effective treatment for this could follow operant principles (i.e., increased attention during better moods or health states, and decreased attention to hypochondriacal complaints), an understanding of the social context from which this behavior emerged can reduce "blaming" of the parent for disabilities and dependency. When the parties involved (especially the younger couple) understand the realities of the role conflict they are involved in, the problem can be seen for what it is: a dilemma to be worked out. The younger couple can make choices on a more rational basis than they could without an understanding that the role conflict is a comprehensible consequence of increased longevity.

ASSESSMENT

The general assessment question to be answered in the social-context model is: To what extent are social pressures, past or present, contributing to the client's problem? When assessing for the applicability of the social-context model to a particular case, four major questions, stemming from our social-learning and role-theory perspective, need to be addressed.

First, is the client currently experiencing social pressures which are proving to be dysfunctional for him or her? Is the client under the influence of models who perform the unwanted behaviors, thus experiencing social reinforcement for performance of these actions? Common examples of this would be a delinquent youth referred to therapy by outside sources, who is still a member of an antisocial milieu, or a woman who is unable to become assertive and independent while living in a very patriarchal family. Knowledge of the client's social situation, friends, and family is essential for the therapist to answer this question.

Is the client experiencing difficulty because of a lack of socialization experience for a particular behavior or set of behaviors? That is, is the client deficient in knowledge about appropriate behaviors? This situation could occur because of a lack of competent models in the client's environment. The therapist should try to elicit the desired (appropriate) behaviors with role-play or hypothetical situations to determine if the client is ignorant (or incapable of performing) the desired functional behavior. For example, if a client has problems with controlling aggression, the therapist could investigate whether any of the person's esteemed peers or family typically react to threats in a nonaggressive manner. The therapist could then attempt to determine if the client is knowledgeable or able to perform a nonaggressive response to a threat or insult. One bright college-educated man was seen for marital therapy. His wife left no ambiguity that she would not tolerate his spanking her; she would leave the marriage even though their relationship was perfectly adequate in other respects. When questioned about the origins of his habit of spanking his wife, it turned out that he had seen Maureen O'Hara adore John Wayne in *The Quiet One* after being spanked. He thought that spanking was an appropriate way of dealing with recalcitrant women. It was the wrong social model, and the client felt silly when the source of his behavior was found. This client was unusual in that he could identify exactly where he learned this misinformation. However, we often adopt social models from similar sources and do not know their appropriateness.

Are the psychological sequelae of past socialization experiences providing the client with difficulties in current functioning? That is, are the psychological deficits associated with socialization experiences of low SES and female children adversely affecting the client? The client can be tested with paper-and-pencil measures for low self-esteem, helplessness, and external locus of control. More indepth interviewing will be necessary to assess for the presence of low personal expectations of efficacy and low personal standards and goals.

Finally, the presence of role conflict should be assessed. In order to do this, the therapist must investigate the client's expectations, the expectations of significant others, and what the client feels about his or her own place in society now. Also of help to the therapist is to find out who the client's heroes were when he or she was young, who are they now, and why. This can sometimes elicit expectations not brought out by direct questioning. The therapist should be aware of groups particularly prone to role conflict (e.g., working women, upwardly mobile minority members, families with adolescents or aging grandparents). However, it is a mistake to assume role conflict on the basis of membership in some group. Corroborating data must be produced.

THERAPEUTIC INTERVENTIONS

The major goals of interventions within the social-context model are to resocialize the client or to change the effect of the social pressures. While resocialization principles are based on social-learning theory, changing the effect of social pressures often may require cognitive techniques. As with all models, the presence of a social-context model as an explanatory mechanism does not necessitate the use of a social intervention. Once the assessment is made, it may be determined for reasons of efficacy and feasibility to use an intervention other than a social one. However, whatever intervention is used is made more effective by the information gained by the models conceptualization. For example, although a young woman experiencing panic attacks and depression as a result of role strain may be helped greatly by desensitization and cognitive therapy for depression, the assessment of role strain informs the therapist as to what the content of those interventions should focus on, and what issues that therapy should focus on after those symptoms have abated.

Resocialization

Probably the most complete therapeutic use of resocialization occurs when clients are removed from their dysfunctional social setting and placed in a new social context with models and social reinforcements designed to promote prosocial behavior. This situation occurs, for example, in group home treatment centers for juvenile delinquents, and with hospital stays for psychiatric patients. Bandura (1973) states that a homestyle treatment program carefully designed to promote prosocial behavior is one of the few effective alternatives for changing delinquent behavior. If such children are not removed from their environment, it is virtually impossible to gain control over the modeling and social-reinforcement forces which affect the client and lead to the delinquency. Within a new social context, however, the child can be effectively reinforced for prosocial behavior while experiencing peer approval for his new actions.

Polansky, Bergman, & DeSaix (1972), after an indepth study of inadequate and neglectful mothers in poor Appalachian communities, concluded that hospitalization was the treatment of choice for the mothers displaying a futile, apathetic behavioral style. Some of the inadequate women studied by Polansky et al. had literally no cooking or child-care skills. They were unable to prepare any hot food, and were overwhelmed by the task of keeping themselves or their children clean and clothed. This inadequacy was largely tolerated by the surrounding society, and other family members sometimes took over the mother's responsibilities. Polansky et al. suggest that removal from the social setting which condones total inadequacy and placement in a hospital program based on realistic contingencies was the only hope for the women most firmly entrenched in apathy.

On a less radical note, it is certaiinly realistic for therapists who see that their client is in a social milieu not conducive to therapeutic change to suggest that the client remove him or herself from that social setting. Thus, the recovering alcoholic who finds new friends to replace his old drinking buddies is providing him- or herself with models of alternatives to drinking, and social reinforcement of nondrinking. This is a major function of Alcoholics Anonymous. Successful prosocial experiences can help the person who has had dysfunctional socialization experiences by displaying the reinforcing properties of prosocial behavior (e.g., money and status in the mainstream society; Bandura, 1973). However, the person's social network must also be changed if this intervention is to work.

Those who have undergone dysfunctional socialization frequently not only perform "bad" behaviors, but have learned few alternative modes of action. Thus, they suffer socialization deficits. Social-learning theory informs us that functional behavior can best be taught to these clients by a combination of modeling and selective reinforcement. Frequently, the therapist serves as a model of behavior for the client, displaying new alternatives for the client to emulate. That this method has its limitations is recalled when we remember that the efficacy of modeling depends upon (among other things) the perceived similarity of the model to the subject. In the opinion-change literature, it has also been shown that when the communicator is similar to the listener in ways that are relevant to the situation at hand, communication effectiveness is increased (Berscheid, 1966). Especially for persons who have lacked positive models, therapy may be enhanced by selecting a therapist who is similar to them in salient ways (age, sex, or race, for example). It may be difficult for a middle-aged male therapist to effectively model assertive responses to a young woman's mother-in-law, simply because the woman may not see the therapist's behavior as possible for her.

A very powerful method for persons to socially learn new behaviors is through a group of peers. Peers are generally seen as more appropriate models (that is, more similar to oneself) than are therapists (Bandura, 1973). Thus, if peers can function to model and reinforce each other for new ways of behaving, it can produce an intense and effective learning experience. Yalom (1970) reported that among the factors seen as "curative" by participants in group therapy were: (1) the experience of recognizing one's similarity to others; (2) being able to see oneself as others do; and (3) witnessing the expression of honesty and emotion in others.

The women's movement borrowed the consciousness-raising group from left-wing politics and used it to promote a feminist political perspective. Along the way, however, the consciousness-raising group took on some therapeutic properties for women experiencing problems because of their roles and social station. First of all, these groups explained many problems, for which the women had previously blamed themselves, in light of the social context (Kirsh, 1974). This in itself can have a tremendous therapeutic effect. The groups then function to resocialize women along nonsexist lines (Kirsh, 1974; Mander & Rush, 1974). To this end, consciousness-raising and women's groups have stressed peer equality and self-expression. The groups eventually gain the power to serve as standard-makers for the women involved, who are then freer to reject societal standards they don't feel are appropriate for them (Kirsh, 1974).

Group therapy has proved effective in many situations in which the traditional therapist/client relationship has been ineffective because of low identification of the client with the therapist. Group therapy is the treatment of choice with Vietnam veterans who are undergoing delayed stress reactions to their military experience (Figley, 1978). Their experiences had been so traumatic as to lead them to mistrust those who did not experience them also. With other men who underwent the same experience, however, they were more able to learn new ways of coping with their difficulties from each other.

Modeling can also serve to disinhibit responses which were previously acquired but, because of social pressures, have been inhibited. For Vietnam veterans, expressions of emotional caring are behaviors which the vets have learned to inhibit during their brutal military experience. This inhibition causes problems for them in forming close relationships. In a veterans' group in which we were involved, one of the biggest changes occurred when the men, modeling after the group leader, were able to express their caring for one another. The leader and the other men were able to disinhibit the response in one another. This result is also consistent with Yalom's (1970) findings on the active ingredients in group therapy mentioned above.

Very often group therapy is more effective than individual therapy in helping people who share common social pressures. We have been active in initiating and running groups for patients and families of people with various severe physical disabilities such as epilepsy and spina bifida (a disorder in which the child is born with an open spinal cord and is frequently incontinent and sometimes paraplegic). In 11 years of activity with the epilepsy group, it was a common occurrence for new members to enter the group feeling anxious. They often reported that they had never told anyone before that they had epilepsy. The group format would be to ask each individual to introduce him or herself and tell about either their seizures or the seizures of their children, what seemed to help, what their experiences were with other people, their response to anticonvulsant medication, and other pertinent issues. New members were introduced towards the end of the session. They frequently reported that it was an enormous relief for them to meet other people with epilepsy who shared their experiences. They seemed to be dubious that perfectly decent people could have epilepsy. Individual therapy could not be as powerful in helping these people be comfortable with their disability.

Singletary, Friend, & Nurse (unpublished) showed that individuals on hemodialysis who participated in support groups for renal patients increased their longevity significantly over those patients who did not participate in such groups. Although the design was a correlational one, other psychological factors which may have accounted for the self-selection were examined and did not account for the difference in survival rates between the two groups.

Specific deficits accruing from socialization experiences can be addressed directly. Low self-esteem and learned helplessness deficits have been identified as resulting from certain socialization methods. Dweck (1975) experimented with an attribution-retraining program to aid children who displayed an extreme learned-helplessness reaction to failure (a strong decrement in performance following failure experience). She compared a success-only treatment, in which the kids had only successful experiences, with an attribution-retraining treatment. This treatment consisted of teaching the children to take responsibility for failures, and to attribute failures to lack of effort (rather than to low ability or some other internal and stable attribute). After training, Dweck found that only the attribution-retraining group maintained or improved their performance following a failure experience. The success-only group persisted in their tendency to decline in performance following failure.

Diener & Dweck (1978) studied the verbalizations produced by children who were classified as helpless or mastery-oriented. They found that the helpless children tended to ruminate on failure, while the mastery-oriented kids' verbalizations were focused on finding the correct solution. Diener & Dweck conclude that, in addition to attribution retraining, helpless children should be aided in controlling their self-punitive ruminations and increasing their self-instruction.

In providing therapy for lower-class clients, Goldstein (1973) suggests that the therapist take into account some of the preferences characteristic of low SES individuals. He concludes that potentially the most effective psychotherapy for lower-class clients may be brief in duration and authoritarian in nature, focusing on behavior change. It should include role-taking training and the therapist should employ concrete examples when explaining new concepts. Additionally, the program should include early and frequent reinforcement. Siassi (1974) emphasizes that the main thrust of therapy for the poor should be to "alleviate the inner helplessness, hopelessness and anger [p. 400]."

Changing the Effects of Social Pressures

One of the clearest ways to change social pressures is to bring other important people into therapy with the client. Thus, family and couples therapy can be utilized to clarify the conflicts placed on the "identified patient" and discover ways in which to decrease those conflicts. It is helpful to examine the demands being placed upon individuals because of their role requirements. Roles within the family may subsequently be modified to reduce the conflict.

Anything which influences the values of our culture has a potentially great effect on the individuals within it. Thus, potent social forces such as television can have a great impact on socialization and role expectations. It has been argued that aggressive behavior can be increased through viewing violence on television (Liebert, Neale, & Davidson, 1973). Although generally children do not model in a sex-typed fashion, there is evidence that they do acquire sex-typed behavior from TV (Stockard & Johnson, 1980). Prosocial effects of TV are also apparent in studies of educational programming such as *Sesame Street* (Liebert et al., 1973). Thus, political and economic pressures as translated into television programming can have a potent effect on individual's functioning.

One of the major functions of the therapist is to clarify past and present causes of a troublesome behavior for a client. This is especially true in cases in which the social-context model is operating. Social pressures are usually too large for clients to apprehend on their own, so the therapist's large-scale analysis is especially helpful in these situations. Attribution of causality to forces outside the individual can be a great help in defusing blame and guilt. It is important that this attribution be followed by concrete problem-solving as to what can be done *within* one's social constraints. Without necessary follow-up action, attribution of problems to uncontrollable social forces can result in learned helplessness, depression, chronic hostility, and/or apathy.

We strongly feel that forces of change directed at larger social systems can be of immense help in changing people's psychological well-being. We know that chronic unemployment or underemployment is degrading and can lead to a learned helplessness type of depression; we know that racism has profound negative consequences on the victims. As psychologists we feel proud of Dr. Kenneth Clarke's role in influencing social legislation; we are aware that inequity can be a powerful, and often negative, social motive (Adams, 1965). We feel that psychologists and other professionals can address attention to changing a social-welfare system that seems to perpetuate class differences and chronic alienation from the mainstream of society. We feel that protection for the disabled can be accomplished by both legislation and by personal awareness of both the disabled and the community about the disability. We also feel that more professional support for the treatment of the chronic psychotic population must be legislated.

These areas are probably more important than many we have discussed at greater length in this book. We have been personally active in most of them, and feel that social workers, social psychologists, and economists all have a great deal to offer in addressing these areas. Addressing these areas is part of psychotherapy, but we personally are not expert enough to include the larger social context in this book. Some therapists may feel that they can be more efficacious in promoting mental health by changing social structures through political or organizational means, than in attempting to alleviate individual's discomfort within an office setting. Social change is certainly another intervention which emerges from the social-context model.

8 Case Studies

Two case studies will be presented to illustrate how the models approach can be utilized in clinical work. Although we have attempted to illustrate principles of the models approach by using case material throughout the book, a more detailed evaluation of cases can point up the advantages and limitations of the approach. Some of the material has been given in a briefer form in other chapters.

THE CASE OF MRS. X

Mrs. X was an attractive 28-year-old mother of two young boys who came into therapy because of recurring anxiety attacks. She was known to us several years before as a student in an undergraduate Abnormal Psychology class. We knew her to be bright and personally effective. Mrs. X described her anxiety attacks as similar to symptoms expected with high sympathetic nervous system activation, with a great deal of trembling and perspiring. She said she felt as though she was about to hear catastrophic news; that her husband was going to leave her or that some harm would befall her children. She reported that these periods of intense anxiety did not occur after any specific event or interaction. They did, however, follow a temporal pattern in that they tended to occur in the morning. She managed to function and take care of her children's needs despite a high degree of discomfort. Her husband was usually out of the house during the anxiety attacks.

Mrs. X was a particularly dynamic woman who participated in a wide range of activities. She enjoyed photography, sewing, swimming, travel, reading, playing tennis, church discussion groups, and modern dance, among other things. Although occasionally her anxiety interfered with these activities, she generally continued with her normal schedule. She sometimes had to push herself to do so, but she did not mention her difficulties to the people around her.

At this point, it was necessary to evaluate the information gathered about the presenting problem in light of various models. Did the information fit an operant model? To answer this, we looked at the consequences to Mrs. X of her anxiety attacks. Frequently, one sees certain patterns of payoffs for dysfunctional behaviors, such as escape or avoidance of unpleasant tasks or a differential attention response from family or friends. These potential reinforcers did not seem to be present in this case. Another clue that the operant model probably did not apply was that Mrs. X did not seem to "savor" her periods of anxiety; they seemed ego-alien to her. We have frequently noted that when dysfunctional behavior is an operant, the client has a degree of positive feeling about the "problem" that may be indirectly expressed. We have seen the indirect expression of such feelings include an apologetic description of the consequences such as, "I know how much difficulty my problems are causing everyone," or the accompaniment of such a description by a surreptitious smile indicating that the person is getting some benefit from the problem. In this case, however, there were neither direct nor indirect indications that the operant model was involved.

The next model that was assessed for was the capacity model. Was Mrs. X overcommitted by responsibilities? Did she take on duties that were beyond her capacities to handle? We enquired about the basic structure of Mrs. X's life: What demands were being placed on her and what evidence did we have about her ability to cope with these demands? Upon investigation, it was found that most of Mrs. X's demands were self-imposed, and those that weren't (such as care of her children and her relationship with her husband) had been successfully handled quite easily for years before the onset of the anxiety attacks. Generally, it appeared Mrs. X's relationships were sound and her abilities were well matched with the demands placed upon her. Since Mrs. X appeared to be having no difficulty fulfilling her roles in her family and in society, the social model also appeared to be irrelevant in this case.

When we looked for the applicability of the respondent model, the investigation of antecedents did show that there were consistent temporal antecedents for the attacks. They occured in the morning and sometimes at midday or late afternoon. However, there seemed to be no psychologically meaningful antecedents—i.e., we could not determine specific external events or stimuli uniquely associated with those times that would lead to an onset of the anxiety attacks.

Mrs. X's cognitions surrounding the anxiety attacks were largely rational and practical (e.g., "I need to calm down, why am I doing this, I need to relax and it will go away"). However, thoughts that she was losing control were beginning to become more and more prevalent as the attacks continued without any explanation. The temporal sequence of the appearance of more and more "irrational" cognitions over time led us to hypothesize that while these cognitions of losing control may be exacerbating the attacks, they were probably not etiological; rather they were reasonable conclusions from her experiences.

In response to the question, "What have you tried that seems to help?," Mrs. X tentatively replied that she frequently felt better after drinking orange juice. This information, in addition to the lack of psychologically meaningful patterns in the rest of the case data, led to a suspicion of a biological component. At the end of the first session, Mrs. X was advised that she might have a metabolic disorder and that a glucose tolerance test was warranted before the next session. There was no next session. Mrs. X was diagnosed by a physician as having hypoglycemia. Her symptoms were relieved by changes in diet.

What made her case relatively clear was the utter lack of psychological function that the anxiety symptoms had. Mrs. X happened to have led an extremely high-functioning life prior to the onset of her anxiety attacks. She was a productive, able person with sound relationships. One can easily see that if she were a poorly-functioning person in a bad marriage, say, the possibility of a biological component to her anxiety attacks would not have presented itself so clearly, since other models would have had to be investigated more fully than in this case. In this instance, however, the absence of evidence for a psychological model, coupled with the somatic nature of the symptoms, led us to make a medical referral which in this case proved fruitful. Even though the reduction in anxiety following intake of orange juice was a clear clue to a possible medical problem in this case, often a medical consultation is requested on the basis of an *absence* of psychological findings alone. The therapist should rule out plausible rival models as part of assessment.

Six years later, Mrs. X returned to therapy with similar episodes of anxiety. She was now a graduate student in history, and, because of her high level of performance, was being encouraged by her advisers to continue beyond her Masters degree. She enjoyed being a graduate student, and looked forward to pursuing more creative approaches in her historical research. Going on for her doctorate would provide that opportunity. Despite her superficially good adjustment to academia, she had developed, over a span of about 2 weeks, anxiety attacks similar topographically to those caused by her hypoglycemia. This time, the attacks were restricted to one specific class she was taking. She reported that before the onset of the attacks, she had enjoyed the course and felt fairly confident about her ability to do well in it. Mrs. X described the attacks as periods of intense dread of being called on in class. Physically, she alternately flushed and blanched, she trembled, and her palms sweated profusely. She found it extremely difficult to concentrate in class, and had cognitions concerning her fear of doing poorly in the class as a result. When we inquired about the possibility that these symptoms were much more noticeable to her than to others, she replied that her reaction was so strong that other students had indeed noticed and had asked if she were feeling ill.

On the basis of the obvious situational specificity of the anxiety episodes, and Mrs. X's sophistication about hypoglycemia, a biological model was ruled out. This point alone emphasizes how similar behaviors, even within the same person, may represent different models.

When we explored changes that had occurred in Mrs. X's life since we had seen her 6 years before, and some of the consequences of those changes, it became apparent that she was in a major conflict. She was experiencing enormous stress as a result of being in a social-role conflict over wanting to advance her career and, at the same time, wanting to be a good mother. Although she clearly enjoyed graduate school, this conflict was increased by the realities of the job market: There were virtually no positions open locally for historians and there were precious few nationally. She was simply not sure that she wanted to continue her education if it meant compromising what she considered to be her responsibilities as a mother and if the reward was uncertain. These thoughts were occasionally in her mind during class. She was caught in a situation replete with significant social-role conflicts: She felt that graduate school was in conflict with her responsibilities as a mother, she felt that her home responsibilities sometimes decreased her ability to perform adequately in graduate school, and these conflicts were compounded because she suspected her graduate education to be mainly recreational since openings for historians were scarce.

Thus, it appeared that Mrs. X's problem fit well into a social model: Her learned social roles were in conflict and producing a great deal of stress. The treatment goal within the social model is to change the person's role behavior or to change the social system which produces the conflict. Although ideal, these are often not feasible in real-life situations. In this case, both roles were highly valued by Mrs. X, and the social system in question was too large to be modified by us. We discussed Mrs. X's situation at length with her, and she became aware that the decisions she had to make should be made in a more rational way. We also discussed the reality that these decisions were difficult, and that when there were conflicting choices she should not expect solutions but rather an evaluation of the relative merit of alternatives. Her expectation that problems have solutions further increased her frustration about her conflict. She then decided that she would continue her graduate education and compromise her standards in both areas of academia and family. It was also clear that she was in no way "neglectful" in either area.

Although it seemed likely that the social conflict produced Mrs. X's general anxiety about her school/home situation, it was also clear that the fullblown anxiety response had become a classically conditioned response to the classroom situation of one particular course. This was clear because of the extreme specificity of the classroom as an eliciting stimulus for the anxiety. The anxiety attacks were disabling in themselves and had to be addressed early in therapy.

The treatment goal, resulting from the fit of the anxiety attacks into a respondent model, was to reduce the stimulus control of the classroom in bringing on the attacks. This could have been done by many techniques (systematic desensitization, in vivo desensitization, or response prevention, for example). Mrs. X was treated by use of paradoxical intentions. She was instructed to experience the anxiety in the classroom and not to fight it. She was further instructed to amplify the anxiety if she could. The more one tries to inhibit anxiety, the more it seems to persist. This intervention was chosen first as a "least intrusive" method, because it takes no elaborate instruction or gradation procedure. In this case, it was appropriate, as the anxiety was reported as being greatly reduced by the next session. She had two classes that she reported were essentially anxiety free. There was no interference with functioning in the class after a paradoxical procedure was used.

In addition, Mrs. X reported that she had developed a phobia of public speaking in her graduate classes and in her undergraduate teaching responsibilities. The signs of the phobia were the general sympathetic signs that she exhibited in class. We developed a heirarchy of "phobic" items, with the items low on the hierarchy being situations such as speaking in front of one person, and moving on to more fear producing items such as speaking in front of large classes. These items were presented after she had learned relaxation techniques. Since Mrs. X. had been in yoga classes, she was able to learn relaxation very rapidly. The last item on the hierarchy was imagining herself *thinking* about losing control over her anxiety while speaking in public, and to imagine herself being calm while having these thoughts about losing control. She was to imagine the public speech in a huge auditorium filled with the most prestigious figures in her academic field.

As mentioned in Chapter 4, we have found that phobias are generally fears of losing control and not just specific fears of stimulus situations. Losing control is generally imagined in these specific situations. Therefore, we always include imagining oneself having thoughts of losing control in every hierarchy. Although we do not have any hard evidence on this, the one time that we had the person imagine actually losing control, the person became considerably worse. We never tried having clients think about actually losing control again. Instead, we emphasize imagining being in the feared situation and *coping* with thoughts of losing control. We also try to amplify the intensity of the phobic situation as much as possible. In fact, we use a combination of desensitization and flooding. Our reasons for doing this are to use adaptation-level theory principles to provide a contrast effect so that the phobic situation looks mild by comparison. We used desensitization for the public-speaking phobia, and not paradoxical intentions, because there were no immediate public-speaking opportunities. We therefore had to resort to use of imagined stimuli. There was, unfortunately, no immediate schedule of Mrs. X having to do public speaking.

When the immediate anxiety of being in the classroom was reduced, we continued to focus on the social conflict that she had. Our goal here was to reduce the conflict by changing role behaviors and expectations wherever appropriate. Her standard in each area of life was extremely high. If she were to give up graduate school, her standard for being a mother and a wife would be met because of her high level of competence and because she regarded these activities as being very rewarding. She liked being with her family a great deal. If she could accept spending significantly less time with her family, her performance in graduate school would improve. Again, although she had misgivings about her level of performance, she was regarded very highly in school. In her case, we were able to modify her standards so that being a mother and a graduate student became more acceptable. Her rather perfectionistic standards made her feel like a failure when she was "merely" extremely competent in all the areas of her life.

We shifted her standards through repeated exposures to a lower standard, one we considered more rational. According to adaptation-level theory, repeated exposures should lead to a different adaptation level. We continually talked with her about her internal standards of perfection, and suggested that a more lenient standard was more appropriate. What added to our confidence in this intervention was "objective" information from her advisor and from her husband that her levels of performance were high.

In some respects, therapy at this point became vocational counseling, working on the difficult career choice she had. She decided that she would always have some regrets if she did not pursue her PhD, but she also decided that it would be better if she took a full-time teaching position while getting her doctorate. It was her feeling that she would be unemployable as a teacher if she had her doctorate, because schools could hire people at lower salary levels. She could, upon receiving her doctorate, apply for a position she found more congruent with her professional objectives, but having a public-school teaching position would be a fail-safe position that was acceptable to her. Her mood improved as these social conflicts were addressed, and as they were reasonably resolved.

The next issue to be addressed was why Mrs. X's standards were so high. It became apparent as we explored the origins of her expectations that a cognitive model was also applicable in explaining her high standards and in guiding treatment. She told us of her background in which her mother was proud of her only when the contingencies were "correct." That is, she and her sister had great pressure to be pretty, to be polite, and to be strong students. When there were "lapses" in performance (which were not frequent), her mother would become extremely distressed and critical of her. She and her sister were always the best-dressed children in church, and she remembers wearing hats and gloves while the other youngsters did not. Disapproval, although infrequent, was considered a threat to the family.

In a very emotional but vague way, Mrs. X. then talked about the background scandal that occurred when she was approximately eight and her sister was about 10-years-old. Although her memories of events were blurred, she remembers talking to the minister about her father having made sexual advances to her. She is quite, although not absolutely, certain that her father had made sexual advances to her sister. Although she is not sure, she had no specific recollection of whether he had made such advances to her. (Such "amnesia" on the part of incest victims is relatively common). She does remember growing up with a cloud of scandal around the family and around the fact that the court ordered her father to stay away from the house. Although he moved back in about a year later, she knew that there was shame attached to the family. As she described these intense events, she was unsuccessfully trying to hold back tears and maintain control. She went on about comments that she had heard from other children and neighbors that she did not know how to interpret, but she did know that there was something dreadfully wrong with her family.

Mrs. X reported feeling more comfortable about herself after she told about the "deep, dark, dirty secrets" that she had never discussed with anyone before. Although the description of what transpired in therapy is consistent with the Freudian view of catharsis or emotional release, it is also consistent with the view of therapy as being a safe haven in which threatening events can be explored. By talking about the anxiety-ridden shame in her family and not receiving any evaluation from the therapist about these events, she is getting the message that these events do not define her in a negative way at all. Desensitization is occurring.

Mrs. X further related that her mother and father still had conflicts after these incidents, and eventually he moved out of the house permanently. She felt vaguely responsible for the failure of her parents' relationship and felt even more of a need to "perform" in public; i.e., be a perfect little girl. By the time we had seen her, her own standards were far removed from the pressures that had determined them. She had not, consciously at least, related any of her current problems to the intense emotional experiences of her childhood. She always did feel that she had to prove worthy in all areas of her life, and she felt it was absolutely terrible not to get approval for all of her actions. After discussion of her background, which she reported had a strong effect of relief, we were able to discuss the forces that influenced her in a rational, indeed Ellisonian rational-emotive, manner (Ellis, 1962, 1970).

The next two sessions were aimed at following up on the consequences of the intense need for approval and on developing alternatives. Mrs. X did see where her need for approval had caused her unnecessary anguish and unnecessary compromises. Several situations had arisen during the course of therapy in which she would have normally been nonassertive for fear of offending people and she had handled them well. One of the situations involved her mother, about whom we had extended discussions; she was able to discuss the demands that her mother was making on her in a productive manner. Her mother asked her to do chores that were well within her own capabilities, and Mrs. X frequently resented doing these chores. During the course of therapy, she was able to say no to her mother in a nonoffensive manner without feeling guilty herself.

In summary, Mrs. X, despite very few therapy sessions, presented a variety of models in the treatment of the same "disorder," an anxiety reaction. She presented a clear biological model on her first appearance at therapy. At her second appearance, her presenting problem (anxiety attacks) fit a respondent model. However, her life situation in general fit well into a social-conflict model, and this model was very helpful in directing treatment. Finally, it appeared that the cognitive model fit the role of etiological model in that unrealistically high standards of approval forged in childhood had "set up" Mrs. X to be at high risk for conflict later.

The case of Mrs. X ended quite well. There were a total of seven sessions for the variety of anxiety problems that she faced. All were successfully resolved. Approximately a year after therapy ended, we saw her and she reported that her phobia of public speaking was also gone. The speed of Mrs. X's improvement is not typical. Usually cognitive restructuring takes considerably longer. We feel that she responded faster to the rational emotive approach than most clients because of two reasons: her high level of personal resources of ability and psychological sophistication, and because her background of assumed incest made her "irrational" high standards understandable. She understood her need to appear perfect.

THE CASE OF JOANN Z

The following case did not end at all well, despite periods of significant improvement during the course of therapy. However, unsuccessful endings are extremely useful for therapists to promote reflection on what they could have done better. Although the answer to that in this case is still not absolutely clear to us, perhaps readers could find better approaches.

Joann Z was a 14-year-old girl who acted out in an intense fashion. Her father owned his own business and her mother was a housewife. She had a 10-year-old brother, whom her parents reported she tormented. The father's business was quite variable, and as a result he had major concerns about wasting money. When she was brought to therapy by her parents, Joann had already had an educational assessment which showed her to have significant learning disabilities in the following areas: gross motor, visual memory, oral comprehension, spelling, and mathematics. She was at a normal level in auditory sequential memory and verbal expression, and did not show any general intellectual deficit. Although she was somewhat overweight in a mesomorphic manner, she was a handsome youngster who made a nice appearance.

Both parents came to the first session without Joann. They had just been notified that she was expelled from a summer camp that she claimed she wanted to attend. She arrived in camp and immediately announced that she sold illicit drugs. After the camp personnel talked to her, she told them that she had just said that for effect but they were wary. She then continued the drug announcement in a highly visible way, so that they were forced to expel her. It is important to note that there was no refund of the relatively high camp tuition.

Mr. Z said it was extremely frustrating to live with Joann. The camp event was typical of her: He had been reluctant to send her to camp because of the expense and the fear that she would get in trouble. She pleaded to go to camp and promised to behave. She was very persuasive and talked about how bored she would be and that she would get in trouble unless she went to camp. He reluctantly agreed after she assured him that she would behave.

Her behavior at home was described as constantly provocative. Among the provocative things she did was to call a neighbor and accuse her of having an affair with her father, to break the lock on the telephone and make many unnecessary long distance phone calls (to Frank Sinatra, among other people), and to walk around the house and the neighborhood making strange noises. She repeatedly said "Voom!" to everyone she came in contact with.

We began therapy with a case conception based on the operant model. Mr. Z was receptive to an analysis that pointed out how much Joann responded to his being angry. It was quite clear to him that however angry he got, and however justified the anger was, it simply did not make Joann's behavior better and in fact seemed to inflame her more. He agreed to be calm when he brought Joann back from camp. He agreed to curb his primary response, which was to yell and threaten, and simply tell Joann that it was a shame that she missed an opportunity for fun that summer. Both parents were also instructed to play to strength, i.e., give Joann attention whenever she was calm and reasonable. It was explained that she may be acting in a way that makes negative attention reinforcing, because she gets angry and wants to retaliate whenever she is punished. Therefore, the more upset her parents become, the more reinforcement power her negative behavior develops. It was also pointed out that punishment habituates; i.e., one "gets used" to it, so that it requires constantly increasing amounts to produce an effect. Her parents could not point to any successes that the punishment created in the sense of reducing undesired behaviors, and they did admit that she had been getting worse despite the escalating punishment.

Although it was clear that there was an element of limited capacities in this case (i.e., the learning disabilities), Joann was already in a special classroom which was aimed at bringing the academic demands placed on her more in line with her abilities. Thus, as in most child misbehavior problems, we first looked to the operant model. After doing a functional analysis of how Joann's acting out functioned in her family, it became clear that the consistent reinforcer for Joann was negative attention from her parents. Her parents, who appeared to be bright and concerned about their daughter, admitted that all attempts at punishment had not only proved ineffective, but were followed by increases in the very patterns of behavior the punishments were aimed at reducing.

It seemed this pattern of behavior fit the reinforcement contingency that we call "warfare in the family": misbehavior by the youngster is followed by punishment, punishment makes the youngster even angrier at the parents, and the child wants to retaliate and to establish a sense of personal freedom. According to reactance theory (Brehm, 1966), people respond to a free behavior being threatened or eliminated by becoming increasingly motivated to restore the free behavior. The youngster therefore becomes increasingly provocative and the cycle continues, often with escalation by both parties. The intervention then, became shifting this reinforcement pattern so that misbehavior was not attended to, while positive behavior was actively reinforced. Later, this plan was instituted at the school as well as at home. The school was advised to ignore Joann as much as possible when she was provocative and to attend to her whenever she was appropriate. When the provocations could not be ignored because they disrupted the classroom, which certainly did occur, Joann was to be quietly led out of the room and seated in the assistant principal's office. No one was to "reason" with her or to attend to these provocations. This intervention was coupled with clear, unambiguous, and matter-of-fact feedback to Joann about the consequences of her behavior by us.

Joann was calmer than her father expected on the way back from camp. She admitted making a mistake and, after a reasonable discussion with her father, she said she would go back to camp and try to get along. Mr. Z called the camp and they agreed to give Joann another chance. This time she lasted one day. She told everyone that the counselors were all interested in having sex with her and with each other. It was more difficult for her father to remain calm when he brought her back the next time, but he managed.

The first time we saw her, she entered the room and said "Voom! Voom! Voom! Voom!" while looking a little disturbed. She had a wild look on her face as if she were about to lose control. Our response was to tell her that she had developed a pattern of behaviors that was producing problems for her in school and at home, and that we wanted to talk about how she could change this pattern. It was necessary to form a therapeutic alliance immediately and to do so directly with Joann. When she responded with a stream of "vooms," we said that we would ask her to leave and we would talk to her parents if she continued, and that therapy required work on her part. We pointed out that it would not be useful to work with someone who only says "voom." She continued until we stood up and started escorting her out. She never "voomed" twice in a session after that. In fact, the alliance was formed. It is always important, but especially with nonvoluntary patients, to form a working relationship in which it is clear that decisions will be made together for a common goal. The therapist first must get the client to agree that there are goals that are in the client's interest. Joann had to understand that her provocative behavior was hurting her. In her case, it was not very difficult for her to see this. It turned out to be difficult to replace her provocative behaviors with more appropriate ways of dealing with people.

Joann could be quite pleasant to talk to after that, but not consistently. She provoked us by pointing a nail file at our neck, putting gum all over the waiting room wall, breaking a reclining chair by jumping on it, and putting graffiti on the bathroom walls. These incidents were not discussed with her parents, because these public violations were beyond their capacity to handle. It was important to Mr. and Mrs. Z to have a positive public image. Joann constantly tested them on this also. Therefore these behaviors were ignored at that time. She spent more time in sessions talking about feeling inadequate in school because of her learning disabilities, and how she acted crazy to cover up her fears of people getting to know her.

However, although her behavior improved substantially in school, she was at least as difficult to deal with at home as she was prior to entering therapy. Although there were still incidents in school, the principal did see major gains. Since the behavior at home was still unacceptable, we decided to institute a time-out procedure for her. We advised the parents to send Joann to her room after one of her provocative actions. This was done only after Joann had agreed in session that time-out was a reasonable response on her parent's part to her outlandish behavior. Joann was included in this discussion because it was felt that if punishment were administered without her consent and without a justification, she would only become angrier and be even more provocative.

The necessity of the justification is based on principles of reactance theory (Brehm, 1966), which states that a motivation for countercontrol would develop if justifications were not provided. Since we had a therapeutic alliance and Joann agreed that her behaviors needed control, she accepted the time-out as a reasonable response. It was also clearly pointed out to her that she would find it very difficult to accept while she was in the middle of her acting-out behaviors. She had to understand that it would be extremely difficult for her to comply when asked to go to her room, and that she would often think that her parents were unfair in asking her to go to her room. Her expectations were shifted by this information so that a contrast effect would occur; going to her room would not seem as bad as the expectations of difficulty that we had created.

Her parents reported some improvement, but her father seemed to be skeptical about therapy. On several occasions, he expressed doubts that the gains would be maintained. He felt that she was always a "little crazy," and that she would always be this way, despite therapy. In order to overcome the skepticism, we arranged for Mr. and Mrs. Z to meet with another parent who had had virtually identical problems with her daughter, and whose daughter was now doing extremely well.

Joann became more open in our private discussions. She talked about fears of ridicule in school, and fears of being stupid. She was a bright, sensitive youngster who needed to develop a behavioral repertoire of appropriate responses to handle social situations. She did not have any friends and she felt that she would not be accepted by peers. At this point, we could see another model was present: the social model. Joann, because of her long history of bizarre behavior, had never developed adequate social skills to gain for herself social reinforcement. As a result, she found it more reinforcing to get negative attention from peers by her acting out than by appropriate social interaction. We needed to give her direct feedback and explicit training on social interactions, as well as facilitate real-life social experiences whenever possible.

About this time, Joann was diagnosed as having an unstable cervical vertabra. At first she refused to accept the treatment because the brace was ugly. Of course, her parents were quite upset by this, and they started to react in a negative punitive way. When we discussed the implications of the disorder in a more rational manner, she seemed amenable to wearing the brace. Once her parents stopped giving her attention for not wearing the brace, or for her threats not to wear it, Joann was able to see that it was simply necessary for her to wear the brace.

It became increasingly apparent that the parents could not accept the fact that Joann responded negatively to controls and punishment. The parents were surprised how well the neck-brace treatment was accepted when explained rationally to Joann. Also, about this time, our notes indicate a surprising development. Joann was getting tacit encouragement from her parents in her acting out towards us. When she "voomed," her father laughed and her mother grinned. When Joann would tell us about some of her acting out in school, both parents, especially her father, seemed to enjoy her descriptions of incidents in school. Their verbal behavior was of disapproval, but they seemed to be giving nonverbal signs of encouragement of acting out. At this time, however, we were not certain this was the case. Joann wrote the following note to explain her behavior at this time:

> Joann is the greates of the great. She is a wonderful funny and a very different human bean. About the weirdest youll ever meat. She isCrazy Joann. She is disturbed because she sits on her seat and vooms her life away. One day shell grow up. The only reason she acts in the way she does is because this is what releives her form her problems. She fakes she is happy and knows it all but she is really crying under that smile. She does not even have children and shes worried about them having cures in their spine and learning disabilities. She knows her behavior is not exceptable but she wants people to know that she has alot of problems Up to her nose and is having trouble dealing with them

Joann's behavior rapidly deteriorated at this time. The principal of the school reported that she was once again disrupting the school with frequent "vooms" and with stupid laughter. Mrs. Z reported that she was tormenting her brother, and yelling and laughing inappropriately. Joann's behavior in the office was congruent with what was reported. She jumped on the chair, laughed, gave silly irrelevent answers to questions and would not remain on a given topic. We asked her to leave saying there was no point in continuing a session if she did not want to work. We set up the next session with her parents only.

We again reviewed principles of reinforcement with her parents. Although they again indicated some misgiving about the efficacy of the principles, they agreed to try. They seemed to understand the principles in general, even though some areas seemed foreign to them. However, as far as we could determine at that time, the principles were being carried out. We also discussed what we called Joann's "nutburger" act with her, and she clearly saw her behavior in a similar manner. We called it the "nutburger" act so it was not glorified. During the next several weeks, there was substantial improvement in Joann, and we started talking about termination.

After 5 weeks of improvement, Joann reverted to her previous pattern of acting out. A school visit indicated that the school had been attempting to minimize attention to the provocative behaviors, but the behaviors simply commanded attention from both the teachers and other youngsters. However, since Joann had been getting a good deal of positive attention from the school, a simple attention model of reinforcement did not seem applicable. Discussion with Joann's parents indicated that she had reverted to being provocative and they had reverted to being punitive. They were once again screaming at her, hitting her, and calling her names when she acted out. Since they were adults and she was still a child, we explained that we had to rely on their being more receptive to change than she. Although they agreed, there seemed to be little, if any, change in their behavior over the next few weeks.

Since we did not see change in their patterns of reinforcement, and since we felt the functional analysis that indicated that their negative response was reinforcing to Joann was still correct, a new set of questions was generated. Why did they not implement the program? What prevented them from responding positively to appropriate behaviors and ignoring negative behaviors? At this point, it was felt that the focus had to shift from Joann's behavior to that of her parents. We hypothesized that her parents had been classically conditioned to respond to her outbursts with great rage and anxiety. We attempted to increase Joann's parents' capacities to deal with her. Thus, as with the parents of hyperactive youngsters in Chapter 4, we instituted a systematic desensitization procedure; desensitizing Joann's parents to incidents of her embarrassing behavior, while teaching them relaxation skills. To top item on the hierarchy was Joann cursing wildly in front of the parish priest. Although they were able to handle the items on the hierarchy with relative ease and showed little anger or anxiety as difficult items were described, the parents' use of reinforcement principles did not become consistent, and Joann did not improve. A revealing event provided evidence that the classical-conditioning model was not applicable, and that another model was operating for the parents.

Joann had been doing poorly in school, and her parents wanted her to be given home tutoring rather than attend school. It was our feeling that this would not be beneficial, because Joann would not have an opportunity to develop social skills while isolated and because it seemed clear that her parents would find it even more difficult to deal with her if she were home more. In fact, we made it clear that we saw virtually no possibility of Joann doing better in the long run if she were not going to school. The parents agreed, but with some reluctance. Finally Mr. and Mrs. Z brought up the question of whether Joann needed institutionalization. This was a shock to us, because Joann's behavior, while intense, had responded well to environmental changes, and had never appeared psychotic in nature. It was also clear that Joann needed as "normal" an environment as possible if she were to improve, as she needed to learn to function effectively at home and school. Although surprised at their question, we were able to bring them back to specific suggestions about reinforcement while discouraging institutionalization, and once again Joann showed some improvement. The improvement continued with some minor setbacks for several months.

A pattern developed in therapy in which Joann would have periods of time of considerable improvement, so much so that we started slowing the frequency of sessions down, and then she would dramatically get worse. Each time she was worse, the antecedent pattern was that she would violate a rule, and her parents would overreact and start punishing her. They were unable to apply the reinforcement principles drawn from the "warfare-in-the-family" pattern in a consistent manner.

Although we repeatedly went over the principles, and the parents seemed to understand them, they simply did not comply with what we regarded as the requirements for change; to ignore provocative behaviors and to attend to positive behaviors. Joann's behavior became even more provocative. Not only did she "voom" in school, but she told people she was a chicken and she would make clucking sounds in class and in the halls. Many of the students encouraged her to disrupt classes, but some told her they did not like that behavior. One seemingly outstanding student took personal responsibility to teach Joann that she did not have to act so bizarre. Joann modified her "chicken" routine, at the encouragement of this student, but she still had incidents. One particularly intense one was when she attacked a teacher with her "wings," all the time making loud chicken-like sounds.

She found it very difficult to maintain any relationship. Her pattern of closeness with us was highly variable; after getting close to a person, she would become afraid of their getting to know her better and therefore rejecting her. She became provocative to keep people at a distance. The principal of the school took her home for a week to create a helping relationship. Joann stole things from the principal's house and disrupted the principal's family. She finally antagonized the student who had befriended her by accusing the student of sleeping with another student's boyfriend.

In each of these cases, Joann stated that she did not know why she acted the way she did, and that she really liked the people involved. Although she was able to gain understanding about the consequences of these behaviors, she still did not change. It seemed that two factors were involved; first, she was afraid that rejection was inevitable; she provoked her rejection in a way that her act, rather than herself, was rejected. She was afraid that she would still be rejected, even if she acted appropriately, so her "nutburger" act protected her "real self" from exposure. The second factor was that the above provocations were most disturbing to her parents. They became very upset and angry when she reported these apparently nonfunctional behaviors. Again, it seemed like negative attention had raised its ugly head. Why could the parents not apply the principles of reinforcement?

It then seemed relatively clear to us. When we applied a functional analysis to the parents' behavior, the consequence seemed to be that it was reinforcing to them to have Joann act out. They seemed to be intimately involved in maintaining the acting-out behaviors. But why?

The family history shed light on this question. Mr. Z felt reluctant to get married at the time he did. He felt he was pressured by his family and by his wife into a relationship that he did not want. Mrs. Z was pregnant and their Catholic upbringing had strongly influenced them against abortion. Mrs. Z wanted to get married, but she had also had reservations about the timing of this marriage. Both parents felt trapped, and both parents admitted that they deeply resented the birth of Joann. Their resentment increased when she was a difficult child to raise. Probably because of the guilt associated with their resentment, Joan was always showered with gifts and always dressed in the best clothes. They needed to hide from themselves and Joann that she was not wanted. When she became hostile and defiant with her parents, they always pointed to the material things that they had given her. They felt that they had been more than responsible parents. As a teenager, Joann understood that this was an attempt to make her feel guilty. She specifically resented the buying of these things as a substitute for acceptance.

After a great deal of soul searching for a variety of models that would explain why Mr. and Mrs. Z would not conform to the contingency-management program, we posed questions such as: Is the reinforcer negative attention? Is there a biological substrate related to the learning disability or to the irritation of the brace that compels Joann to act out? What can we do to increase Mr. and Mrs. Z's capacities to handle Joann's provocation? Does the younger brother have a role that we are not aware of in provoking Joann? Could there be other biological factors like allergies or metabolic difficulties that we had not considered?

The model that seemed to fit the best was a form of the operant model, focusing on the reinforcement patterns for Mr. and Mrs. Z. Because of the circumstances of her birth, Joann's parents could not tolerate her, and wanted her to leave the family and be institutionalized. In addition, Joann's behavior was extremely irritating. Through classical conditioning she had become a CS for their CR, which was a strong negative emotional response. Her presence alone aroused them. Since institutionalization was so much against cultural norms, they wanted this recommendation to be initiated by the psychologist. They then were reinforced by her acting out behavior, and they were threatened by her appropriate behavior. After we agonized about how to handle this, we felt that being direct would be the best way. We could assess their reaction to the confrontation, in which information that is discrepant from their perception would be presented. We would simply tell them that it seems that they wanted Joann institutionalized, and they were not carrying out our recommendations because they were afraid that she may not need residential care if she improved.

We talked with both parents about how their behavior had played a role in "provoking" Joann. We specifically said that we thought that they wanted Joann institutionalized. We also told them that they seemed more afraid of her doing well than of her failing to improve. We told them that they were contributing to her bizarre behavior as an attempt to justify their need to have her out of the house. We did so in a direct and nonevaluative way. They calmly agreed. They said that they had been convinced for a long time that Joann had not "been dealt a full deck" and that she needed institutional care. They had no emotion as they said this.

We were surprised by their acceptance of our interpretation. We expected an emotional response of either strenuous denial or of painful acceptance. The lack of emotion in their response indicated that we made no impact. When one confronts a client with information that is discrepant from the client's beliefs, and the beliefs are salient, there is an emotional response indicating that the therapist has made a change. It is important for therapists to be aware that effectiveness does not mean that the client agrees with the new information. Once a point is made and acknowledged by an emotional response, change will occur. In several similar situations in which clients disagreed, they stated that it was as if the therapist was looking over their shoulder when similar situations occurred. We expected, and hoped, that Joann's parents would feel that we were looking over their shoulders when they disciplined Joann.

It then seemed that it was beyond the existing capabilities of her parents to apply discipline in a manner that would lead to positive gains. They had a long pattern of overreacting to admittedly provocative incidents and little pattern of "playing to strength" or reinforcing positive behaviors. After approximately 1 year of therapy, it was clear that even with the insight about their motivational pattern, it was still too difficult for them to change. If there had been a strong emotional response to our presenting them with our belief that they wanted their daughter institutionalized, we would have continued the contingency-management program, hoping that the parents could now run such a program. Since their motivational patterns had not changed, but had remained the same as before the "insight," we decided on a risky strategy. We took direct responsibility for discipline. Joann's parents were told that when she engaged in provocative behaviors, they were to walk away from her and say that they will tell the doctor about what happened. Although there was no doubt that we could not administer discipline at all, we felt that it was better to have no punishment than to have punishment that was making an angry youngster even angrier.

Although Mr. and Mrs. Z were not perfect about not punishing Joann, it appeared as though they punished her considerably less. Still, we could not be sure, and in retrospect, we are doubtful about the effectiveness of this intervention, given the parents' motivations.

Therapy continued with major gains coming mainly from working with Joann and helping her to realize the implications of her negative behavior. We specifically taught her alternative ways of dealing with people. For example, she simply did not know that she did not have to be noticed at all times. She felt awkward when a group of people were in a conversation and she did not contribute. We would then explain that listeners were contributers although in a different way from speakers, and that it was all right to be quiet. It did not mean that she was stupid or shy. We covered much detail, since she had little in social-skill practice. However, since she had always observed people, she was able to see skills to emulate.

Also, the school did a wonderful job in continuing the contingency-management program of ignoring provocations and playing to strengths. The gains in school were remarkable, and she was taken out of most classes for the learning disabled and placed in regular classes. Her grades and her conduct improved remarkably. She even won an award for being the most improved student in the school. We terminated therapy feeling pride in being involved in such positive changes. The improvement that Joann demonstrated was a tribute to the power of the operant model and to using principles from the Blank Trials Law to teach Joann appropriate social and academic behavior. We also strongly feel that the relationship we had with her provided feedback that she was a valued person. The therapeutic relationship also provided her with a safe haven, so that she could act more freely in situations that she would normally avoid because they were threatening to her.

For over a year, we would hear from Joann periodically either directly by phone or from school personnel. Although there were incidents reported, she seemed to be doing adequately. We had no reason to suspect that her adjustment was falling apart.

The next time we heard from Joann's parents, they reported that she had to be hospitalized. They reported that she bragged to her brother about performing oral sex with several boys in the schoolyard. Her brother, predictably, told her parents and the warfare cycle escalated. We do not know what preceded this episode. Apparently her behavior became more bizarre and she needed hospitalization. She called us, very upset and crying, from the hospital and we recommended that she stop her performing. Although she promised to do so, her behavior was described by the hospital as being among the most intense acting out they had seen.

Her therapist called us and described what he considered among the most intense sessions he had. Joann, he described, pleaded with him to let her perform oral sex with him, and had a wild-eyed, out-of-control expression on her face. He was absolutely convinced that she was schizophrenic. Since we had seen similar types of episodes previously, we felt it was an extention and intensification of the "vooms" that we had seen previously. We felt the behavior was operant and was reinforced by the massive attention it received and by how upset it made her parents and other authority figures. She was placed on sedating neuroleptics and she did calm down. During this time, she called to tell us that we were correct; that her actions now placed her in situations that she could no longer control.

The last call that we received was about 2 months after she was released from the hospital. She called in the middle of an intense fight with her father. Suddenly, with a background of screams, there was a thud, and Joann cried over the phone that her nose was broken. We talked to Mr. Z and pointed out that we were legally obliged to report this incident to Child Protective Services, the New York State agency that must investigate alleged child abuse. We did and have not had any further direct contact with the family. They were reported to be angry at us for forcing them to be investigated. They felt betrayed.

A number of questions are raised by this case. Was the operating model biological? Was Joann schizophrenic and we were simply wrong? Although we still think about this, the biological model could not have predicted the improvement that existed once the behavioral management was taken away from the parents. Once the punishment decreased, Joann became a competent student and also performed better in social situations. However, biological factors may have simply lowered her threshold for stresses; she may have been more vulnerable to acting bizarre when under pressure than most people.

Should we have conducted a more formal systems-type approach to family therapy? It seems clear that it would have been very helpful to have Mr. and Mrs. Z's hidden agenda of institutionalizing Joann out on the table nearer the beginning of therapy. As it was, their goal seemed to be to prove that Joann was indeed unmanageable. Obviously, this was detrimental to therapy. In retrospect, we feel that it would have been useful to have the whole family involved in all sessions (unless there were a specific and compelling reason for individual sessions), and to have all members address problems of the family. We still have virtually no information about the role that the younger brother played in the distress of this family. We cannot predict what would have emerged, but having the entire family in therapy would have provided additional alternative points of intervention. We now also feel that Joann's bizarre behavior helped her parents relationship: It was one of the precious few areas they had in common. Together they could discuss the "Joann problem."

Should we have recognized that the family environment was too hostile for Joann to develop and recommended another placement? We absolutely would handle this differently now. In retrospect, it is clear that Joann's parents asked us for permission to place Joann in a residential setting on a number of occassions and in a number of ways. We feel we should have recommended a residential school for normal children. Joann would then not be exposed to frequent hostility at home, and she would not get the same response to her frequent and intense provocations. Given the history of the parents' never accepting her, it was beyond their capacities to keep her at home.

Since Joann's behavior improved considerably in the course of therapy and did so in a way consistent with the operant and cognitive models, we did not feel at the time that these other issues were as important as they turned out to be. We learned from this case that improvement alone is not sufficient to confirm the operations of a given model. Unless basic issues, which still may involve the same model, are considered, the changes may not be stable. In this case, the reinforcement system involved in the development of the difficulty was not addressed (i.e., the fundamental difficulty the parents had accepting the fact that they had a daughter, and their need to eliminate her from family life) and the pattern of the problem re-emerged. As pointed out by Levine and Fasnacht (1974), superimposing a reinforcement system upon an inappropriate reinforcement system will lead to changes, but the changes will not last unless the underlying inappropriate system is also modified. It was clear that an accurate assessment of the capacities of the parents to keep Joann at home was essential. Because of her history of constantly punishing them, she had become a conditioned stimulus for a very negative conditioned response. She was beyond their capacity to deal with at a calmer level.

We are ending with a note that Joann sent while she was progressively doing better while in High School:

My Poem

Joann

If a man does not keep pace with his companions, Perhaps it is because he hears a different Drummer. Let him step to the music which he hears.
However measured or far away.
It is not important that he should mature as soon as an apple tree or an oak.

Henry David Thoreau

this applies to me. It is not important that I mature as fast as an apple tree or oak. Let me step to the music I hear. My mother said I have six more months to mature and grow up then its all over for me.

9 Armchair Speculations on the Models Approach

While we have found the models approach very helpful as a guide to conceptualization and intervention in psychotherapy, there are other areas of clinical psychology in which we have speculated that the approach might prove useful. We acknowledge that the ideas proposed here are not fully developed and are speculative. Nonetheless, we feel this approach can aid progress in three areas: psychological diagnosis, clinical research, and clinical training. It is our hope that others will find these notions stimulating.

PSYCHOLOGICAL DIAGNOSIS

Diagnosis in the field of psychopathology has traditionally consisted of categorizing sets of abnormal behaviors into abstract classes on the basis of theoretical or empirical similarities. Diagnosis has usually been assumed to be more than descriptive; it has been used to direct thinking about both etiology and intervention. These assumptions follow from a "medical model" of psychological distress. In medicine, it is logical and necessary for diagnosis to precede intervention, since diagnosis informs the physician about the disease process. For this reason, medical texts place heavy emphasis upon diagnosis, because a correct diagnosis leads to correct treatment and increases understanding of the disorder (e.g., Holvey, 1972; Miller, 1960). The application of the medical model to psychological "diagnosis" has not been as fruitful in informing us about etiology and intervention in the psychological realm. Traditional psychiatric diagnosis has not, in effect, succeeded in informing us about the nature of the psychological *process* behind dysfunctional behavior.

Psychological classification systems differ in their reliance upon theory. On the one hand, some behaviorists (e.g., Krasner & Ullmann, 1973) have advocated dropping traditional psychiatric diagnosis altogether, to be replaced with a purely empirical, descriptive system of classification. On the other hand, the second Diagnostic and Statistical Manual of the American Psychiatric Association (DSM II; American Psychiatric Association, 1968) was replete with psychoanalytic theory. DSM II made diagnoses on the basis of the tenets of psychoanalytic theory, while ignoring behavioral topography. For example, DSM II grouped together behaviorally disparate conditions (such as hysterical paralysis, mild depression, and hypochondriasis) under the name "neurosis" because of their theoretically similar etiology (they were all thought to occur because of anxiety stemming from the repression of childhood impulses), rather than because of similarities inherent in the behaviors themselves. Thus, psychoanalytic theory gave information about the etiology and appropriate treatment of disorders diagnosed under this system.

DSM III (American Psychiatric Association, 1980) has largely removed psychoanalytic theory from its classification system, and relies much more heavily than did DSM II upon data, both observational and epidemiological. DSM III has grouped syndromes together on the basis of topographical similarities of the behaviors involved, and on the basis of longitudinal data concerning typical course. Additionally, it has generally adopted the specific, observation-based language of the behaviorists. Thus, DSM III has done a service in gathering together much data concerning description and projected course of psychiatric syndromes.

In eliminating the strong influence of psychoanalytically-based personality theory which pervaded DSM II, DSM III has also divested itself of much of the power—however spurious—of the earlier diagnostic system to determine etiology and treatment of psychopathologies. DSM III is largely atheoretical and its usefulness as a guide to treatment suffers because of it. Diagnosis without some conceptual base does not guide treatment.

Spitzer (1975) lists the purposes of psychiatric diagnosis as: (1) enabling professionals to communicate effectively; (2) aiding in our comprehension of pathological processes; and (3) allowing control of psychiatric disorders via prediction, prevention, and treatment. Given these criteria, we would evaluate DSM III most positively for its role as a descriptive classification system because it simplifies large amounts of complex data (Becker, 1974) and thus promotes effective communication among professionals. We feel that, in terms of its success at aiding comprehension of disorders or directing research to increase comprehension of disorders, it has not been helpful. A purely descriptive classification system without a theoretical base does not have the power to increase knowledge about the nature of the entities described within it.

Most importantly, we feel that DSM III is totally inadequate and frequently misleading in directing treatment, except perhaps with pharmacological therapy for the severe disorders. DSM III has been criticized for not making discriminations fine enough to guide treatment decisions (Harris, 1979; Karasu & Skodol, 1980), and for not including response to treatment data (Eysenck, Wahefield, & Friedman, 1983; Harris, 1979). In the whole of DSM III (over 450 pages), there are two paragraphs devoted to determining treatment, and these merely suggest that each therapist treat according to his or her theoretical predilection (i.e., the systems therapist will choose family therapy, the behavioral therapist will choose behavior therapy, the medically-oriented therapist will give pharmacotherapy, and so on). We regard those recommendations as being fundamentally inadequate. The unique psychological, biological, and/or social mechanisms operating within a given person are ignored under these treatment recommendations. The recommendations that therapists treat according to their theoretical allegiance can be made without any diagnostic procedure. Obviously, we feel that a conceptual analysis is required of all cases, irrespective of what diagnostic group a person's symptoms fall into. As it stands, DSM III fails in the central purpose of diagnosis, from the clinician's (and the client's) standpoint, which is to direct treatment.

The models approach is a systematic method of integrating theories with empirical support for purposes of psychodiagnostic conceptualization and intervention. In this sense, whenever a conceptualization is made within the models approach, a theoretical framework is selected. The theory then guides thinking about intervention. Thus, when a behavioral pattern that would fall under the DSM III diagnosis of "obsessive-compulsive disorder" is conceptualized as having a strong operant component, it is operant theory which then guides our thinking about etiological and maintaining factors and supplies us with direct points of intervention: rearranging the reinforcement contingencies.

A case was seen that illustrates this point. A woman client found her life increasingly restricted by repetitive, compulsive rituals. Finally, her rituals were so pervasive that they required that she not leave a particular seat in the kitchen. She rarely left the seat and even voided in it several times, as she was not able to get up to use the bathroom. Her behavior certainly fit the DSM diagnosis for obsessive-compulsive disorder. Assessment (guided by models; see flow chart on p. xii–xiii for a schematic representation of this process) indicated that this woman was ignored by her husband, except when he pleaded with her to move from the chair. This strongly indicated the presence of an operant component to her behavior. Operant theory would then dictate that the contingencies in this woman's life must be changed in order for her behavior to change. Her husband was directed to give her attention for adaptive behavior, and to show minimal concern about her dysfunctional behavior. They were told to spend more time doing interesting activities together when she was behaving appropriately. This intervention led to major gains. Traditional diagnosis, even when there is little dispute as to its accuracy, does not lead to treatment. Meyer and Turkat (1979) strongly emphasize this point, stating that "traditional psychiatric diagnosis is at best irrelevant and at least inadequate in the behavioral conceptualization of clinical phenomena [p. 266]."

The diagnosis of obsessive-compulsive disorder in this case did not indicate what intervention would be appropriate. To say that the behavioral therapist should treat this case behaviorally, while the psychoanalytic therapist should treat it psychoanalytically, simply ignores the person to be treated. Treatment must be determined by the conceptualization of the specific dynamics of a case, and not by the theoretical preferences of the therapist. It is analogous to a physician declaring that he or she belongs to the "penicillin school" of treatment. Therefore cancer, colds, and collitus would all be treated with penicillin (with, of course, different dosages and ways of administration of the drug).

The use of conceptualizations based upon models necessarily leads to treatment implications, and does so irrespective of traditional diagnosis. Thus, a models conceptualization of an "obsessive-compulsive disorder," which was found to have a strong operant component, would lead to one type of treatment procedure (e.g., rearranging contingencies so that the person was reinforced for nonobsessive behavior), whereas a models conceptualization of another "obsessive-compulsive disorder," which was found to be respondent in nature, would lead to a very different treatment procedure (e.g., desensitization and response prevention to eliminate the anxiety maintaining the disorder).

Traditional diagnosis does provide us with a common language, and, as stated previously, supplies us with a great deal of descriptive data concerning the *typical* course and symptoms of diagnostic groups (although the very validity of such diagnostic groups is sometimes questionable; see Spitzer, 1975). We suggest that traditional diagnosis is more appropriately used as a starting point for further evaluation rather than as a guide to treatment or an impetus for research.

Whereas traditional diagnosis emphasizes nomothetic classification, the models approach emphasizes idiographic classification, and as such, is much more attuned to appropriate treatments for specific individuals. A nomothetic classification system emphasizes common characteristics of a group, and an idiographic approach focuses on the unique individual features of a specific individual. We suggest that there is no contradiction in using both traditional diagnostic categories and the further conceptualization provided by a models analysis. As Meehl (1959) stated, there is no inconsistency in classifying a patient as a member of a certain taxonomic group and concurrently attempting to understand the "content" of the patient's personality (which will of necessity differ from individual to individual within taxonomic group). This is analogous to the concurrent use of traditional diagnosis and a models conceptualization. Thus, traditional diagnostic categories could be crossreferenced to include the pertinent model(s).

Without including diagnosis on all axes, a depression could be diagnosed variously as Depression, Operant Type; or Depression, Capacity Overload; or Depression, Biological Type. The treatment would then be guided by the amended diagnosis using the principles of conceptualization. It is very clear that our knowledge of models is still primitive, so that the list must be further refined as we gain more experience in the categorization of disorders in this way. Multiple-model diagnoses would be used when applicable, just as multiple-traditional diagnoses are now encouraged where appropriate. There may be many cases in which the primary model, even when accurately pinpointed, cannot lead to intervention. As an example, we are counseling a man who is experiencing a great deal of anxiety because his wife is critically ill. Although his anxiety is not biologically caused, we recommended anti-anxiety medication to simply increase his coping capacities. Although the primary model here is cognitive (in that his cognitions about his wife are making him extremely anxious), the intensity of the current situation requires immediate reduction in his anxiety level. Cognitive interventions cannot be used at this point, because the client is too anxious to engage in the reflection required by cognitive restructuring. Although the cognitive model is proposed as the functional model, intervention in this case followed the biological model.

In addition, use of a subscript diagnosis that emphasizes the particular model can be further refined. For example, there are advances in biological psychiatry taking place that have potential for increasing biological specificity. The advent of the Computerized Axial Tomography (CAT) scan can help pinpoint the location of brain injuries, and the Dexamethasone Suppression Test (e.g., Carrol, 1982) can help determine the appropriateness of antidepressant pharmacotherapy. Rather than stating only that a client is "Depressed, Biological Type," the diagnosis can be made still more specific. Thus, the diagnosis might be Depression, Biological Type, resulting from specific allergies (or catecholamine deficiency, etc.). These subtypes could be used for each of the models.

An operant disorder may be subclassified according to the type of reinforcement operating. A diagnosis of "Anxiety reaction, Operant type, reinforcement: avoidance of social interactions" will quite specifically guide intervention. Intervention would then be directed at changing the reinforcement power of social avoidance for that person. This might be done by teaching social skills, by rewarding social interaction externally, or by increasing the aversiveness of social avoidance, among other things. The particular intervention would be determined by the practicalities of the case. Such a classification immediately suggests intervention strategies. A traditional diagnosis of anxiety reaction alone provides no indication of which of many techniques reported in the literature as useful in treating anxiety might be appropriate for this individual.

We wish to make it very clear that we are not proposing a new diagnostic system to replace DSM III. We do feel that the models approach does lend itself to a diagnostic system that can direct intervention. The current DSM diagnostic system correctly does not claim to lead to intervention strategies. There is a need for a clinical diagnostic system to direct intervention, and a models approach could be the basis of such a system.

An example of a good attempt at detailed, intervention-oriented classification of a specific subset of clinical problems is the Schover, Friedman, Weiler, Heiman, & LoPiccolo (1982) multiaxial system for coding sexual problems. Sexual problems are classified along different axes, such as the phase of the sexual act during which the problem is experienced, generality of the problem across situations, and the duration of the problem. A woman who does not experience orgasm would not simply be diagnosed inorgasmic, but her problem would also be coded according to the length of time she has not had orgasm, and in what situation she does have orgasm. Although the authors do not attempt to make inferences about etiology with this system, an implied learning model (both operant and respondent) guides treatment decisions once the correct classification is made. Schover et al. have improved on the DSM III classifications of sexual disorders by including data that direct intervention.

In the field of education, some researchers have attempted to individualize instruction on the basis of classification of personality and ability characteristics of the student (Cronbach & Snow, 1977; McCord & Wakefield, 1981; Wakefield, 1979).

CLINICAL RESEARCH

The models approach has implications for the manner in which clinical research is conceptualized and conducted. Because the approach is new, we are not attempting to present a comprehensive system of research which incorporates the models viewpoint. We do have general, preliminary recommendations about clinical research which emerge from a models approach. First, we discuss research strategies which could empirically validate the models approach and expand our knowledge of psychological disorders. Next we talk about how, if validated, the models approach could aid clinical outcome research.

The clearest way for the models approach to obtain research validation is through demonstrations that its use can lead to increased effectiveness in determining intervention and etiological schemata, as compared to the existing classification system. Case studies would be an initial step in demonstrating utility of the approach, when the cases are being treated in a different way than that customarily consistent with the "standard" diagnostic scheme. This is what we have attempted to do in this book, by presenting case material in which successful treatment emerged from a models conceptualization of the case that frequently differed from what one would consider "typical" for that diagnostic entity (i.e., reported in the literature).

Although case studies are correctly criticized for lacking controls and for their generally subjective assessments of change, we feel that they also have compelling strengths. For one, they are real. Case studies are not arranged to isolate variables of interest, but reflect the myriad of variables with which the therapist is confronted. The good clinician should be treating every client as an experimental case study in the sense that the therapist is constantly testing hypotheses. The therapist should be especially sensitive to those cases that have negative outcomes. Whenever we do not have results, we become obsessed about the applicability of different models or whether we personally made mistakes. We try to develop new hypotheses. It is important to learn from those cases that do not respond. We also can see the relationship between our interventions and behavioral change, although not in a way that is as unbiased as controlled research. There are also times when improvement occurs in therapy that seems unrelated to specific treatments. This should lead to considerations about what the effective ingredients of therapy are. We have come to respect changes that occur as a result of time and/or of having a safe haven.

Just as the clinician should be aware of the limitations of case studies, the clinician must also have a healthy skepticism of research. Often, measuring instruments are not sensitive enough to detect significant clinical findings. Above all, research is a human endeavor with the same motives for claimed success as other human endeavors. Researchers can also be wrong. For example, during our lives, claims have been made for successful treatment of schizophrenia by frontal lobotomy, psychoanalysis, electroconvulsive therapy, client-centered therapy, carbon-dioxide therapy, megavitamin therapy, behavior modification, and neuroleptic medications. All of these treatments were backed by some empirical research. Research trends are also subject to fashion.

However, research has the enormous advantage of being subject to replication and therefore it can be verified. It is easier to disconfirm incorrect experimental conclusions than to disconfirm conclusions drawn from case studies. Case studies, however, are the single most definitive criterion of the utility of a therapeutic program. If the therapist does not find the program leading to gains for the client in actual application, either the therapeutic program does not work or it was explained in a way that did not help the therapist. Success with clients is the critical test.

Case studies are also extremely valuable as sources of hypotheses for more rigorous research. Single-subject research designs could be very useful in showing the efficacy of a models assessment for directing treatment. It has been argued (e.g., Leitenberg, 1973; Sidman, 1960) that group designs obscure the actual behavior of individuals, and that single-subject designs are therefore preferable. Leitenberg points out that this is especially important for the evaluation of psychotherapy research, as clients receiving therapy show more of *both* positive and negative changes than do untreated controls. Thus, group designs may obscure individual differences that are of great importance to the practicing clinician. A random time-series single-subject design (Campbell & Stanley, 1963) could be of use in showing the efficacy of a models approach. The assessment could provide the therapist with a hypothesis of which model was primary at a given time. The time of introducing the intervention based on the model would then be determined randomly. If the intervention was a short one and if the change produced was fairly rapid, it would be possible to demonstrate the effectiveness of several disparate models within a diagnostic category using this research design.

Multivariate research methods have the potential for the discovery of models, if used in a different way than is now conventionally done. The usual method for multivariate assessment to be conducted is to give a large sample of items to as wide a population as possible, and to see whether clusters of items have a common factor underlying them. Often if specific behaviors cluster together, it is thought that there may be evidence for a clinical syndrome (e.g., Cattell, 1978). The models approach lends itself to a factor analysis within a specific diagnostic category. The goal is to determine whether there are different factors operating *within* the category.

An excellent example of the use of a factor analytic approach in clinical diagnosis is the multivariate work of Quay and Peterson (Peterson, Quay & Cameron, 1959; Quay & Peterson, 1958; Quay, Peterson & Consalvi, 1960; Quay, 1964). These researchers approached the area of juvenile delinquency from the standpoint that it is not a discrete phenomenon, but is a constellation of very different disorders. A questionnaire was developed that was given to a large number of youths who were diagnosed as being delinquent (Quay & Peterson, 1958). A factor analysis was completed of the results and it showed that there were three different types of delinquents. They named these types the sociopathic delinquent, the neurotic delinquent, and the subcultural delinquent. Most importantly, they found that these types of delinquents were fairly distinct in the method and purpose of their delinquent behavior, and that they required different treatment approaches. Their findings that there were different types of factors under the general rubric of "delinquency" is prototypic of what a models approach could do. We expect similar independence of types of anxiety states, depressions, and other conditions.

We are currently conducting an exploratory factor analysis on a group of obese people. If items such as, "I often overeat before exams," "Food seems to calm me down," and "I eat too much when I feel stressed" all have high loadings on a given factor, then the items that should have high loadings on a cross-validation factor analysis could be, "I overeat when I am anxious," and "Whenever I feel upset, I tend to overeat." If there are robust factors operating within a given diagnostic classification, then a multivariate analysis can be a helpful assessment procedure for determining the existence of models, and may be helpful in determining the validity of these conceptions.

F. M. Levine (1967) suggested a simple technique for determining whether factor titles reflect the meaning of the factor that may have use within a models analysis. This technique—the empirical-anchor technique—simply requires that after the exploratory factor analysis is complete and factor titles are designated, these titles be translated into direct statements of the factor. For example, if a factor seems to measure extroversion, a cross-validation sample would be given the items, "I am an extrovert," and "I am outgoing." If the factor was extroversion, these items would have high loadings on the extroversion factor and low loadings on other factors. We can speculate that, by constructing items designed to measure specific factors, there could be developed more precise analytic techniques for understanding a symptom category. If we want to measure whether there is an operant model within—e.g., hypochondriasis—we should ask items such as, "I get more attention from my spouse whenever I am sick." These items may lead to the discovery of an operant factor.

Findings from multivariate research can now become a point of departure for single case or for factorial designs. Presumably these factors should have implications for differential intervention. An important method of validating the practical implications of the factors would be to see if they lead to specific intervention strategies. Other research approaches must be used to confirm these findings.

Factorial-research designs could be used productively to examine the differential benefit of adding a models assessment in defining treatment parameters. As an example, in the case of obesity, it is clear that virtually all overweight people would benefit from reducing their caloric intake or increasing their energy expenditure. However, a multivariate analysis may indicate that there are many different models operating in obesity. Some cases may be due to poor nutritional information, while others are due to anxiety. A factorial design can test whether there would be an incremental effect of a subdivision into models. In the case of the treatment of obesity, a factorial design will allow a 2 × 2 design of anxious obese and "bad-habits" obese to be assigned to two groups. One of the groups could emphasize relaxation training and desensitization, while the other group could be given training in stimulus-control procedures. It could be predicted that the anxious-obese group would have a differential benefit from the relaxation-based intervention, and the "bad-habits" group could benefit from the stimulus-control training. Factorial designs lend themselves to the differential predictions that specific models connote.

Once particular models within diagnostic classes are validated, this has implications for clinical-outcome research in the manner in which clinical research subjects are selected. The dominant procedure currently is the selection of subjects based on the diagnosis or the presence of the behaviors of interest. Many investigations of the treatment of phobias are based upon the presence of an "irrational fear." Therefore, when studies were conducted on phobias of public speaking and on the ubiquitous rat phobia, all of the subjects selected shared behaviors indicating significant discomfort in the presence of the phobic stimuli.

Due to this diagnosis-based method of selection of subjects, there are periodic disputes in the literature about what type of treatment is the most effective for a given disorder. Is, for example, desensitization more effective for phobics when conducted *in vivo* than when used imaginally (Sherman, 1972)? Is modeling more effective than desensitization (Bandura, Blanchard, & Ritter, 1969), or is implosion preferable (Hogan & Kirchner, 1977; Mealiea, 1967)? These questions are simply not as useful as the question of under which conditions or with whom is desensitization, for example, the treatment of choice. Only if it can be demonstrated that desensitization is better for all people under all conditions, or not as good for all people under all conditions, can simple comparisons be truly useful. Otherwise the research question must be made more specific.

The current diagnostic system, DSM III, has been criticized for its inability to guide research as well as for its lack of direction in intervention. Rachman and Wilson (1980) recommended that the nature of outcome research be changed so that medical (DSM III) diagnoses of psychological problems be replaced by psychological definitions of the problems. Both Rachman and Wilson and Kiesler (1966) have criticized researchers' exaggerated assumptions of generality across individuals and situations. Rachman and Wilson point out that a shift must take place in clinical research towards an emphasis on both specificity of the problem and specificity of the situational determinants. That is, they think that traditional medical diagnoses as the bases of research obscure the effect of intervention. Medical (psychiatric) diagnoses are too broad to take into account the specificity of a particular person's problem. These diagnoses assume that people have similar problems across different situations. Thus, individual differences in the nature and temporal pattern of problems are obscured when research is conducted according to psychiatric diagnoses. Research criteria which select subjects according to their membership in gross diagnostic categories will not, according to Rachman and Wilson, yield useful information about either the nature of psychopathology or about treatment.

The current use of the diagnostic criteria for the selection of research subjects does not take into account that a similar behavioral description of a category may reflect a wide variety of different models being involved in the etiology and/or maintenance of those behaviors. As we have pointed out numerous times in this book, the presence of particular symptoms does not necessarily indicate how similar or dissimilar two persons' problems are.

If we wanted to determine whether allergy treatments are appropriate for depression, we may make an operational definition of depression (e.g., a score on a depression inventory) and then compare an allergy treatment group with a control nontreated group. Almost certainly there would be little or no effect. However, it is known that some allergies can present as depression (Strickland, 1980), and for that small fraction of the depressed population who are victims of allergies, the conclusion that allergy shots are not an effective treatment for depression would be unfortunate. The research question must be changed from "Is X an effective treatment for Y diagnosis" to "With whom within Y diagnosis does X work?"

Several researchers have discussed the difficulty in conducting "pure" outcome research because of ethical considerations; their clinical obligation to people in distress precedes the obligation to conform to a predesignated treatment plan. Thus, they are confronted with research subjects who meet the criteria for inclusion in a research group, yet who are clearly in need of different treatment than that which is being evaluated. A subject's dysfunction falls into another model, even though diagnostically the subject's problem is similar to the disorder the researcher is investigating. This puts the researcher in a bind: should the researcher include this person in the study, even though the investigator "senses" the treatment is not right for the subject? The subject's participation will probably dilute the group effect, as well as fail to alleviate that person's discomfort. If the individual is excluded from the project, what reason can be legitimately given in terms of research strategy? If the models were designated a priori within the diagnostic class to be investigated, more sensitive outcome studies could be designed that better fulfill research and clinical goals.

The point to be made is that, in contrast to the current strategy of research groups being determined by diagnostic categories, the models approach would dictate that these diagnostic groups be broken down further into subcategories according to the psychological mechanism (model), and, where appropriate, different treatments evaluated within the diagnostic category.

There will always be very rare and idiosyncratic models at work for a given individual. We do not imply that all possible models which could underlie a certain constellation of symptoms must be specified before productive research can be done, but at least the main model of interest must be specified so that individuals who have symptoms which can be conceptualized using other models can be legitimately excluded from the research project. For example, we are currently conducting research on a treatment of stuttering that combines elements of motor learning with elements of anxiety reduction (Levine, Sandeen, & Ramirez, 1981; Levine & Ramirez, 1985). The approach, contingent negative practice, has produced positive results with 18 of 19 youngsters studied. This experiment represents the typical clinical research paradigm in that the subjects were selected according to their behavioral topography (i.e., all subjects stuttered). The same treatment was applied to all and the results were analyzed and compared to baseline in a multiple-baseline design.

We were made aware of the necessity of specifying the model within the diagnostic class when we were confronted with a potential research subject who showed clear evidence of the operant model being involved in his stuttering problem. This child had begun stuttering at age 3. Generally, stuttering is not considered of clinical significance until about age 7, since many children simply outgrow the difficulty. In this case, however, the child's parents were told by their pediatrician that the stuttering was a sign that the child needed attention and that the best response was for the parents to drop whatever they were doing and give the child their total attention when he stuttered. Needless to say, the child was massively reinforced for stuttering. If he had been included in the research program, which would not address the operant component of his behavior, it is unlikely he would have made progress. The implied model that we were working with using the contingent negative practice treatment was a limited capacities model: i.e., the child simply did not have the motor control to speak clearly. Stuttering which emerged from any other psychological mechanism (e.g., operant) would not be appropriately included in this study.

CLINICAL TRAINING

The models approach has direct implications on the training required by clinicians. The models expanded upon in this book are acknowledged to be in their infancy, but what is emphasized is the connection between data-supported theories and clinical work. We agree with Kalish (1981) that a basic general knowledge of psychology is necessary for the clinician. Use of the models approach presupposes a strong background in many aspects of psychological theory and research findings. A clinician who has successfully incorporated the general models strategy into his or her work will not be afraid to test out "new" models—that is, to try to apply a novel psychological theory to the contents of a specific case, and to do so systematically and logically.

In recent years, there has been considerable controversy about how effective clinical psychology programs are in training clinicians. Some of these criticisms have direct relevance to the implications of the models approach for training.

Carkhuff (1969, 1972) has conducted studies comparing the efficacy of lay persons trained briefly as counselors with professionally-trained therapists. He concludes that lay helpers are able to effect significant changes in clients, at a level above or equal to that of professionals. Carkhuff (1969) faults professional training programs for being "often apparently self-neutralizing admixtures of science and art and research and practice [which] frequently offer little to bridge the gap between the two [p. 9–10]." While he doesn't believe it is necessarily the case that lay helpers are inherently better than professionals, he states that the current state of professional training does not include aspects of concrete skill acquisition necessary to increase professional trainees' helping ability.

The debate within the discipline of clinical psychology over the emergence of professional schools awarding the Doctor of Psychology (PsyD) degree has also brought some basic training issues to light. The 1949 Boulder conference (Raimy, 1950) on clinical training proposed a model of training which gives equal emphasis to the dual roles of scientist and practitioner. This model stood, basically unchallenged, until the 1973 clinical training conference in Vail (Korman, 1974). The Vail conference proposed the establishment of professional schools dedicated to the training of practitioners, which would award the PsyD degree rather than the PhD.

The PsyD programs have been criticized for not providing a scholarly, research-oriented approach to clinical practice (Perry, 1979). Perry states that the research training which is absent from PsyD programs provides the trainee with a method of problem-solving which is as applicable to clinical practice as it is to formal research. Stricker (1975) makes the point that service and science are (or should be) intimately intertwined, and the PsyD programs promotes an already-apparent schism between the basic and applied branches in psychology.

Peterson (1976) defends the PsyD system, stating that clinicians must use scientific methods of thought in solving clinical problems, and that professional practice must be based upon scholarly knowledge—and that this is what is provided by PsyD programs. He states that "broadly defined scholarly inquiry [as Peterson says is offered in PsyD programs] offers a strong advantage over narrowly defined research [p. 793]."

While we have no opinion on the existence of professional schools or the PsyD degree per se, the issues raised are relevant to a discussion of the training requirements necessitated by a models approach. First of all, it is clear that in order to be able to use the models approach effectively, students must be well-educated in psychological theory and data. However, for this material to be of use to the student in clinical practice, care should be taken by teachers to, in Carkhuff's (1969) words, "bridge the gap" between "science and art and research and practice." Similarly, research design training in graduate school should include techniques for evaluating the efficacy of clinical interventions. We strongly agree with Stricker's (1975) comment about the interdependence between service and science, and feel that research training, if not too narrowly provided, can make for better clinicians.

Teaching the models approach requires more emphasis on conceptual rather than concrete thinking. Rather than learning and memorizing various techniques which have been used for problem X, a student must learn how to evaulate problem X for model dynamics, and how to determine intervention on the basis of this conceptualization. This conceptual training has several concrete advantages for the student. First, it provides a systematic framework which enables the student to incorporate new theoretical and empirical data into therapy. This allows for more creative thought and less slavish imitation in beginning therapists. (However, this does not mean that we regard interpersonal skills as unimportant. We do feel that as we can conceptualize cases more accurately, therapy will become less dependent upon style and more upon content. We are advocating conceptual teaching for the assessment and planning of intervention.) Thus, a student learns the meaning and purpose of interventions rather than only the technique. Once the purpose of an intervention is understood, it is easier for the student to use any technique or style which accomplishes that purpose.

We are constantly surprised by the variety of conditions that can produce similar symptoms. We treated a 14-year-old boy who was experiencing difficulty in school. Not only were his grades poor, but he was frequently leaving class. Our initial assessment indicated that the young-ster was peer victimized; he was frequently being teased and threatened. Although we have had a good deal of success in the treatment of young-sters like this, he showed no significant improvement. His parents indi-cated that he often left church when it was crowded because he felt ill. Further questioning showed that the youngster had a phobia of crowds; the respondent model was indicated in school. He responded quickly to desensitization. His symptoms of anxiety had been perceived by his peers as signs of being a victim, and teasing therefore decreased as he became less anxious. If we treated by symptoms, we would not have been able to conceptualize the dynamics of this unusual case. Because of many "un-usual" cases like this, it is important to transmit our conceptualization skills to students. The ability to conceptualize accurately and creatively enables therapists to "catch" unusual dynamics and intervene effectively.

We are quite traditional in the belief that a psychologist should know psychology; a rigorous program of basic psychology is essential in the training of psychologists who can conceptualize in a creative way. We have seen too many students who mechanically use techniques without knowing the underlying principles. These students frequently quote the literature that the technique is effective. We would rather have students who can generate novel techniques that are based on demonstrated princi-ples than ones who treat on the basis of what technique has been shown "effective" in the literature. Thorough training in learning, problem solv-ing, cognitive psychology, neuropsychology, and social psychology are among the requirements of a good training program. We frankly feel that this training is frequently more valuable than classroom training in psychotherapy.

Teaching the models approach is an effective way of teaching clinical skills that cannot be learned from journal reports of techniques. We pro-pose that a models-type conceptualization is what most good clinicians learn on their own by years of clinical experience. To be successful, a clinician must learn a method for matching patient to treatment. A good conceptualization of a case enables clinicians to pick a certain treatment for a client. Conceptualization skills are not taught, or even mentioned, in most texts or journal articles on behavior or cognitive therapy (Meyer & Turkat, 1979). We feel that supervised therapy is a more powerful way to learn than sitting in classrooms. Consistent with the cognitive skill-acquisition theory of Anderson (1982), we believe that learning the words does not necessarily mean knowing the operations. It takes hours of repetitive experience to become proficient in the skill of therapy.

A student trained in the models approach will not undergo "culture shock" when entering a different theoretical milieu or when beginning work with a new population of clients. While new information will certainly have to be learned in such cases, the basic models approach can still remain intact and function well for the student.

We would like to re-emphasize here that the models approach is *not* atheoretical. It is, rather, a systematic way of incorporating various theories into the practice of psychotherapy. It is eclectic *only* in the sense that no particular treatment technique will be eschewed because of its previous association with a particular "school" of therapy or theoretical orientation. Any technique can be appropriated to fulfill the treatment requirements made explicit by a models conceptualization. Because of this, training in the models approach would be a good form of "retraining" for therapists who want to break out of their narrowly defined orientation, yet are wary (with good reason) of leaving behind theory.

Applying the models approach necessitates a good general knowledge of psychology, a scientific orientation to planning and evaluating treatments, and a conceptual understanding of how and why treatment decisions are made. We are hoping that good psychotherapy programs emphasize these issues.

The implications of the models approach for diagnosis and treatment call for multidisciplinary training and cooperation. Although all therapists should attempt to incorporate knowledge from relevant fields into their training, the scope of this task is overwhelming, and some division of responsibility and expertise according to background is appropriate. In such a system, medicine would be primarily concerned with addressing biological disorders which affect behavior; psychology would have the major responsibility for the operant, respondent, and cognitive models; social work and counseling would deal with the capacities model; and social psychology and sociology would address the social model.

It is important for therapists to know their limitations. The effects of biological forces on behavior is a growing area, and an area that few nonmedical therapists can hope to master. It is, therefore, necessary for therapists to refer to physicians when there is a reasonable doubt as to whether the behavioral pattern in question has biological causes or mediators. There have been a number of occasions when we suspected that the behavior in question had a biological cause and that intervention in the biological area was necessary. We routinely refer to neurologists when signs of neurological damage are present (e.g., violent and otherwise inexplicable mood changes or severe memory or attention problems). We have also referred clients to psychiatrists for psychopharmacological evaluations, as well as to endocrinologists for metabolic workups. It is clearly in the domain of medicine to make biological diagnoses and interventions, and we are obliged to consult when there is evidence for a biological model.

In a similar way, we have often referred clients to social workers and vocational counselors when we thought that the model in question was the limited-capacity model. For example, when working in a rehabilitation unit at a hospital, we will find patients that have reached maximal hospital benefit and, upon discharge, do not have the resources to find themselves an appropriate place to live. Many patients need vocational rehabilitation after changes in their lives due to trauma or disease. We find that social workers and guidance counselors simply know more about these problems. Psychological testing may be very helpful in determining the individual's vocational capacities. The counselor also has detailed knowledge about the employment market. We have erred in making vocational recommendations that were not in line with the realities of job opportunities. It is also quite apparent how vital residential or job placement is in a person's life. We do not mean to suggest that social workers or guidance counselors are limited to these specific roles, just that they have better training in dealing with these problems than most other therapists.

We do feel that psychologists are in the best position to utilize the operant, the respondent, and the cognitive models. These models are central to the field of psychology. Psychologists are the ones who are developing and distributing knowledge in these areas. A good program in clinical psychology requires or encourages students to train in these areas. In fact, it is command of these areas that is required for a rich conceptualization of cases rather than administration of psychological techniques, often (unfortunately) on the basis of diagnosis. Certainly these areas alone contain more information than virtually all practitioners can know. However, the classroom and laboratory training that psychology provides allows psychologists to be in the best position to relate these sciences to human behavior.

References

Abramson, L. Y., Seligman, M. E. P., & Teasdale, J. D. (1978). Learned helplessness in humans: Critique and reformulation. *Journal of Abnormal Psychology, 87*(1), 49–74.

Adams, J. S. (1963). Toward an understanding of inequity. *Journal of Abnormal and Social Psychology, 67*(5), 422–436.

Adams, J. S. (1965). Inequity in social exchange. In L. Berkowitz (Ed.), *Advances in experimental social psychology* (Vol. 2). New York: Academic Press.

Ainsworth, M. D. S., & Bell, S. M. (1970). Attachment, exploration, and separation: Illustrated by the behavior of one-year-olds in strange situations. *Child Development, 41,* 49–67.

American Psychiatric Association. (1968). *Diagnostic and statistical manual of mental disorders* (2nd ed.). Washington, DC: American Psychiatric Association.

American Psychiatric Association. (1980). *Diagnostic and statistical manual of mental disorders* (3rd ed.). Washington, DC: American Psychiatric Association.

Ames, S. M. (1976). *Techniques for treating temper tantrums in young children: A comparative outcome study.* Unpublished doctoral dissertation, State University of New York at Stony Brook.

Anastasi, A. (1982). *Psychological testing.* New York: Macmillan.

Anderson, J. R. (1982). Acquisition of cognitive skill. *Psychological Review, 89*(4), 369–406.

Appley, M. .H. (Ed.). (1971). *Adaptation-level theory: A symposium.* New York: Academic Press.

Archibald, W. P. (1978). *Social psychology as political economy.* New York: McGraw-Hill.

Aronson, E., Turner, J., & Carlsmith, M. (1963). Communicator credibility and communicator discrepancy as determinants of opinion change. *Journal of Abnormal and Social Psychology, 67,* 31–36.

Atthowe, J. M., & Krasner, L. (1968). A preliminary report on the application of contingent reinforcement procedures (token economy) on a "chronic" psychiatric ward. *Journal of Abnormal Psychology, 73,* 37–43.

Ayllon, T., & Azrin, N. H. (1965). The measurement and reinforcement of behavior of psychotics. *Journal of the Experimental Analysis of Behavior, 8,* 357–383.

Azrin, N. H., & Holz, W. C. (1966). Punishment. In W. K. Honig (Ed.), *Operant behaviour.* New York: Appleton-Century Crofts.

Azrin, N. H., Naster, B. J., & Jones, R. (1973). Reciprocity counselling: A rapid learning based procedure for marital counselling. *Behaviour Research and Therapy, 11,* 365–382.

Bailey, C. (1977). *Fit or fat?* Boston: Houghton-Mifflin.

Bandura, A. (1969). *Principles of behavior modification.* New York: Holt, Rinehart & Winston.

Bandura, A. (Ed.). (1971). *Psychological modeling: Conflicting theories.* Chicago, IL: Aldine.

Bandura, A. (1973). *Aggression: A social learning analysis.* Englewood Cliffs, NJ: Prentice-Hall.

Bandura, A. (1977). *Social learning theory.* Englewood, Cliffs, NJ: Prentice-Hall.

Bandura, A., Blanchard, E. B., & Ritter, R. (1969). The relative efficacy of desensitization and modeling approaches for inducing behavioral, affective, and attitudinal changes. *Journal of Personality and Social Psychology, 13,* 173–199.

Bandura, A., & Walters, R. H. (1963). *Social learning and personality development.* New York: Holt, Rinehart & Winston.

Bart, P. (1972). Depression in middle-aged women. In V. Gornick & B. K. Moran (Eds.), *Woman in sexist society.* New York: Signet.

Baucom, D. H. (1981). *Cognitive behavioral strategies in the treatment of marital discord.* Paper presented at the 15th annual convention of the Association for the Advancement of Behavior Therapy, Toronto, Canada.

Baum, W. M., & Rachlin, H. C. (1969). Choice as time allocation. *Journal of the Experimental Analysis of Behavior, 12*(6), 861–874.

Beach, S. R. H., Abramson, L. Y., & Levine, F. M. (1981). Attributional reformulation of learned helplessness and depression: Therapeutic implications. In J. F. Clarkin & H. I. Glazer (Eds.), *Depression: Behavioral and directive intervention strategies.* New York: Garland.

Beach, S. R. H., & O'Leary, K. D. (1985). The current status of outcome research in marital therapy. In L. L'Abate (Ed.), *Handbook of family psychology and psychotherapy.* Homewood, IL: Dow Jones-Irving.

Beck, A. T. (1972). *Depression: Causes and treatment.* Philadelphia, PA: University of Pennsylvania Press.

Beck, A. T. (1976). *Cognitive therapy and the emotional disorders.* New York: International Universities Press.

Beck, A. T., & Rush, A. J. (1978). Cognitive approaches to depression and suicide. In G. Serban (Ed.), *Cognitive defects in the development of mental illness.* New York: Brunner/Mazel.

Beck, A. T., Rush, A. J., Shaw, B. F., & Emery, G. (1979). *Cognitive therapy of depression.* New York: Guilford.

Becker, J. (1974). *Depression: Theory and research.* Washington, DC: Winston.

Bee, H. L. (1978). Overview: The effects of poverty. In H. L. Bee (Ed.), *Social issues in developmental psychology* (2nd ed.). New York: Harper & Row.

Bem, D. J. (1967). Self-perception: An alternative interpretation of cognitive dissonance phenomena. *Psychological Review, 74,* 183–200.

Berscheid, E. (1966). Opinion change and communicator-communicatee similarity and dissimilarity. *Journal of Personality and Social Psychology, 4,* 670–680.

Berscheid, E., & Walster, E. (1974). Physical attractiveness. In L. Berkowitz (Ed.), *Advances in experimental social psychology.* New York: Academic Press.

Bernstein, D. A., & McAlister, A. (1976). The modification of smoking behavior: Progress and problems. *Addictive Behaviors, 1,* 89–102.

Beutler, L. E. (1983). *Eclectic psychotherapy: A systematic approach.* New York: Pergamon Press.

Beutler, L. E., Johnson, D. T., Neville, C. W., Jr., Elkins, D., & Jobe, A. M. (1975). Attitude similarity and therapist credibility as predictors of attitude change and improvement in psychotherapy. *Journal of Consulting and Clinical Psychology, 43,* 90–91.

Bexton, W. H., Heron, W., & Scott, T. H. (1954). Effects of decreased variation in the sensory environment. *Canadian Journal of Psychology, 8,* 70–76.

Biddle, B. J. (1979). *Role theory: Expectations, identities, and behaviors.* New York: Academic Press.

Bockar, J. A. (1976). *Primer for the nonmedical psychotherapist.* New York: Spectrum.

Bootzin, R. R. (1972). Stimulus control treatment for insomnia. *Proceedings of the Annual Convention of the American Psychological Association, 7,* 395–396.

Bowen, M. (1978). *Family therapy in clinical practice.* New York: Aronson.

Bregman, E. (1934). An attempt to modify the emotional attitudes of infants by the conditioned response technique. *Journal of Genetic Psychology, 45,* 169–195.

Brehm, J. (1966). *A theory of psychological reactance.* New York: Academic Press.

Brehm, S. S. (1976). *The application of social psychology to clinical practice.* New York: Wiley.

Brenner, M. H. (1973). *Mental illness and the economy.* Cambridge, MA: Harvard University Press.

Brickman, P., & Campbell, D. (1971). Hedonic relativism and planning the good society. In M. Appley (Ed.), *Adaptation level theory: A symposium.* New York: Academic Press.

Broverman, I. K., Broverman, D. M., Clarkson, F. E., Rosenkrantz, P., & Vogel, S. R. (1970). Sex role stereotypes and clinical judgments of mental health. *Journal of Consulting and Clinical Psychology, 34,* 1–7.

Brown, R. S. (1978). Jogging may be therapeutic for psychiatric patients. *Clinical Psychiatry News, 6*(5), 1.

Brown, S. L., & Schwartz, G. E. (1980). Relationships between facial electromyography and subjective experience during affective imagery. *Biological Psychology, 11,* 49–62.

Brozek, J. (1955). Nutrition and behavior: Psychological changes in acute starvation with hard physical work. *Journal of the American Dietetic Association, 31,* 703–707.

Bruch, H. (1973). *Eating disorders: obesity, anorexia nervosa, and the person within.* New York: Basic Books.

Burkart, M., & Levine, F. M. (1982, April). *Modification of a rat phobia using a cognitive intervention based on adaptation-level theory.* Paper presented at the British Psychological Society meeting, York, England.

Buss, A. H., & Plomin, R. (1975). *A temperament theory of personality development.* New York: Wiley.

Cairns, R. B. (1979). *Social development: The origins and plasticity of interchanges.* San Francisco: Freeman.

Campbell, D. T., & Stanley, J. C. (1963). *Experimental and quasi-experimental designs for research.* Chicago, IL: Rand McNally.

Carey, M. P., Flasher, L. V., Maisto, S. A., & Turkat, I. D. (in press). One a priori approach to psychological assessment. *Professional Psychology: Research and Practice.*

Carkhuff, R. R. (1969). *Helping and human relations: Vol. 1. Selection and training.* New York: Holt.

Carkhuff, R. R. (1972). New directions in training for the helping professions: Toward a technology for human and community resource development. *Counseling Psychologist, 3*(3), 12–30.

Carrol, B. J. (1982). Clinical applications of the dexamethasone suppression test for endogenous depression. *Pharmacopsychiatria, 15,* 19–24.

Cattell, R. B. (1978). *The scientific use of factor analysis in behavioral and life sciences.* New York: Plenum.

Cautela, J. R. (1971). Covert conditioning. In A. Jacobs & L. B. Sachs (Eds.), *The psychology of private events.* New York: Academic Press.

Chesler, P. (1972). *Women and madness.* New York: Avon.

Cohen, A. R. (1964). *Attitude change and social influence.* New York: Basic Books.

Cooper, C. L., & Marshall, J. (1976). Occupational sources of stress: A review of the literature relating to coronary heart disease and mental ill health. *Journal of Occupational Psychology, 49*(1), 11–28.

Cooper, K. H. (1969). *Aerobics.* New York: Evans.

Cronbach, L. J., & Snow, R. E. (1977). *Aptitudes and instructional methods.* New York: Wiley.

Dargis, J. J. (1978). Postpartum adjustment and exercise. *Dissertation Abstracts International, 38*(11-B), 5634.

Davison, G. C., & Valins, S. (1969). Maintenance of self-attributed and drug-attributed behavior change. *Journal of Personality and Social Psychology, 11*(1), 25–33.

Diener, C. I., & Dweck, C. S. (1978). An analysis of learned helplessness: Continuous changes in performance, strategy, and achievement cognitions following failure. *Journal of Personality and Social Psychology, 36*(5), 451–462.

DiLoreto, A. O. (1971). *Comparative psychotherapy.* New York: Aldine-Atherton.

Dimond, R. E., Havens, R. A., & Jones, A. C. (1978). A conceptual framework for the practice of prescriptive eclecticism in psychotherapy. *American Psychologist, 33*(3), 239–248.

Dollard, J., & Miller, N. E. (1950). *Personality and psychotherapy: An analysis in terms of learning, thinking, and culture.* New York: McGraw-Hill.

Dollard, J., Miller, N. E., Doob, L. W., Mowrer, O. H., & Sears, R. R. (1939). *Frustrations and aggression.* New Haven: Yale University Press.

Duhl, B. S., & Duhl, F. J. (1975). *Cognitive styles and marital process.* Paper presented at the annual meeting of the American Psychiatric Association.

Dunham, H. W. (1980). *Social systems and schizophrenia: selected papers.* New York: Praeger.

Dunlap, K. (1932). *Habits: Their making and unmaking.* New York: Liveright.

Dweck, C. S. (1975). The role of expectations and attributions in the alleviation of learned helplessness. *Journal of Personality and Social Psychology, 14*(3), 268–276.

Dweck, C. S., & Bush, E. S. (1976). Sex differences in learned helplessness: I. Differential debilitation with peer and adult evaluators. *Developmental Psychology, 12* (2), 147–156.

Dweck, C. S., Davidson, W., Nelson, S., & Enna, B. (1978). Sex differences in learned helplessness: II. The contingencies of evaluative feedback in the classroom and III. An experimental analysis. *Developmental Psychology, 14*(3), 268–276.

Dweck, C. S., Goetz, T. E., & Strauss, N. L. (1980). Sex differences in learned helplessness: IV. An experimental and naturalistic study of failure generalization and its mediators. *Journal of Personality and Social Psychology, 38*(3), 441–452.

D'Zurilla, T., & Goldfried, M. (1971). Problem-solving and behavior modification. *Journal of Abnormal Psychology, 78*(1), 107–126.

Effron, D. M. (1978). *Cardiopulmonary resuscitation.* Pamphlet published by American Heart Association, Oklahoma Affiliate.

Ellis, A. (1962). *Reason and emotion in psychotherapy.* New York: Stuart.

Ellis, A. (1970). *The essence of rational psychotherapy: A comprehensive approach to treatment.* New York: Institute for Rational Living.

Ellis, A. (1972). *Executive leadership: A rational approach.* Secaucus, NJ: Citadel Press.

Ellis, A. (1977a). The rational-emotive approach to sex therapy. In A. Ellis & R. Grieger (Eds.), *Handbook of rational emotive therapy.* New York: Springer.

Ellis, A. (1977b). The basic clinical theory of rational emotive therapy. In A. Ellis & R. Grieger (Eds.), *Handbook of rational emotive therapy.* New York: Springer.

Ellis, A., & Grieger, R. (Eds.). (1977a). *Handbook of rational emotive therapy.* New York: Springer.

Ellis, A., & Grieger, R. (1977b). The present and future of rational emotive therapy. In A. Ellis & R. Grieger (Eds.), *Handbook of rational emotive therapy.* New York: Springer.

Emery, G. Hollon, S. D., & Bedrosian, R. C. (Eds.). (1981). *New directions in cognitive therapy: A casebook.* New York: Guilford.

English, H. B. (1929). Three cases of "conditioned fear response." *Journal of Abnormal and Social Psychology, 34,* 221–225.

Evans, R. I. (1975). *Carl Rogers: The man and his ideas.* New York: E. P. Dutton.

Eysenck, H. J., Wahefield, J. A., & Friedman, A. F. (1983). Diagnosis and clinical assessment: The DSM III. *Annual Review of Psychology, 34,* 167–193.

Farberow, N. L., & Schneidman, E. F. (1965). Statistical comparisons between attempted and committed suicides. In N. L. Farberow & E. F. Schneidman (Eds.), *The cry for help.* New York: McGraw-Hill.

Feingold, B. F. (1973). *Introduction to clinical allergy.* Springfield, IL: Charles C. Thomas.

Ferster, C. B., Nurnberger, J. I., & Levitt, E. B. (1962). The control of eating. *Journal of Mathetics, 1,* 87–110.

Figley, C. R. (Ed.). (1978). *Stress disorders among Vietnam veterans.* New York: Brunner/ Mazel.

Flavell, J. H. (1977). *Cognitive development.* Englewood Cliffs, NJ: Prentice-Hall.

Fling, S., & Manosevitz, M. (1972). Sex typing in nursery school children's play interests. *Developmental Psychology, 7* (2), 146–152.

Fordyce, W. E. (1976). *Behavioral methods in chronic pain and illness.* St. Louis, MO: Mosby.

Fordyce, W. E. (1978). Learning processes in pain. In R. A. Sternbach (Ed.), *The psychology of pain.* New York: Raven.

Foulkes, W. D. (1966). *The psychology of sleep.* New York: Scribner.

Frank, J. D. (1961). *Persuasion and healing: A comparative study of psychotherapy.* Baltimore, MD: John Hopkins University Press.

Franks, C. M. (1976). Foreward. In A. Lazarus, *Multimodal behavior therapy.* New York: Springer.

Freud, S. (1960). *The psychopathology of everyday life.* New York: Norton.

Garcia, J., Ervin, F. R., & Koelling, R. A. (1966). Learning with a prolonged delay of reinforcement. *Psychonomic Science, 5*(3), 121–122.

Garcia, J., & Koelling, R. A. (1966). Relation of cue to consequence in avoidance learning. *Psychonomic Science, 4,* 123–124.

Garfield, S. L. & Kurtz, R. (1974). A survey of clinical psychologists: Characteristics, activities, and orientations. *The Clinical Psychologist, 28,* 7–10.

Garfield, S. L., & Kurtz, R. (1977). A study of eclectic views. *Journal of Consulting and Clinical Psychology, 45*(1), 78–83.

Goldfried, M. R. (1971). Systematic desensitization as training in self-control. *Journal of Consulting and Clinical Psychology, 37*(2), 228–234.

Goldfried, M. R. (1980). Toward the delineation of therapeutic change principles. *American Psychologist, 35*(11), 991–999.

Goldfried, M. R. (Ed.). (1982). *Converging themes in psychotherapy: Trends in psychodynamic, humanistic, and behavioral practice.* New York: Springer.

Goldfried, M. R., & Davison, G. C. (1976). *Clinical behavior therapy.* New York: Holt, Rinehart, & Winston.

Goldfried, M. R., & Padawer, W. (1982). Current status and future directions in psychotherapy. In M. R. Goldfried (Ed.), *Converging themes in psychotherapy: Trends in psychodynamic, humanistic, and behavioral practice.* New York: Springer.

Goldiamond, I. (1965). Self-control procedures in personal behavior problems. *Psychological Reports, 17,* 851–868.

Goldstein, A. P. (1962). *Therapist-patient expectancies in psychotherapy.* New York: Macmillan.

Goldstein, A. P. (1973). *Structured learning therapy: Toward a psychotherapy for the poor.* New York: Academic Press.

Goldstein, A. P., & Stein, N. (Eds.). (1976). *Prescriptive psychotherapies.* New York: Pergamon.

Golin, S., Sweeney, P. D., & Shaeffer, D. E. (1981). The causality of causal attributions in depression: A cross-lagged panel correlational analysis. *Journal of Abnormal Psychology, 90,* 14–22.

Goodenough, F. L. (1931). *Anger in young children.* (Institute of Child Welfare Monograph No. 9). Minneapolis, MN: University of Minnesota Press.

Gottesman, I. I., & Shields, J. (1972). *Schizophrenia and genetics: A twin study vantage point.* New York: Academic Press.

Gottman, J. M., Notarius, C., Gonso, J., & Markman, H. (1976). *A couple's guide to communication.* Champaign, IL: Research Press.

Gruneberg, M. M. (1979). *Understanding job satisfaction.* London: Macmillan.

Haley, J., & Hoffman, L. (1967). *Techniques of family therapy.* New York: Basic Books.

Harlow, H. F., & Suomi, S. J. (1970). Nature of love—simplified. *American Psychologist, 25,* 161–168.

Harlow, H. F., & Zimmerman, T. (1959). Affectional responses in the infant monkey. *Science, 130,* 421–432.

Harris, S. L. (1979). DSM III: Its implications for children. *Child Behavior Therapy, 1,* 37–46.

Hay, D. F. (1977). Following their companions as a form of exploration for human infants. *Child Development, 48,* 1624–1632.

Hays, P. (1976). Etiological factors in manic-depressive psychoses. *Archives of General Psychiatry, 33*(10), 1187–1188.

Helson, H. (1964). *Adaptation level theory: A systematic and experimental approach to behavior.* New York: Harper & Row.

Helson, H. (1971). Adaptation-level theory: 1970—and after. In M. Appley (Ed.), *Adaptation level theory: A symposium.* New York: Academic Press.

Heron, W., Doane, B. K., & Scott, T. H. (1956). Visual disturbances after prolonged perceptual isolation. *Canadian Journal of Psychology, 10,* 13–18.

Herrnstein, R. J. (1970). On the law of effect. *Journal of Experimental Analysis of Behavior, 13,* 243–266.

Herrnstein, R. J. (1974). Derivatives of matching. *Psychological Review, 86,* 486–495.

Hess, B. B., & Waring, J. M. (1978). Parent and child in later life. In R. M. Lerner & G. B. Spanier (Eds.), *Child influences on marital and family interaction: A lifespan perspective.* New York: Academic Press.

Hetherington, E. M. (1965). A developmental study of the sex of the dominant parent on sex-role preference, identification, and imitation in children. *Journal of Personality and Social Psychology, 2,* 188–194.

Higdon, H. (1978). Running and the mind. *Runner's World,* 36–43.

Hilgard, E. R., & Bower, G. H. (1975). *Theories of learning.* Englewood Cliffs, NJ: Prentice-Hall.

Hogan, R. A., & Kirchner, J. H. (1967). Preliminary report of the extinction of learned fears via shortterm implosive therapy. *Journal of Abnormal Psychology, 72,* 106–109.

Hoiberg, A. (1978). Effects of participation in the physical conditioning platoon. *Journal of Clinical Psychology, 34*(2), 410–416.

Holvey, D. N. (Ed.). (1972). *The Merck manual of diagnosis and therapy* (12th ed.). Rahway, NJ: Merck, Sharp, & Dohme Research Laboratories.

Jacobson, N. S., & Margolin, G. (1979). *Marital therapy: Strategies based on social learning and behavior exchange principles.* New York: Brunner/Mazel.

James, W. (1890). *Principles of psychology.* New York: Holt, Rinehart & Winston.

Janis, I. L. (1974). *Psychological stress: Psychoanalytic and behavioral studies of surgical patients.* New York: Academic Press.

Jarvik, M. E., & Brecher, E. M. (1977). Drugs and sex: Inhibition and enhancement effects. In J. Money & H. Musaph (Eds.), *Handbook of sexology.* New York: Elsevier.

Johnson, J. E., & Leventhal, H. (1974). Effects of accurate expectations and behavioral instructions on reactions during a noxious medical examination. *Journal of Personality and Social Psychology, 29*(5), 710–718.

Kalish, H. I. (1981). *From behavioral science to behavior modification.* New York: McGraw-Hill.

Kallmann, F. J. (1953). *Heredity in health and mental disorder: Principles of psychiatric genetics in the light of comparative twin studies.* New York: Norton.

Karasu, T. B., & Skodol, A. E. (1980). VIth Axis for DSM III; psychodynamic evaluation. *American Journal of Psychiatry, 137,* 607–610.

Karen, R. L. (1974). *An Introduction to behavioral therapy and its applications.* New York: Harper & Row.

Katzman, L. S. (1977). A study to investigate the relationship between physical activity and frequency of sexual behavior among selected males, ages 45 to 74. *Dissertation Abstracts International, 35,* 2573A–2574A.

Kazdin, A. E. (1974). Self-monitoring and behavior change. In M. J. Mahoney & C. E. Thoreson (Eds.), *Self-control: Power to the person.* Monterey, CA: Brooks/Cole.

Kazdin, A. E. (1978a). *History of behavior modification: Experimental foundations of contemporary research.* Baltimore, MD: University Park Press.

Kazdin, A. E. (1978b). The application of operant techniques in treatment, rehabilitation, and education. In S. L. Garfield & A. E. Bergin (Eds.), *Handbook of psychotherapy and behavior change* (2nd ed.). New York: Wiley.

Keefe, F. J., & Brown, C. J. (1982). Behavioral treatment of chronic pain syndromes. In P. A. Boudewyns & F. J. Keefe (Eds.), *Behavioral medicine in general medical practice.* New York: Addison-Wesley.

Kelly, E. L. (1961). Clinical psychology—1960. Report of survey findings. *Newsletter of the Division of Clinical Psychology of the APA, 14*(1), 1–11.

Kelman, H. (1961). Processes of opinion change. *The Public Opinion Quarterly, 25,* 57–78.

Kety, S. S., Rosenthal, D., Wender, P. H., & Schulsinger, F. (1971). Mental illness in the biological and adoptive families of adopted schizophrenics. *American Journal of Psychiatry, 128*(3), 302–306.

Keys, A., Brozek, J., Henschel, A., Michelson, O., & Taylor, H. L. (1951). *The biology of human starvation.* Minneapolis, MN: University of Minnesota Press.

Kiesler, D. J. (1966). Some myths of psychotherapy research and the search for a paradigm. *Psychological Bulletin, 65*(2), 110–136.

King, D. S. (1980). *Food and chemical sensitivities can produce psychological symptoms.* Paper presented at the annual convention of the American Psychological Association, Montreal, Canada.

Kinsey, A. C., Pomercy, W. B., & Martin, C. E. (1948). *Sexual behavior in the human male.* Philadelphia: W. B. Saunders.

Kirsch, B. (1974). Consciousness raising groups as therapy for women. In V. Franks & V. Burtle (Eds.), *Women in therapy: New psychotherapies for a changing society.* New York: Brunner/Mazel.

Klerman, G. L. (1972). Drug therapy of clinical depression: Current status and implications for research on neuropharmacology of the affective disorders. *Journal of Psychiatric Research, 9*(3), 253–270.

Kopel, S., & Arkowitz, H. (1975). The role of attribution and self-perception in behavior change: Implications for behavior therapy. *Genetic Psychology Monographs, 92,* 175–212.

Korman, M. (1974). National conference on levels and patterns of professional training in psychology: the major themes, *American Psychologist, 29,* 441–449.

Krasner, L., & Ullmann, L. P. (1973). *Behavior influence and personality: The social matrix of human action.* New York: Holt, Rinehart, & Winston.

Ladd, G. W., & Mize, J. (1982). Social skills training and assessment with children: A cognitive-social learning approach. *Child and Youth Services, 5*(3–4), 61–74.

Lazarus, A. A. (Ed.). (1970). *Multimodal behavior therapy.* New York: Springer.

Lazarus, A. A. (1981). *The practice of multimodal therapy.* New York: McGraw-Hill.

Lee, M. W. (1976). *Social reinforcement: A reanalysis.* Unpublished manuscript, University of North Carolina at Chapel Hill.

Leitenberg, H. (1973). The use of single-case methodology in psychotherapy research. *Journal of Abnormal Psychology, 82,* 87–101.

Levine, F. M. (1966). Relation of stimulus-seeking behavior and arousal level. *Psychological Reports, 18*(3), 743–746.

Levine, F. M. (1967). The empirical anchor technique: A simple experimental method for testing the construct validity of factor titles. *Multivariate Behavioral Research, 2*(2), 251–254.

Levine, F. M. (1982, November). Intruder in the bedroom (Previously titled: TV, intimacy, and environmental design). *McCalls Working Mother,* pp. 108, 117.

Levine, F. M., Broderick, J. E., & Burkart, M. (1983). Attribution and contrast: Two explanations for the effects of external rewards on intrinsic motivation. *British Journal of Psychology, 74,* 461–466.

Levine, F. M., & Fasnacht, G. (1974). Token rewards may lead to token learning. *American Psychologist, 29* (11), 816–820.

Levine, F. M., & Ramirez, R. (1985, March). *Contingent negative practice as a successful treatment of stuttering.* Paper presented at the annual convention of the Eastern Psychological Association, Boston, MA.

Levine, F. M., Sandeen, E. E., & Ramirez, R. R. (1981), Contingent negative practice as a treatment of stuttering: preliminary results. Unpublished manuscript, State University of New York at Stony Brook.

Levine, F. M., & Sheff, H. (1979, April). *Contingent negative practice as a successful treatment of stuttering.* Paper presented at the annual convention of the Eastern Psychological Association, Boston, MA.

Levine, F. M., & Tursky, B. (1972, April). *Psychophysiological and movement responses of chronic schizophrenic patients and controls to high stimulation and sensory restriction.* Paper presented at the annual convention of the Eastern Psychological Association, Atlantic City, NJ.

Levine, M. (1966). Hypothesis behavior by humans during discrimination learning. *Journal of Experimental Psychology, 71*(3), 331–338.

Levine, M. (1971). Hypothesis theory and nonlearning despite ideal S-R reinforcement contingencies. *Psychological Review, 71*(2), 94–103.

Levine, M., Leitenberg, H., & Richter, M. (1964). The blank trials law: the equivalence of positive reinforcement and nonreinforcement. *Psychological Review, 71* (2), 94–103.

Lewinsohn, P. M. (1974). A behavioral approach to depression. In R. M. Friedman & M. M. Katz (Eds.), *The psychology of depression: Contemporary theory and research.* Washington, DC: Winston.

Lewinsohn, P. M., & Atwood, G. E. (1969). Depression: A clinical-research approach. *Psychotherapy: Theory, Research, and Practice, 6,* 166–171.

Lewinsohn, P. M., Graf, M. (1973). Pleasant activities and depression. *Journal of Consulting and Clinical Psychology, 41,* 261–268.

Lewinsohn, P. M., & Libet, J. (1972). Pleasant events, activity schedules, and depressions. *Journal of Abnormal Psychology, 79,* 291–295.

Lichtenstein, E., & Danaher, B. G. (1976). Modification of smoking behavior: A critical analysis. In M. Hersen, R. M. Eisler, & P. M. Miller (Eds.), *Progress in behavior modification* (Vol. 3). New York: Academic Press.

Lidsky, T., Labuszewski, T., & Levine, F. M. (1981). Are movement disorders the most serious side effects of maintenance therapy with antipsychotic drugs? *Biological Psychiatry, 16,* (12), 1189–1194.

Liebert, R. M., Neale, J. M., & Davidson, E. S. (1973). *The early window: Effects of television on children and youth.* New York: Pergamon Press.

London, P. (1964). *The modes and morals of psychotherapy.* New York: Holt.

LoPiccolo, J., & Hogan, D. R. (1979). Sexual dysfunction. In O. F. Pomerleau & J. P. Brady (Eds.), *Behavioral medicine: Theory and practice.* Baltimore, MD: Williams & Wilkins.

Lovaas, O. I., & Simmons, J. Q. (1969). Manipulation of self-destruction in three retarded children. *Journal of Applied Behavior Analysis, 2,* 143–157.

Luce, G. G. (1971). *Body time: Physiological rhythms and social stress.* New York: Pantheon Books.

Maccoby, E. E., & Jacklin, C. N. (1974). *The psychology of sex differences.* Stanford, CA: Stanford University Press.

MacCulloch, M. J., Feldman, M. P., Orford, J., & MacCulloch, M. L. (1966). Anticipatory avoidance learning in the treatment of alcoholism. A record of therapeutic failure. *Behaviour Research and Therapy, 4,* 187–196.

MacCulloch, M. J., Feldman, M. P., & Pinschof, J. M. (1965). The application of anticipatory avoidance learning to the treatment of homosexuality. II. Avoidance response latencies and pulse rate changes. *Behaviour Research and Therapy, 3,* 21–44.

Maher, B. A. (1966). *Principles of psychopathology.* New York: McGraw-Hill.

Mahoney, M. J. (1977a). Reflections on the cognitive-learning trend in psychotherapy. *American Psychologist, 32,* 5–13.

Mahoney, M. J. (1977b). Personal science: A cognitive learning therapy. In A. Ellis & R. Grieger (Eds.), *Handbook of rational emotive therapy.* New York: Springer.

Mahoney, M. J., & Arnkoff, D. (1978). Cognitive and self-control therapies. In S. L. Garfield & A. E. Berhin (Eds.), *Handbook of psychotherapy and behavior change* (2nd ed.). New York: Wiley.

Maier, S. F., & Seligman, M. E. P. (1976). Learned helplessness: Theory and evidence. *Journal of Experimental Psychology: General, 105*(1), 3–46.

Mander, A. V., & Rush, A. K. (1974). *Feminism as therapy.* New York: Random House.

Marks, I., & Gelder, M. (1967). Transvestism and fetishism: Clinical and psychological changes during faradic aversion. *British Journal of Psychiatry, 119,* 711–730.

Marmor, J., & Woods, S. M. (Eds.). (1980). *The interface between the psychodynamic and behavioral therapies.* New York: Plenum Books.

Martin, M. J. (1983). A brief review of organic diseases masquerading as functional illness. *Hospital and Community Psychiatry, 34*(4), 328–332.

Maslow, A. H. (1966). *The psychology of science: A reconnaissance.* New York: Harper & Row.

Masserman, J. H. (1943). *Behavior and neurosis: An experimental psychoanalytic approach to psychobiologic principles.* Chicago: The University of Chicago Press.

Masters, W. E., & Johnson, V. E. (1966). *Human sexual response.* Boston, MA: Little-Brown.

McCord, R. R., & Wakefield, J. A. (1981). Arithmetic achievement as a function of introversion-extraversion and teacher-presented reward and punishment. *Personality and Individual Differences, 2,* 145–152.

McDowell, J. J. (1982). The importance of Herrnstein's mathematical statement of the Law of Effect for behavior therapy. *American Psychologist, 37*(7), 771–779.

McGoldrick, M., & Carter, E. A. (1982). The family life cycle. In F. Walsh (Ed.), *Normal family processes.* New York: Guilford.

McNamara, M. J. (1978). The effects of three conditioning programs on selected physical and psychological parameters of college students. *Dissertation Abstracts International, 38,* 7212A.

Mealiea, W. L. (1967). *The comparative effectiveness of systematic desensitization and implosive therapy in the elimination of snake phobia.* Unpublished doctoral dissertation, University of Missouri.

Mednick, S. A. (1970). Breakdown in individuals at high risk for schizophrenia: Possible predispositional perinatal factors. *Mental Hygiene, 54*(1), 50–63.

Meehl, P. E. (1959). Some ruminations on the validation of clinical procedures. *Canadian Journal of Psychology, 13,* 102–128.

Mehrabian, A., & Williams, M. (1969). Nonverbal concomitants of perceived and intended persuasiveness. *Journal of Personality and Social Psychology, 13,* 37–58.

Meichenbaum, D. H. (1977). *Cognitive-behavior modification.* New York: Plenum.

Meichenbaum, D. H., & Cameron, R. (1977). The clinical potential of modifying what clients say to themselves. In A. Ellis & R. Grieger (Eds.), *Handbook of rational emotive therapy.* New York: Springer.

Meichenbaum, D. H., Gilmore, J., & Fedoravivius, A. (1971). Group insight versus group desensitization in treating speech anxiety. *Journal of Consulting and Clinical Psychology, 36,* 410–421.

Meichenbaum, D. H., & Goodman, J. (1971). Training impulsive children to talk to themselves: A means of developing self-control. *Journal of Abnormal Psychology, 77,* 115–126.

Merbaum, S. (1973). The modification of self-destructive behavior by a mother-therapist using aversive stimulation. *Behavior Therapy, 4,* 442–447.

Metalsky, G. I., Abramson, L. Y., Seligman, M. E. P., Semmel, A., & Peterson, C. (1982). Attributional styles and life events in the classroom: Vulnerability and invulnerability to depressive mood reactions. *Journal of Personality and Social Psychology, 43*(3), 612–617.

Mettee, D. R., & Wilkins, P. C. (1972). When similarity "hurts": Effects of perceived ability and a humorous blunder on interpersonal attractiveness. *Journal of Personality and Social Psychology, 22*(2), 246–258.

Meyer, V., & Crisp, A. (1964). Aversion therapy in two cases of obesity. *Behaviour Research and Therapy, 2,* 143–147.

Meyer, V., & Turkat, I. D. (1979). Behavioral analysis of clinical cases. *Journal of Behavioral Assessment, 1*(4), 259–270.

Miller, J. B., & Mothner, I. (1981). Psychological consequences of sexual inequality. In E. Howell & M. Bayes (Eds.), *Women and mental health.* New York: Basic Books.

Miller, N. E. (1948). Studies of fear as an acquirable drive: I. Fear as motivation and fear reduction as reinforcement in the learning of a new response. *Journal of Experimental Psychology, 38,* 89–101.

Miller, S. E. (Ed.). (1960). *A textbook of clinical pathology.* Baltimore: Williams & Wilkins.

Minuchin, S. (1974). *Families and family therapy.* Cambridge, MA: Harvard University Press.

Mischel, W. (1966). A social-learning view of sex differences in behavior. In E. Maccoby (Ed.), *The development of sex differences.* Stanford, CA: Stanford University Press.

Miskimins, R. W., & Baker, B. R. (1973). *Self-concept and the disadvantaged.* Brandon, VT: Clinical Psychology.

Mowrer, O. H. (1960). *Learning theory and behavior.* New York: Wiley.

Murray, E. J., & Jacobson, L. I. (1978). Cognition and learning in traditional and behavioral psychotherapy. In S. L. Garfield & A. E. Bergin (Eds.), *Handbook of psychotherapy and behavior change* (2nd ed.). New York: Wiley.

Neale, J. M., & Oltmanns, T. F. (1980). *Schizophrenia.* New York: Wiley.

They shall overcome. (1983, May 23). *Newsweek,* pp. 60–62.

Nisbett, R. E. (1972). Hunger, obesity, and the ventromedial hypothalamus. *Psychological Review, 79,* 433–453.

Novaco, R. (1975). *Anger control: The development and evaluation of an experimental treatment.* Lexington, MA: Heath.

O'Banion, D., Armstrong, B., Cummings, R. A., & Stange, J. (1978). Disruptive behavior: A dietary approach. *Journal of Autism and Childhood Schizophrenia, 8*(3), 325–337.

Ober, D. C. (1968). Modification of smoking behavior. *Journal of Consulting and Clinical Psychology, 32,* 543–549.

O'Leary, K. D., & Wilson, G. T. (1975). *Behavior therapy: Application and outcome.* Englewood Cliffs, NJ: Prentice-Hall.

Orbach, S. (1978). *Fat is a feminist issue.* New York: Berkley Medallion.

Ossofsky, H. J. (1976). Affective and atopic disorders and cyclic AMP. *Comprehensive Psychiatry, 17*(2), 335–346.

Palmore, E. B. (1969). Physical, mental, and social factors in predicting logevity. *Gerontologist, 9*(2), 103–108.

Paris, G., & Cairns, R. B. (1969). An experimental and ethological analysis of social reinforcement with retarded children. *Child Development, 40,* 213–235.

Paul, G. L. (1966). *Insight versus desensitization in psychotherapy.* Stanford, CA: Stanford University Press.

Pavlov, I. P. (1928). *Lectures on conditioned reflexes* (W. H. Gantt, Trans.). New York: International.

Perry, N. W. (1979). Why clinical psychology does not need alternative training models. *American Psychologist, 34*(7), 603–611.

Peter, L. J., & Hull, R. (1969). *The Peter principle.* New York: W. Morrow.

Peterson, C., Semmel, A., von Baeyer, C., Abramson, L. Y., Metalsky, G. I., & Seligman, M. E. P. (1982). The attributional style questionnaire. *Cognitive Therapy and Research, 6*(3), 287–300.

Peterson, D. R. (1976). Need for the doctor of psychology degree in professional psychology. *American Psychologist, 31,* 792–798.

Peterson, D. R., Quay, H. C., & Cameron, G. R. (1959). Personality and background factors in juvenile delinquency as inferred from questionnaire responses. *Journal of Consulting and Clinical Psychology, 23,* 395–399.

Physicians' desk reference 38th ed. (1984). Oradell, N. J.: Medical Economics Co.

Polansky, N. A., Borgman, R. D., & DeSaix, C. (1972). *Roots of futility.* San Francisco, CA: Jossey-Bass.

Quay, H. C. (1964). Personality dimensions in delinquent males as inferred from the factor analysis of behavior ratings. *Journal of Research in Crime and Delinquency, 1,* 33–37.

Quay, H., & Peterson, D. R. (1958). A brief scale for juvenile delinquency. *Journal of Clinical Psychology, 14,* 139–142.

Quay, H. C., Peterson, D. R., & Consalvi, C. (1960). The interpretation of three personality factors in juvenile delinquency. *Journal of Consulting Psychology, 24,* 555.

Rachlin, H. (1976). *Behavior and learning.* San Francisco, CA: Freeman.

Rachlin, H., & Green, L. (1972). Commitment, choice, and self-control. *Journal of the Experimental Analysis of Behavior, 17,* 15–22.

Rachman, S., & Teasdale, J. (1969). *Aversion therapy and behavior disorders: An analysis.* Coral Gables, FL: University of Miami Press.

Rachman, S. J., & Wilson, G. T. (1980). *The effects of psychological therapy.* New York: Pergamon.

Raimy, V. C. (Ed.) (1950). *Training in clinical psychology.* New York: Prentice-Hall.

Rescorla, R. A. (1967). Pavlovian conditioning and its proper control procedures. *Psychological Review, 74*(1), 71–80.

Rescorla, R. A. (1968). Probability of shock in the presence and absence of CS in fear conditioning. *Journal of Comparative and Physiological Psychology, 66*(1), 1–5.

Reynolds, G. S. (1975). *A primer of operant conditioning*. Glenview, IL: Scott, Foresman.

Rimm, D. C., DeGroot, J. C., Boord, P., Reiman, J., & Dillow, P. V. (1971). Systematic desensitization of anger response. *Behaviour Research and Therapy, 9*, 273–280.

Rimm, D. C., & Masters, J. C. (1979). *Behavior therapy: Techniques and empirical findings* (2nd ed.). New York: Academic Press.

Rodriguez, R. (1982). *Hunger of memory*. Boston, MA: David R. Godine.

Rogers, C. R. (1951). *Client-centered therapy: Its current practice, implications, and theory*. Boston, MA: Houghton-Mifflin.

Rogers, C. R. (1961). *On becoming a person*. Boston: Houghton-Mifflin.

Rogers, C. R. (Ed.). (1967). *The therapeutic relationship and its impact: A study of psychotherapy with schizophrenics*. Madison, WI: University of Wisconsin Press.

Rotter, J. B. (1966). Generalized expectancies for internal versus external control of reinforcement. *Psychological Monographs: General and Applied, 80*(1), 1–28.

Ryan, W. (1971). *Blaming the victim*. New York: Pantheon.

Sager, C. J., Brayboy, T. L., & Waxenberg, B. R. (1970). *Black ghetto family in therapy: A laboratory experience*. New York: Grove.

Sarbin, T. R. (1954). Role theory. In G. Lindzey (Ed.), *Handbook of social psychology: Vol. 1. Theory and method*. Reading, MA: Addison-Wesley.

Schofield, W. (1964). *Psychotherapy: The purchase of friendship*. Englewood Cliffs, NJ: Prentice-Hall.

Schönpflug, W., & Schultz, P. (1979) *Larmwirkungen bei tatigkeiten mit komplexer informationsverarbeitung*. Forschungsbericht 79-105 01 201, Berlin, West Germany: Umweltbundesamt.

Schover, L. R., Friedman, M. S., Weiler, S. J., Heiman, J. R., & LoPiccolo, J. (1982). Multiaxial problem-oriented system for sexual dysfunctions: An alternative to DSMIII. *Archives of General Psychiatry, 39*, 614–619.

Schultz, P. (1979). Regulation und fehlregulation im verhalten II. Stess durch fehlregulation. *Psychologisch Beitrage, 21*, 597–621.

Schultz, P., & Schönpflug, W. (1982). Regulatory activity during states of stress. In W. Krohne & L. Laux (Eds.), *Achievement, stress, and anxiety*. New York: Wiley/Hemisphere.

Sears, R. R., Maccoby, E. E., & Levin, H. (1957). *Patterns of child rearing*. New York: Harper & Row.

Seligman, M. E. P., Abramson, L. Y., Semmel, A., & von Baeyer, C. (1979). Depressive attributional style. *Journal of Abnormal Psychology, 88*, 242–247.

Seligman, M. E. P., & Maier, S. F. (1967). Failure to escape traumatic shock. *Journal of Experimental Psychology, 74*, 1–9.

Selye, H. (1976). *The stress of life*. New York: McGraw-Hill.

Settin, J. M., & Bramel, D. (1981). Interaction of client class and gender in biasing clinical judgments. *American Journal of Orthopsychiatry, 51*(3), 510–520.

Shaw, B. F., & Beck, A. T. (1977). The treatment of depression with cognitive therapy. In A. Ellis & R. Grieger (Eds.), *Handbook of rational emotive therapy*. New York: Springer.

Shaw, M. E., & Costanzo, P. R. (1970). *Theories of social psychology*. New York: McGraw-Hill.

Sheff, H., & Levine, F. M. (1981). *Warfare in the family: A behavioral-cognitive model of child abuse*. Unpublished manuscript, State University of New York at Stony Brook.

Sherman, A. R. (1972). Real-life exposure as a primary therapeutic factor in the desensitization treatment of fear. *Journal of Abnormal Psychology, 79*, 19–28.

Siassi, I. (1974). Psychotherapy with women and men of lower classes. In V. Franks & V. Burtle (Eds.), *Women in therapy: New psychotherapies for a changing society*. New

York: Brunner/Mazel.

Sidman, M. (1960). *Tactics of scientific research*. New York: Basic Books.

Singer, J. (1974). *Imagery and daydream methods in psychotherapy*. New York: Academic Press.

Singletary, Y., Friend, R., & Nurse, H. (unpublished). *Group participation and survival among hemodialysis patients*.

Skinner, B. F. (1974). *About behaviorism*. New York: Knopf.

Sloane, R. B., Staples, F. R., Cristol, A. H., Yorkston, N. J., & Whipple, K. C. (1975). *Psychotherapy versus behavior therapy*. Cambridge, MA: Harvard University Press.

Snyder, W. U. (1961). *The psychotherapy relationship*. New York: Macmillan.

Sowell, T. (1981). *Ethnic America: A history*. New York: Basic Books.

Spitzer, R. L. (1975). More on pseudoscience in science and the case for psychiatric diagnosis. *Archives of General Psychiatry, 33,* 459–470.

Stampfl, T. G., & Levis, D. J. (1967). Essentials of implosive therapy: A learning-theory-based psychodynamic behavioral therapy. *Journal of Abnormal Psychology, 72*(6), 496–503.

Starr, P. (1982). *The social transformation of American medicine*. New York: Basic Books.

Staub, E., & Kellett, D. S. (1972). Increasing pain tolerance by information about aversive stimuli. *Journal of Personality and Social Psychology, 21*(2), 198–203.

Staub, E., Tursky, B., & Schwartz, G. E. (1971). Self-control and predictability: Their effects on reactions to aversive stimulation. *Journal of Personality and Social Psychology, 18*(2), 157–162.

Steinmann, A. (1974). Cultural values, female role expectancies, and therapeutic goals: Research and interpretation. In V. Franks & V. Burtle (Eds.), *Women in therapy: New psychotherapies for a changing society*. New York: Brunner/Mazel.

Sterner, R. T., & Price, W. R. (1973). Restricted riboflavin: Within-subject behavioral effects in humans. *American Journal of Clinical Nutrition, 26,* 150–160.

Stockard, J., & Johnson, M. M. (1980). *Sex roles: Sex inequality and sex role development*. Englewood Cliffs, NJ: Prentice-Hall.

Stricker, G. (1975). On professional schools and professional degrees. *American Psychologist, 30,* 1062–1066.

Strickland, B. R. (1979, August). Depression as a concomitant of physical disorders: Difficulties of differentiation. In (Chair), *Neglected aspects in the treatment of depression and schizophrenia*. Symposium conducted at the annual convention of the American Psychological Association, New York.

Strickland, B. R. (1980, August). *Implications of food and chemical susceptibilities for clinical psychology*. Paper presented at the annual convention of the American Psychological Association, Montreal, Canada.

Stuart, R. B. (1967). Behavioral control of overeating. *Behavioural Research and Therapy, 5,* 357–365.

Stuart, R. B. & Davis, B. (1972). *Slim chance in a fat world: Behavioral control of obesity*. Champaign, Illinois: Research Press.

Sullivan, H. S. (1954). *The psychiatric interview*. New York: Norton.

Thomas, A., & Chess, S. (1977). *Temperament and development*. New York: Brunner/Mazel.

Thomas, A., Chess, S., & Birch, H. G. (1968). *Temperament and behavior disorders in children*. New York: New York University Press.

Thomas, A., Chess, S., & Birch, H. G. (1970). The origin of personality. *Scientific American, 223* (2), 102–109.

Tinklepaugh, O. L. (1928). An experimental study of representative factors in monkeys. *Journal of Comparative Psychology, 8,* 197–236.

Tredway, V. A. (1978). Mood and exercise in older adults. *Dissertation Abstracts International, 39,* 2531B.

Turkat, I. D., & Maisto, S. A. (in press). Application of the experimental method to the formulation and modification of personality disorders. In D. H. Barlow (Ed.), *Behavioral treatment of adult disorders.* New York: Guilford.

Turkat, I. D., & Meyer, V. (1982). The behavior-analytic approach. In P. Wachtel (Ed.), *Resistance: Psychodynamic and behavioral approaches.* New York: Plenum.

Ullman, L., & Krasner, L. (1965). *Case studies in behavior modification.* New York: Holt, Rinehart, & Winston.

Valentine, C. A. (1968). *Culture and poverty: Critique and counter-proposals.* Chicago, IL: University of Chicago Press.

Vaughan, K. B., & Lanzetta, J. T. (1980). Vicarious instigation and conditioning of facial expressive and autonomic responses to a model's expressive display of pain. *Journal of Personality and Social Psychology, 38*(6), 909–923.

Wachtel, P. L. (1977). *Psychoanalysis and behavior therapy: Toward an integration.* New York: Basic Books.

Wakefield, J. A. (1979). *Using personality to individualize instruction.* San Diego, Ca: EDITS Publishers.

Wallace, J. (1966). An abilities conception of personality: Some implications for personality measurement. *American Psychologist, 21,* 132–138.

Walters, G. C., & Grusec, J. E. (1977). *Punishment.* San Francisco, CA: Freeman.

Watson, J. B., & Rayner, R. (1920). Conditioned emotional reaction. *Journal of Experimental Psychology, 3,* 1–14.

Weinberg, J. C., Mandel, H. P., & Miller, G. H. (1979). The relationship between various dietary factors and MMPI subscales: Implications for clinical practice. *Journal of Clinical Psychology, 35*(4), 880–886.

Weissman, M. M., & Klerman, G. L. (1981). Sex differences and the epidemiology of depression. In E. Howell & M. Bayer (Eds.), *Women and mental health.* New York: Basic Books.

Williamson, R. C. (1970). Marriage roles, American style. In G. H. Seward & R. C. Williamson (Eds.), *Sex roles in changing society.* New York: Random House.

Winokur, G., & Clayton, P. (1967). Family history studies: II. Sex differences and alcoholism in primary affective illness. *British Journal of Psychiatry, 113*(502), 973–979.

Wolpe, J. (1952). Experimental neuroses as learned behavior. *British Journal of Psychology, 43,* 243–268.

Wolpe, J. (1958). *Psychotherapy by reciprocal inhibition.* Stanford, CA: Stanford University Press.

Wolpe, J. (1965). Conditioned inhibition of craving in drug addiction. *Behaviour Research and Therapy, 2,* 285–287.

Wooley, S. C., Wooley, O. W., & Dyrenforth, S. R. (1979). Theoretical, practical, and social issues in the behavioral treatments of obesity. *Journal of Applied Behavior Analysis, 12,* 3–25.

Yalom, I. D. (1970). *The theory and practice of group psychotherapy.* New York: Basic Books.

Yates, A. J. (1958). The application of learning theory to the treatment of tics. *Journal of Abnormal and Social Psychology, 56,* 175–182.

Young, R. J., & Ismail, A. H. (1978). Ability of biochemical and personality variables in discrimination between high and low fitness levels. *Journal of Psychosomatic Research, 22*(3), 193–199.

Author Index

Subject Index